Next Wave

CULTURES

Critical Youth Studies

Series Editor: Greg Dimitriadis

Next Wave

CULTURES

Feminism,

Subcultures,

Activism

Edited by Anita Harris

Routledge
Taylor & Francis Group

New York   London

Routledge
Taylor & Francis Group
711 Third Avenue
New York, NY 10017

Routledge
Taylor & Francis Group
2 Park Square
Milton Park, Abingdon
Oxon OX14 4RN

© 2008 by Taylor & Francis Group, LLC
Routledge is an imprint of Taylor & Francis Group, an Informa business

International Standard Book Number-13: 978-0-415-95710-6 (Softcover) 978-0-415-95709-0 (Hardcover)

Library of Congress Cataloging-in-Publication Data

Next wave cultures : feminism, subcultures, activism / edited by Anita Harris.
       p. cm. -- (Critical youth studies)
    Includes bibliographical references and index.
    ISBN 978-0-415-95709-0 (hb : alk. paper) -- ISBN 978-0-415-95710-6 (pb : alk.
    paper)
    1. Teenage girls. 2. Young women. 3. Subculture 4. Feminist theory. I. Harris,
Anita, 1968-

    HQ798.N49 2008
    305.235'2--dc22

                                                                    2007009025

Visit the Taylor & Francis Web site at
http://www.taylorandfrancis.com

and the Routledge Web site at
http://www.routledge.com

Contents

Part III   New Activisms: Cultural and Political

Acknowledgments

For permission to reprint images, thanks to Beyond Media, Jessica, and Randi. For their intellectual and practical help, thanks to all the contributors, as well as Catherine Bernard, Gill Cohen, Greg Dimitriadis, Michelle Fine, Catherine Harris, Hilary Pilkington, Josh Roose, Deborah Tolman, Judy Webb, and above all, Michael and Lucius. This book was supported by the Outside Studies Program at Monash University.

Series Editor Introduction

Anita Harris's new collection *Next Wave Cultures: Feminism, Subcultures, Activism*, powerfully engages with the contemporary lives of young women around the globe, taking the reader to the furthest edges of subculture and feminist theory—and transcending both. In doing so, Harris and her contributors underscore the ways such theoretical and conceptual constructs must always be put into critical dialogue with the demands of complex and ever-evolving social, material, and cultural realities. This empirical impulse has come to mark the volumes in this series so far—and it is an impulse "worked" here for its maximum import and impact.

As this volume's contributors make clear, both "subculture" and "feminist" theories were generated at historical moments in some ways distinct from our own. Both were tied to a perhaps more stable set of social structures and relationships than those that exist today. Subculture theory tended to assume that particular groups—the now paradigmatic "skinheads," "mods," "punks," and "lads" of Dick Hebdige, Paul Willis, and others—emerged from particular notions of class identity that mapped neatly onto extant capitalist relations. These groups had seemingly stable boundaries that could be explained both in terms of their resistance to and incorporation in an industrial economy. With the rise of postindustrial, neoliberal economic regimes, and the destabilizing cultural effects of globalization, however, much more is "up for grabs" today. As Harris and her contributors all make clear, a more rhizomatic set of "neotribes, lifestyles, scapes, scenes, networks, communities, and citizenships," now proliferate in unpredictable ways. The political location(s) of these groups are located in more dispersed sets of commitments.

Of course, much of this early work on subcultures was also called into question by feminist critics such as Angela McRobbie. As McRobbie powerfully argued, the stress on "punks," "lads," and others often ignored the more private spaces (such as bedrooms, etc.) where young women carved out their own identities. Although McRobbie and others highlighted the masculine biases that marked this early work on subcultures, they also fell back onto and assumed stable notions of gender. Young women's experiences, in short, were largely "flattened out" and even homogenized. Here, too, much more is "up for grabs" today. The (often invisible) advances of second-wave feminism, as well as the proliferation of new, global media forms, technologies, and cultures, have allowed (at least some) young women a broader "palate" of ways to live out their gendered lives. As Harris makes clear, so-called third-wave feminism has largely destabilized monolithic notions of gender in ways that researchers can only understand from "the ground up."

Enter *Next Wave Cultures: Feminism, Subcultures, Activism*. The volume's great effort here is to pull together a wide span of research that looks at the lives of young women, research that is informed by subculture and feminist theory but is not blinded by it. That is to say, these pieces take up the kinds of questions taken up by Hebdige, McRobbie, and others, questions like: What are the practices, identities, or interests around which young people affiliate? How are these processes gendered? And what are their political implications? But they have removed the blinders often a part of any calcified field of study. We see a much wider range of affiliations, around a much more expansive set of issues. In Part I, "Hustling, Fighting, Surfing, and Sex: Infiltrating Masculine Domains," we see young women taking on and working through a plethora of cultural practices often associated with men—"gangsterism" and surfing, for example. In Part II, "Creating Spaces," we see young women carving out safe spaces in subtle and unpredictable ways, through a range of issues such as disability, technology, and religion.

All of this allows us to see new political possibilities in oft ignored places and spaces. Indeed, in Part III, "New Activisms: Cultural and Political," the authors look toward the ways young women are collectively generating new kinds of political activisms from "the ground up." We see a range of ways civic engagement can happen through music, 'zine writing, street art, as well as other practices. All of this challenges traditional notions of feminism as well as civic engagement more broadly. As the contributors to this section underscore, a great challenge to new century activism is to decenter notions of "citizenship" as it has been traditionally defined and open it up to new possibilities.

Next Wave Cultures: Feminisms, Subcultures, Activism, in closing, is a profound collection that signals new directions for the emergent field of critical youth studies as well as gender studies more broadly. It will prove indispensable to teachers, researchers, activists and others—anyone interested in locating the complex lives of young women today.

Greg Dimitriadis

Introduction
Youth Cultures and Feminist Politics

This book provides a new take on the debate in the West about young women's cultural and political action. A familiar lament about youth in general, and girls in particular, is that they are no longer socially aware, politically active or critical of popular culture. There is a considerable amount of research that indicates young people's move away from both formal political engagement and resistance politics as expressed through subcultural formations (for an overview, see Manning and Ryan 2004; Bennett and Kahn-Harris 2004). Curiously, this research is not typically gender-differentiated, and with just a few exceptions, very little has been said about either the political participation or nonparticipation of young women in particular. An important exception to this has been the interrogation of young women's specifically feminist engagements. Since the eruption of the so-called "generation wars" within the women's movement, there has been a focus on young women's shift from traditional feminist activism to something more diffuse and less organized (Harris 2001; Bulbeck 2006). At the same time, there is an acknowledgment that young people today live in times and under conditions that make political activity and cultural critique difficult to engender (see Furlong and Cartmel 1997). New ways of thinking about cultural and political engagement face the challenge of understanding the impact on youth cultures of the forces of fragmentation and decollectivization that characterize social and political life in late modernity. As many social theorists have illustrated, the contemporary late modern socioeconomic order mitigates against social action by dismantling the social ties that were once forged through clear class identities, requiring individuals to make personal and disembedded projects of their lives in order to succeed, and absorbing critique into popular culture (see Giddens 1991; Beck 1992; Klein 2001). Whereas once young people's resistance politics, and young women's feminist activism in particular, could be easily identified, today these seem obscure, transitory and disorganized. This book demonstrates that young women have new ways of taking on politics and culture that may not be recognizable under more traditional paradigms, but deserve to be identified as socially engaged and potentially transformative nonetheless. These engagements reflect the changing times within which they live by highlighting both the limitations and opportunities afforded by the globalization of youth consumer culture, the co-option of styles of youth resistance by the market (for example grrrlpower, hip hop culture), the emergence of new technologies and media, and the decentralization and dispersal of power and resistance from the national to the global.

In order to understand these changes it is useful to outline the frameworks through which young women's cultural and political cultures have typically been interpreted. These are subculture theory and feminism. Both of these have been central to theorizing and taking seriously young women's political and cultural action. A key concept for both of these paradigms is "resistance," but this idea has come under considerable pressure from forces that have complicated modes of social change activities. Here I identify the ways these frameworks have evolved and adapted to the new conditions that young women live in that shape their possibilities for new kinds of "resistance" today.

Youth Subcultures and "Resistance"

In Western youth studies, one of the commonest ways to analyze young people's cultural and political action has been through the "subculture" paradigm. Scholars have recognized that young people are often alienated from formal political institutions and processes, not least because they are not entitled to vote until reaching the age of majority, and therefore look to other ways to express social and political concerns. Guidikova and Siurala (2001, 9) write that "youth culture scenes often create a quasi-political space of their own, shaped in their own terms." The gathering of young people into a self-conscious collective has been perceived as a way that a disenfranchised group comes together to empower themselves, develop a distinctive group identity, and express critique about their marginalization. Thornton (1997) argues that subculture theory shows how young people resist authority and do not passively accept the culture and roles imposed on them. Subcultures are active, creative, and resistant.

The first major studies of youth subcultures came out of the Chicago School, based in the Sociology and Anthropology Department at the University of Chicago in the United States from the 1920s to the 1950s. Researchers here studied youth on the streets and concluded that young people formed street gangs as a rational response to their deprived social and material circumstances. The street gangs gave them a sense of safety, fun, pride, and location, providing temporary, collective solutions to broader social problems of poverty, disenfranchisement, racism, and marginalization (see for example, Whyte 1943). Some of these ideas about the meanings of subcultures to young people themselves were then developed at the Centre for Contemporary Cultural Studies, known as the CCCS or the Birmingham School, established at Birmingham University, United Kingdom in 1964, but reaching its heyday in the 1970s. Scholars at the CCCS argued not simply that subcultures were a means for marginalized and especially working-class youth to accommodate their social and economic disadvantage, but that they were a way of collectively resisting this situation and enacting class conflict (see Hall and Jefferson

1976). They saw young people's engagement with and undermining of popular culture in the invention of subcultures as a negotiation of class relations and especially resistance to consumer ideology that tried to seduce working-class youth into passive consumption. They argued that subcultures were ways that young people opposed or undermined dominant culture by appropriating or negating its images.

Subculture theory has thus been foundational to work on young people's cultural and political action because it is centered in the notion of resistance and focuses on young people's cultural agency. However, in recent times the concept of resistance has been decoupled from subculture, especially as class has diminished as a key marker of identity for young people. One consequence of deindustrialization and the decline or offshoring of manufacturing has been the splintering and obfuscation of the class structure. Further, as Weinzierl and Muggleton (2003, 14) write, "as … changes wrought by capitalist globalization have intensified, one side effect has been the disappearance of many niches that subcultural-related formations used to occupy for themselves." In other words, spaces for resistance, class-based or not, have also diminished. Critics have also suggested that earlier theorists may have overinterpreted the political meaning or efficacy of subcultural practice in any case. So for example, Nayak (2003, 20) notes that "postmodernist approaches to subculture have asserted that such youth formations are organized as much through commercial enterprise as in 'resistance' to the capitalist economy." Subculture theory, which marked out youth cultures as flamboyant expressions of resistance enacted within clearly demarcated groups, has collapsed under the weight of forces of individualization, the breakdown of class-based identifications, and the emergence of a global, technologized commercial youth market. New ways of thinking about how young people organize socially, express their identities culturally, and engage in consumption and leisure have reflected these changes. Conventional subculture theories of young people's social groupings and cultural affiliations have been displaced in favor of new frameworks of neotribes, lifestyles, scapes, scenes, networks, communities, and citizenships (see Bennett and Kahn-Harris 2004 for an overview).

As Nilan and Feixa (2006, 6) write,

> The idea has been to replace the original "heroic" notion of resistant subcultures with less romantic approaches, originally inspired in part by Bourdieu's concepts of habitus and distinction, by Maffesoli's tribalism, by McRobbie's feminist critique and by Castells' informational theories. These latter-day approaches certainly better reflect the fluidity, variety, and hybridity present in contemporary youth cultures…

Nowadays, subcultures are not perceived simply as singular, fixed categories that youth are affiliated to in order to work out their class identities or to resist dominant culture. Instead, theorists talk about neotribes, youth lifestyles, scenes, new communities, and so on as momentary and changeable expressions of identity. They do not necessarily argue that subcultures are no longer political, but rather they suggest that they are not simple expressions of class politics. As Nayak (2003, 20) writes, "the focus on class at the expense of other 'subordinated' identities can lead to an unabashed celebration of white masculinity." It can also mean that other kinds of political expressions and cultural negotiations that take place within youth cultures are not acknowledged.

For example, Maffesoli's (1996) concept of neotribes denotes the ways in which young people's forms of association have become more transitory, fluid, and inclusive. Neotribes, exemplified by groups of young people involved in club or rave scenes, are not conventionally political because they are not organized around a single resistant identity, and they are not trying to assert themselves against dominant culture in an activist way. However, they do provide a fleeting sense of creative community for the young people involved. For example, Brabazon (2002, 19) sees the rave, and in particular dancing, "as an act of social change, a politics absorbed through the feet" because it brings young people together as an embodied collective. Miles' (2000) concept of lifestyles is another way in which youth culture theorists have tried to explain what has happened to youth subcultures today. He argues that consumption and leisure are where young people now express their creativity, but that this is somewhat problematic. Youth subcultures or lifestyles today are the product of an ongoing process of a negotiation between consumer culture and youth creativity. Young people are constantly negotiating the styles that are sold to them with their capacity to create and produce their own; whether this be music, clothes, or lingo. There is no longer any such thing as the truly "resistant" youth subculture, because youth style and cultures have been appropriated by the consumer industries, depoliticized and packaged back to youth. Others again argue that youth subcultures still remain and are still political forces, although the kind of politics they are about is inevitably filtered through the forces of individualization and consumption that characterize youth identities in late modernity. For example, Guidikova and Siurala (2001) suggest that subcultures today might not be simply "resistant" any more, but they are examples of youth citizenship, in that they represent ways young people can get together and debate social issues, enact alternative social arrangements, and create spaces for alternative transitions and alternative political forums. The suggestion is that as formal politics becomes more alienating to young people, and as consumer industries have taken over their creative resistant expressions such that their spaces for production diminish, they are turning to subculture as a form of new citizenship, if not resistance.

These new ways of thinking about subculture are focused on understanding young people's cultural and political action in changing times. They suggest that some key features of late modern life have brought about a shift from conventional subcultural resistant practice. These include deindustrialization, globalization, the growth of transnational youth culture industries, and the breakdown of old-style protest politics. Although these approaches demonstrate a greater openness to the contemporary complexities of youth cultural action and to a range of young people's identifications beyond class, there remains a gap in terms of young women's gendered experiences and constructions of new subcultural forms. It is necessary to turn to another theoretical tradition in order to center young women in new thinking on youth cultures and resistance. This tradition is feminism.

Feminism and the Third Wave

If subculture theory has been the major paradigm through which youth resistance has been analyzed in the West, feminism has been the key theoretical framework to bring young women into these debates about young people's action for social change. Subculture theory has been widely criticized for excluding the experiences of young women by focusing on publicly visible subcultures populated mainly by young men. Feminist scholars at the CCCS such as McRobbie (2000) and Griffin (1985) highlighted how this approach inevitably positioned girls as insufficiently resistant because they were excluded from public space. At the time of the emergence of subculture theory, young women tended to be marginalized from spectacular public subcultures and instead spent time together at home or engaging in more modest and less confrontational leisure activities. The feminist attention to the domestic realm and the subtle arts of subversion led to closer analyses of the cultural spaces that young women occupy. For example, McRobbie and Garber (1976) argue that the female-dominated teeny bopper culture of the 1970s was an important site of resistance to authoritarian control. During the 1980s, feminist work on young women's agentic use of both popular culture and subculture to negotiate their subordination flourished (see, for example, Griffin 1985; Campbell 1984; Lees 1986; Roman 1988). These studies investigated how young women use and resist dominant ideologies about femininity within their local milieux or how they actively position themselves within masculinist subcultures (for example punk or street gangs). However, by the late 1980s and early 1990s, at the same time that subculture theory was adapting to the late modern conditions that were changing the face of youth cultures, feminism was also shifting to accommodate changes in young women's experiences. In the context of young women's cultural and political action, this was manifested in two significant ways: first, young women emerged as central actors in highly visible subcultures, and second, new ways of doing feminist politics, captured in the umbrella term "third wave," were being claimed by young women themselves. I will discuss each of these developments in turn.

During the late 1980s and early 1990s female-centered youth cultures emerged, most notably female-positive hip hop and riot grrrl and their spinoffs, including the broader grrrlpower movement. Davis (1995, 131) writes that for young women, "Afrocentric racial consciousness and progressive gender politics joined hands in hip hop," and Rose (1990, 114) argues that female rap artists, such as Queen Latifah, MC Lyte, and Salt-N-Pepa, offered "young black women a small but potent culturally-reflexive space" integral to critique and empowerment. Similarly, riot grrrl, with its origins in the U.S. punk scene of the late 1980s and early 1990s, linked feminist ideology with alternative music and a do-it-yourself philosophy. For example, in 1992 the editors of Riot Grrrl zine wrote "we're tired of being written out—out of history, out of the 'scene', out of our bodies ... for this reason we have created our zine and scene ... be proud of being a grrrl..." (Devosby et al. 1992, quoted in Duncombe 2002, 179). In these ways, young women's own gender politics and the space of sub-culture began to coalesce. Whereas previously, feminist scholars had studied young women's cultures looking for covert strategies of resistance, during the 1990s young women actively expressed feminist sensibilities through subcul-tural practice. Alongside female-positive hip hop and riot grrrl, other subcul-tures emerged that, while not explicitly political, did signal that young women were creating their own publicly visible cultures or that more fluid gender sys-tems were being developed within youth cultures. For example, Carlip (1993) documents the emergence of cultures of girl "surfers and sk8rs" in the early 1990s. The rave and club scenes were also notable for their large female mem-berships, emphasis on shared experience and openness to others, and unisex attire. These features have led scholars to argue that such cultures have "recon-figured new modes of feminine and masculine performativity" (Carrington and Wilson 2004, 69; see also Pini 2001). Young women also took a role in claiming a new space for subculture, creative expression and activism: the Internet. Although it is widely noted that Internet knowledge and use is deeply gendered, a huge range of "girls-only" or "girl-friendly" Web sites, e-zines, and chat rooms proliferated in the 1990s, so much so that Takayoshi, Huot and Huot (1999) describe the Internet as a potential "clubhouse for girls."

At the same time that these developments in young women's subcultural activities occurred, feminist analysis of young women's resistance to or nego-tiations of dominant culture has also been advanced by the emergence of so-called third-wave feminism. As with new theorizing about subculture, third-wave feminism seeks to expand notions of resistance. In particular, straightforward ideas of feminist resistance to patriarchal oppression are re-thought by third wavers because gender identity is not experienced by them as a monolithic, categorical, or even primary position (see Walker 1995). This analysis of gender mirrors that of class undertaken by critics and revisionists of subculture theory. Third wavers note that in the late modern Western world, power is dispersed. A fixed dichotomy of dominant versus subordi-nated groups becomes harder to identify because people can occupy a shift-ing range of positions in a power structure owing to their multiple subject positions. At the same time, the traditional state apparatus which had been so much a focus for earlier feminist agitation has been radically altered, from the contraction of the public sphere to the growth of transnational corporate power blocs (Klein, 2001). For these reasons, third wavers argue that feminist concepts and modes of resistance need to expand.

A range of texts that can be identified as "third wave" suggests that young women's cultural and political action is taking on new forms accordingly, although they note that these may be unrecognizable if interpreted through more traditional paradigms of activism. For example, in the introduction to their book on young feminisms, Mitchell, Rundle, and Karaian (2001, 22) state that "we're broadening the sense of what action is." This shift from more straightforward styles of resistance, third wavers argue, has occurred along several axes. First, earlier waves of feminism had already made significant gains for women, necessitating a change in focus for feminism today, for example, from legislative reform or political inclusion to cultural representation, especially as young women have had to grapple with the explosion of the culture industries (see Walker 1995; Heywood and Drake 1997). Third wavers suggest that young women have complex relationships with popular culture that require them to negotiate, infiltrate, play with, and undermine feminine cultural forms rather than simply reject them. Second, the broader trend towards individualization and decollectivization that characterizes late modernity has made the level of the personal rather than the structural a more compelling site of change and traditional social movement activism more difficult to sustain. Budgeon (2001) has described this individual focus as feminist "micropolitics," and Baumgardner and Richards (2000, 48) depict it as simply "living feminist lives." Third, young women's identities have become more fluid, hybrid, and multiple than earlier feminisms could account for, which has made relations of power and therefore resistance more complex, and requires identifications with a series of movements and sites. Walker (1995) argues that young women's feminism can be characterized by its avoidance of simplistic dichotomies in analyzing the oppression of women and its attention to women's ethnic, sexual, and economic diversity. For example, the U.S. young feminist organization Blackgrrrlrevolution encapsulates this in its proclamation that "the pro Black grrrl movement is a queer movement, it is a Marxist movement, it is a social movement, it is a labor movement, it is a civil rights movement, it is a gay rights movement, it is every movement" (Blackgrrrlrevolution quoted in Aapola, Gonick, and Harris 2005, 215). Finally, the third-wave perspective suggests that young women have had to contend with the partial absorption and depoliticization of feminist ideas and images by government, big business, and consumer culture. The concept of "grrrlpower" has been particularly vulnerable to misuses (see Harris 2004). For example, Taft (2005, 69) writes, "by the late 1990s, the discourse of Girl Power had ... been deployed by various elements of popular culture and the mainstream media in a way that constructed a version of girlhood that excludes girls' political selves." Third wavers argue that now that feminism has been at least partially colonized, resistance has to be craftier and more subtle than was previously the case.

Next Wave Cultures

Subculture theory and feminism have been the key theoretical paradigms to take seriously young women's cultural and political critique and action. Each of these frameworks has been challenged in recent times to respond to the conditions of late modernity that have altered the ways young women engage with dominant culture, express themselves and "resist." Once so pivotal, it is this notion of "resistance" in particular that has come under pressure. Maira and Soep (2005, xxxi) note that a too narrow definition of youth resistance, and particularly a focus on dichotomous framing (oppositionality versus appropriation and so on), "can lead to a semantics game of sorting particular actions into very subtle abstract categories, … in the process losing touch with the actual, complex meanings and consequences of these actions in the lives of youth." In order to remain in touch with the complexity of "resistant" action in the late modern context of young people's lives, it is important to attend to the site of culture as a mutable, creative, negotiated space. Duncombe (2002, 5), who interprets culture in this manner as a process, offers a broad definition of cultural resistance as "culture that is used, consciously or unconsciously, effectively or not, to resist and/or change the dominant political, economic, and/or social structure." He argues that this kind of resistance can provide a "free space" for ideas and practices, that it can offer a path into political activity, but that it can also be a political activity in itself. He points out that as culture is generally shared, the work of cultural production is the foundation of community building.

New ways of thinking about youth cultural and political action along these lines have emerged through the post-subculture frameworks of lifestyles, neotribes, scenes, and citizenships and through third-wave feminism. These take a contemporary approach to understanding how current times are engaged with by young women in their emergent cultures and communities. This book contributes to these efforts to interpret how young women are organizing themselves both politically and socially; how they position their identities within new youth cultures; how they conceive of their relationships and networks with other young women in the absence of older style feminist frameworks; and what their experiences can offer for the development of more relevant explanations of youth social and political identities and cultures in a late modern world. It tackles the question of how we might best understand the ways that young women today carve out cultural spaces for connection, community, and identity that move beyond the limits of old-style "resistance," but are still deeply concerned with political and social identifications, connections, and transformations.

The book opens with a section entitled "Hustling, Fighting, Surfing, and Sex: Infiltrating Masculine Domains" that explores the ways that young women negotiate cultural resistance in traditionally masculine spaces or styles. Young women have always existed in male-dominated cultures, but their position today has become more complex. Since the emergence of third-wave feminism and the increased visibility of young women in popular culture, conventionally masculine activities and images have been available to girls in new ways in their identity work. Young women are making their way into youth cultures previously dominated by boys, such as street life, sports, and music. In these sites they are also taking on broader roles than the traditional ones of girlfriend, behind-the-scenes supporter, and onlooker. They are also drawing on and negotiating masculine tropes such as sexual confidence, aggression, and strong physical presence to stake a claim in contemporary youth cultures. At the same time, traditionally feminine concerns such as beauty and care for others and of the self continue to circulate in these sites. The chapters in this section demonstrate how these images and activities are used by young women, at times ironically, to construct identifications with other young women and to generate cultural resistance. They pay particular attention to how young women use and present their bodies and their sexualities to make claims about new forms of feminist and youth politics in the twenty-first century, as well as analyzing how these activities are regulated. In the opening chapter, Angie Colette Beatty analyses the "gangstress" figure in rap culture to show how alternative interpretations of female aggression in rap can highlight young women's agency and resourcefulness. She demonstrates that hustling, as exemplified by the image, language, and behavior of the gang-stress, is a strategy for economic mobility lifted from young women's experience of street survival and played out in the context of the male-dominated entertainment industry. The following chapter, by Dorothy Bottrell, examines how young women's take up of traditionally masculine street culture, including fighting, drinking, and petty crime, can be an important expression of cultural resistance and connection. It illustrates how young women's street cultures can have important social and political meanings of community building and sorority that are often overlooked, especially when regarded through frameworks of problem behavior or "at-risk" youth. Leslie Heywood then considers young women's place in surf culture, arguing that female surfers represent the successful articulation of third-wave feminism in taking up positions beyond gender binarism, in particular by linking beauty culture with physical skill and independent sexuality. However, she also suggests that the image of the female surfer is complicit with neoliberalism and the erasure of structural inequality. In the final chapter in this section, Sara I. McClelland and Michelle Fine consider the extent to which sexual independence has been realized for young women by documenting the new (and old) discourses and spaces that enable and delimit young women's desire. They analyze young women's expressions of sexual wanting and describe cultural practices and research methodologies that facilitate its release.

The second section, entitled "Creating Spaces," looks at the ways and places in which young women construct what has been described as "free spaces" (see Boyte and Evans 1992, quoted in Fine and Weis 1998) for self-expression, connection with others, and cultural resistance. This section highlights the impact of new technologies and new media in facilitating young women's productive cultures. It showcases the opportunities and challenges for young women to use such mechanisms and sites to express themselves, organize, and develop networks and communities. Young women's use of emerging technologies and media can be interpreted as an attempt to create cultures that remain at some remove from the mainstream. The Internet has been a particularly important site for young women to construct unregulated spaces for self-expression and communication with other young people. It is an important resource in bringing young people together who are geographically distant and helping them to organize, interact, and speak out. However, more conventional technologies, for example, face-to-face support groups, can sit alongside media such as camcorders, to facilitate young women in their construction of spaces for empowerment and cultural resistance. The first chapter in this section, by Susan Nussbaum, describes the significance of constructing a safe place for young women with disabilities. She documents the creation of the Empowered Fe Fes: a Chicago-based organization for both support and activism. She discusses the rise of this group and its activities, from group workshops to the production of a film, *Beyond Disability: The Fe Fe Stories*, and suggests that spaces for personal empowerment as well as public sites for recognition are central to young women's feminist disability work. The next chapter, by Amy Dobson, analyses the phenomenon of camgirls: young women who create live streaming Web sites to express themselves. She theorizes the ways that feminine archetypes are employed and exploited by camgirls, and argues that while some of these uses are examples of cultural resistance to norms of femininity, others are more consistent with self-commodification. The final chapter in this section, by Feda Abdo, Rayann Bekdache, Samah Hadid, Mehal Krayem, and Tara Pengilly, the young women editors of the online magazine *Reflections*, describes the importance of young women constructing creative spaces of their own. They describe the purpose and process of the creation of a magazine by young Muslim women for young people of all backgrounds and religions. They argue that both the medium and the message of *Reflections* enables young Muslim women to express themselves, connect with community and develop positive identities for themselves, beyond the imposition of stereotypes and prejudices of mainstream culture.

The last section of the book, entitled "New Activisms: Cultural and Political," looks at young women's involvement in more overt political and cultural activism. As the book as a whole makes a case for the enmeshment of culture and politics for youth, this section highlights the ways that young women both critique and enact activism as both a cultural and political tool. It also considers how young women involved in creative art and politics negotiate the global youth market and its perceived depoliticization of such activities. As discussed, a new challenge for young people today is the complex relationship between cultures of production and the consumer industries. This issue is addressed in the first chapter on young women's music and zine cultures by Kristen Schilt and Elke Zobl. Here, they explore the appropriation of Riot Grrrl politics, as well as the ongoing reverberations of Riot Grrrl into the 2000s as a global feminist force of cultural resistance. They document the rise of feminist art, music, and activist festivals and the importance of these activities in the creation of an international community of young feminists. In the following chapter, Carly Stasko examines creative resistance communities and DIY cultures to consider other new ways young women engage in social action. These include culture jamming, zines, street art, music, and grassroots media literacy work. She argues that it is as a result of the positioning of young women as consumers and the co-option of youth civic engagement that she and others have become involved in new modes of cultural resistance. The next chapter, by Chilla Bulbeck and Anita Harris, analyzes young women's opinions and actions regarding politics and feminism from the perspective of the diminution of sociopolitical structures that support participation for youth. It is a dialogic discussion of the generation debate within feminism that considers new ways to interpret young women's concerns with contemporary politics. The final chapter, by Debi Roker, looks at social action on the part of young British women involved in new groupings and new movements for social change. She argues that the youth citizenship debate in Britain (that resonates globally) is limited by its failure to engage with young people, and especially young women, who participate in social action.

This book contributes to new ways of thinking about youth cultures and subcultures, feminism and gender politics, activism and social and political engagements. It asks, what are the cultures that young women are creating and engaging in, how do these cultures articulate young women's contemporary strategies for connection and social action, and do these cultures express the next wave of (feminist) organization and politics? Duncombe (2002, 7) notes that "the first act of politics is simply to act." This book identifies how young women act now to create next wave cultures.

References

Aapola, S., M. Gonick, and A. Harris. 2005. *Young femininity: Girlhood, power and social change*. London: Palgrave.

Baumgardner, J. and A. Richards. 2000. *Manifesta: Young women, feminism and the future*. New York: Farrar, Straus and Giroux.

Beck, U. 1992. *Risk society: Towards a new modernity.* London: Sage.

Bennett, A. and K. Kahn-Harris. 2004. Introduction. In *After subculture: Critical studies in contemporary youth culture,* ed. Andy Bennett and Keith Kahn-Harris, 1–18. London: Palgrave.

Brabazon, T. 2002. Dancing through the revolution. *Youth Studies Australia* 21(1):19–24.

Budgeon, S. 2001. Emergent feminist (?) identities: Young women and the practice of micropolitics. *European Journal of Women's Studies* 8(1):7–28.

Bulbeck, C. 2006. Explaining the generation debate: Envy, history or feminism's victories? *Lilith* 15:35–47.

Campbell, A. 1984. *The girls in the gang.* Oxford: Blackwell.

Carlip, H. 1995. *Girlpower: Young women speak out.* New York: Warner Books.

Carrington, B. and B. Wilson. 2004. Dance nations: Rethinking youth subcultural theory. In *After subculture: Critical studies in contemporary youth culture,* ed. Andy Bennett and Keith Kahn-Harris, 65–78. London: Palgrave.

Davis, E. 1995. Sexism and the art of feminist hip-hop maintenance. In *To be real,* ed. Rebecca Walker, 127–142. New York: Anchor.

Duncombe, S. 2002. Introduction. In *Cultural resistance reader,* ed. Stephen Duncombe, 127–142. London: Verso.

Fine, M. and L. Weis. 1998. *The unknown city: Lives of poor and working-class young adults,* 127–142. Boston: Beacon Press.

Furlong, A. and F. Cartmel. 1997. *Young people and social change: Individualisation and risk in late modernity.* Buckingham: Open University Press.

Giddens, A. 1991. *Modernity and self-identity.* Cambridge: Polity Press.

Griffin, C. 1985. *Typical girls.* London: Routledge and Kegan Paul.

Guidikova, I. and L. Siurala. 2001. Introduction: A weird, wired, winsome generation: Across contemporary discourses on subculture and citizenship. In *Transitions of youth citizenship in Europe,* ed. Andy Furlong and Irena Guidikova, 5–16. Strasbourg: Council of Europe.

Hall, S. and T. Jefferson, eds. 1976. *Resistance through rituals.* London: Hutchinson.

Harris, A. 2001. Riding my own tidal wave: Young women's feminist work. *Canadian Women's Studies Journal.* Special issue: *Young women: Feminist, activists, grrrls* 20/21(4/1):27–31.

Harris, A. 2004. *Future girl: Young women in the twenty-first century.* New York: Routledge.

Heywood, L. and J. Drake, eds. 1997. *Third wave agenda.* Minneapolis: University of Minnesota Press.

Klein, N. 2001. *No logo.* London: Flamingo.

Lees, S. 1986. *Losing out: Sexuality and adolescent girls.* London: Hutchinson.

Maffesoli, M. 1996. *The time of the tribes: The decline of individualism in mass society.* London: Sage.

Maira, S. and E. Soep. 2005. Introduction. In *Youthscapes: The popular, the national, the global,* ed. Sunaina Maira and Elisabeth Soep, xv–xxxv. Philadelphia: University of Pennsylvania Press.

Manning, B. and R. Ryan. 2004. *Youth and citizenship.* Canberra: National Youth Affairs Research Scheme.

McRobbie, A. 2000. *Feminism and youth culture.* London: Macmillan.

McRobbie, A. and J. Garber. 1976. Girls and subcultures. In *Resistance through rituals*, ed. Stuart Hall and Tony Jefferson, 209–222. London: Hutchinson.

Miles, S. 2000. *Youth lifestyles in a changing world*. Buckingham: Open University Press.

Mitchell, A., L. B. Rundle, and L. Karaian. 2001. Introduction: A conversation with Allyson, Lisa and Lara. In *Turbo chicks*, ed. Allyson Mitchell, Lisa Bryn Rundle, and Lara Karaian, 11–26. Toronto: Sumach Press.

Nayak, A. 2003. *Race, place and globalization: Youth cultures in a changing world*. Oxford: Berg.

Nilan, P. and C. Feixa. 2006. Introduction: Youth hybridity and plural worlds. In *Global youth? Hybrid identities, plural worlds*, ed. by Pam Nilan and Carles Feixa, 1–13. Abingdon, UK: Routledge.

Pini, M. 2001. *Clubcultures and female subjectivity: The move from home to house*. New York: Palgrave.

Roman, L. G. 1988. Intimacy, labor and class: Ideologies of feminine sexuality in the punk slam dance. In *Becoming feminine: The politics of popular culture*, ed. Leslie G. Roman and Linda K. Christian-Smith with Elizabeth Ellsworth, 143–184. East Sussex: Falmer Press.

Rose, T. 1990. Never trust a big butt and a smile. *Camera Obscura* 23 (May):109–131.

Taft, J. 2005. Girl power politics: Pop-culture barriers and organizational resistance. In *All about the girl: Culture, power and identity*, ed. Anita Harris, xx-xx. New York: Routledge.

Takayoshi, P., E. Huot, and M. Huot. 1999. No boys allowed: The World Wide Web as a clubhouse for girls. *Computers and Consumption* 16:89–106.

Thornton, S. 1997. General introduction. In *The subcultures reader*, ed. Ken Gelder and Sara Thornton, 1–10. London: Routledge.

Walker, R. 1995. Being real: An introduction. In *To be real: Telling the truth and changing the face of feminism*, ed. Rebecca Walker, xxix–xi. New York: Anchor.

Weinzierl, R. and D. Muggleton. 2003. What is "post-subcultural studies" anyway? In *The post-subcultures reader*, ed. David Muggleton and Rupert Weinzierl, 3–26. Oxford: Berg.

Whyte, W. F. 1943. *Street corner society: The social structure of an Italian slum*. Chicago: University of Chicago Press.

Part I
Hustling, Fighting, Surfing, and Sex: Infiltrating Masculine Domains

1

What Is This Gangstressism
in Popular Culture?

ANGIE COLETTE BEATTY

In 1992, Stuart Hall posed the question, "What is this 'black' in black popular culture?" (1996, 465). More than one decade later—amidst head-locking identity politics, postfeminist powergrrrl puffery, and an ambiguous "keepin' it real" credo; amidst the fallout from yet another explosion of Black panache in entertainment media; and amidst the continued struggle for cultural hegemony, which according to Hall, is "waged as much in popular culture as anywhere else" (1996, 468)—I pose a similar question. What is this gangstressism in popular culture?

Previous studies (Bost 2001; Emerson 2002; Keyes 2002, chap. 7; Roberts 1991; Rose 1994, chap. 5; Skeggs 1993) have primarily focused on the sexual politics of female rappers while minimally attending to their uses of violence and aggression as agency, if at all. This is both understandable and warranted given the history of Black female sexual oppression in America and its accompanying sexualized media images of Black women and girls (Bobo 1995, chap. 1; Crenshaw 1993, chap. 5; Harris 1996, chap. 1; hooks 1992, chap. 4; James 1999, chap. 6; Keyes 1993, 203–220; Projansky 2001, chap. 5; Rose 1994, 152; Wyatt 1997, chap. 2; Young 2001, chap. 15). However, because Black women, and women in general, are recipients of violence far more often than they are perpetrators, it is important to explore and make meaning of the rage of contemporary female rappers in ways that parallel analyses of male gangsta rappers and their artistic discourse.

Thus, the aim of this chapter is to investigate the commercial rise of the hip hop gangstress,[1] particularly the gangstress emcee (rapper)—a figure who represents an otherwise socially hidden subgroup of women and girls. Because female gangstaism in hip hop is an understudied phenomenon, this chapter opens by briefly outlining the ways in which both academic and popular writings have characterized, and oftentimes mischaracterized, female gangsta rappers and their discourse when they are recognized at all. I then introduce a framework of gangstressism, which centers the female voices of both street hustlers and commercially successful gangstress rappers, with a focus on hustling as a strategy for economic mobility. In doing so, I make a case for a hip hop feminist epistemology to investigate the subjugated thought and behavior of young Black women that simultaneously addresses gender, race/ethnicity, sexuality, class, culture, and historical context.

Constructions of Gangstaism in Popular and Academic Writings

Prior to the mid-1990s, female rap discourse was characterized by gender and race conscious voices of artists whom scholar Tricia Rose describes as "politically correct underdogs" (1994, 147), and who many hip hop fans endearingly refer to as "strong Black women." These artists include Roxanne Shanté, Salt-N-Pepa, MC Lyte, Queen Latifah, Monie Love, Yo-Yo, Ms. Melody, and Harmony (Rose 1994, chap. 5). Also popular during that time is what ethnomusicologist Cheryl Keyes (2002, 189–194) identifies as the "Queen Mother" style or category of female rappers. Considerably overlapping with the feminist category, Queen Mothers include Queen Kenya of hip hop's Zulu Nation (the first women to adopt the Queen qualifier, but not to record under it), Queen Latifah, Sister Souljah, Harmony,[2] Yo-Yo, Nefertiti, Isis, and Queen Mother Rage. Adorning their bodies with African headdresses, hairstyles, cloth, and jewelry, Keyes asserts that these artists may be aware of the historical significance of African queens. Additionally, she argues that, "Their rhymes embrace black female empowerment and spirituality, making clear their self-identification as African, woman, warrior, priestess, and queen. Queen Mothers demand respect not only for their people but for black women by men" (2002, 189–190).

Although the conscious-style discourse remained popular for both men and women in the early 1990s, so-called gangsta rap (or reality rap as it sometimes called), became popular, first on America's West coast in the late-1980s, and later grabbed a mainstream toehold by the early 1990s (George 1998, 42–44; Rose 1994, 58–59). Because this genre of rap is predominated by young African American men and characterized by violence, nihilism, hypersexuality, materialism, leisure drug use, misogyny, homophobia, and occasional race/class political protest, unsurprisingly, male gangsta rappers have become the primary subjects of debate in political arenas, the popular press, and academic inquiry.

In mainstream rhetoric, such inquiry has often functioned to confirm stereotypical beliefs about Black men and Black people in general, and to justify racially and class-based discriminatory practices (Binder 1993; Fried 1996; Lusane 1993; Rose 1994, 124–145). For example, in 1995, Bob Dole attacked the film and music industries for insinuating "nightmares of depravity" (Lacayo 1995, 26) into America's dreams. Particularly, he singled out rap music and media giant Time Warner, which had previously distributed the controversial song "Cop Killer."[3] One day following Dole's speech, former Education Secretary and drug czar William Bennett contacted Time Warner board members requesting that the company cease distribution of rap music that contains offensive lyrics (Lacayo 1995). Moreover, although "Cop Killer," which Ice-T's speed metal band Body Count recorded, was clearly a metal or even a hard rock song, mainstream discourse, nonetheless, referred to it as gangsta rap and used it as a weapon against rap music in general (Rose 1994, 130, 183).

Unsurprisingly, members of the hip hop community have fired back against this race and class bias to provide more accurate depictions of hip hop culture. However, these writings, most of which are male-authored, depict not only gangsta rap, but also rap music in general, as Black male and heterosexual (Rose 1994, 152; McLaren 1995). Moreover, when these writings (LaGrone 2000; Pinn 1999; Quinn 1996; Ro 1996; George 1998, 184–186) do not completely erase women artists from gangsta rap history or reduce them to their sexuality, they often sideline them in a revisionist male narrative in a variety of ways.

Noteworthy is Clarence Lusane's (1993) acknowledgment of the substantive nature of some gangstress protest. Nevertheless, he appears somewhat intolerant of their approach. He writes, "While addressing important themes such as date rape and adultery, their solutions, more often than not, are to just blow the suckers away. The bottom line is that women should act as doggish and reactionary as men" (41). This is in contrast, however, with Lusane's perspective on male gangstaism. He asserts,

> It's a pedagogy necessitated by the abandonment of black youth by the nation's political institutions and leaders of all colors. As Kelley notes, rap reflects and projects "the lessons of lived experiences (1992, 796)." One does not have to agree with the rantings and rage of Ice-T, Sister Souljah or other rappers to unite with their sense of isolation, anger, and refusal to go down quietly. Ignored and dissed by both major political parties and much of what passes for national black leadership, is it any wonder that Ice Cube reflects the views of so many youth. (Lusane 1993, 38)

What is most interesting here is Lusane's inclusion of Sister Souljah among various male gangsta rappers (including NWA, Geto Boys, and MC Ren), whom he admits are notoriously misogynist. Although the hip hop community regards Souljah as a woman who advocates for justice and respect for Black people, generally, as Patricia Collins (2000) notes, both Sister Souljah's music and autobiography have been "dismissed within feminist classrooms in academia as being 'nonfeminist'" (p. 16) because of Souljah's failure to critique Black patriarchy, particularly within Black nationalist ideology and practice. Also key is the fact that Lusane aligns male gangsta rappers with politics and leadership, whereas he associates gangstress rappers with themes. Consequently, women's stories are devalued, as he does not deem these artists as political.

While I concur that the extreme approaches taken by both male and female gangsta rappers to address various social issues and inequalities, although sometimes necessary, are often fraught with problems, my point is that analyses that recognize only the protest of "positive" or "strong" women as legitimate, function to penalize women who transgress gender norms. Moreover, as women's studies scholar Gwendolyn Pough (2004) argues, these types of representations of Black womanhood "help remix the classic Madonna/whore split" (p. 93). Consequently, the pain, sense of isolation, and anger that many poor urban women of color experience are denied.

Feminist Perspectives on Gangstressism

Analyses of gangstress rappers and their artistic discourse, as well as serious acknowledgment of their pain and anger as young Black lower-class females, remain conspicuously marginalized not only in the popular press, but also in academic literature. Nonetheless, a small but developing body of feminist and women-authored works provides the basis for a gangstress framework. Either through textual analysis of women's hip hop music (Bost 2001; Skeggs 1993) and their music videos (Emerson 2002; Shelton, 1997), or through ethnographic and historiographic methods (Keyes 1993, 203–220, 2000, 2002, chap. 7; Rose 1994, chap. 5), these authors convincingly argue that gangstress emcees are far more than pale imitators of male rappers. Says Keyes (2002), who categorizes gangstresses as "Sistas with Attitude,"[4] these female emcees

> value attitude as a means of empowerment and present themselves accordingly. Many of these sistas have reclaimed the word "bitch," viewing it as positive rather than negative and using the title to entertain or provide cathartic release. … As an "aggressive woman who challenges male authority" … the Sista with Attitude revises the standard definition of "bitch" to mean an aggressive or assertive female who subverts patriarchal rule. … Because the element of signifying is aesthetically appealing in this style of rap, these terms may have both negative and positive meanings, depending on the context. (200)

Similar to Keyes, regarding the ways gangstresses resist dominant ideologies, Shelton adds that female gangstas subvert the traits of the nuclear family structure. She argues that their "lyrics and video narratives represent women bearing children without the sanction of marriage in order to debunk the negative mythos surrounding single African American mothers" (1997).

Regarding gangstresses' violent approaches or "revenge fantasies" for countering sexism, like Rose (1994, 174–175), Beverley Skeggs (1993) offers that although such approaches may not be ideal, they might give men who believe they have unconditional access to women pause. Additionally, she argues:

> By using masculine subject positions and using the techniques of masculinity, the female rappers expose the unequal gendered access to power and the concomitant process that normalizes inequality. Just as

Ice T uses his music to "threaten" the police into accountability, BWP etc. use their music to make men equally accountable. (317)

Although these works make important contributions regarding the ways in which gangstresses negotiate their identities in a predominantly Black masculine space within a larger predominantly White and male space, most of them either focus on earlier gangstress rappers or briefly attend to them, while focusing on "feminist" rappers (such as Queen Latifah) who were more popular during the mid-1980s to early 1990s. This is an important point because, although the gangstressism of earlier (such as H.W.A. and BWP) and later rappers (such as Lil' Kim and Foxy Brown) do not necessarily diverge thematically, the meaning of their music, as a function of the increasing commodification of gangsta rap specifically and of hip hop music and culture in general, necessarily changes. Additionally, a consideration of the role of commercialism in gangstressism (as well as gangsta rap in general) serves to question the utility of gangstress practice as a strategy to attain and sustain success in the music and broader entertainment industries. These points are most intriguing to me because, not only has gangstress rap displaced so-called conscious or political discourse, but also the latter has virtually disappeared in commercial rap music, situating artists who self-identify as gangsta bitches as unchallenged voices of young Black womanhood (Dodd 2001; Morgan 1997). As writer Joan Morgan (1997) notes in an *Essence* magazine article, entitled "The Bad Girls of Hip Hop,"

> It would have been easier if the honors had gone to Lyte, Latifah, Salt-N-Pepa or Yo Yo. Then we could have waxed eloquent about Afro-feminine regality, refined sensuality and womanist strengths. But it didn't go down like that. The history makers were DaBrat, the first female rapper to have her premier album go platinum, and Foxy Brown and Lil' Kim, both of whom debuted at the top of the Billboard chart—sistas with the lyrical personas of stay-high juvenile delinquents and hypersexed (albeit couture-clad) hoochie mamas. And while I hardly consider this a feminist victory, the success of these baby girls speaks volumes about the myths shrouding feminism, sex and Black female identity. (77)

Recognizing this commercial shift or changing of the guard between feminist/womanist- and gangstress-oriented discourse, the latter of which was marginalized in rap music prior to this time, Morgan addresses key questions in the debate regarding the utility, meaning, and consequences of gangstress practice for public consumption. Regardless of whether one identifies as feminist, womanist, or otherwise, concern regarding the encroaching ramifications in one's daily life, such as how one will be treated by men and boys at a social event, while walking down the street or in a shopping mall, or during a job interview, is understandable. It is no surprise then, that many women and girls, especially Black women and girls (perhaps more privately than publicly), receive this newer Teflon-veneered[5] female face of rap with mixed emotions (Keyes 2002, 200).

"This Is All To Come Up": Hustling as a Strategy for Economic Mobility

A Hip Hop Feminist Epistemology

Because hip hop gangstressism remains largely unexplored in academic writings, *Gangstresses* (Pitts and Davis 2000), a raw and uncensored 90-minute video documentary heavily informs the framework I develop here. Filmed over the course of a two-year period, the documentary chronicles the lives of poor urban young Black women and girls who have resorted to unconventional means of survival. Interviewing more than fifty women, director Harry Davis traveled to various densely African American populated urban areas across the United States, such as Detroit, Chicago, and Brooklyn. The women range from commercially successful hip hop artists such as Mary J. Blige and Lil' Kim, to underground emcees[6] and adult film entertainers. Additionally, hip hop mogul Russell Simmons and male emcees such as Tupac Shakur provide brief commentary.

Aside from *Gangstresses'* focus on women who struggle to survive in inner-city America, rather than on celebrities, another noteworthy feature is its distinct representation of women of the hip hop generation. Writer Bakari Kitwana (2002, xiii) establishes the birth years 1965 to 1984 as the defining range for this cohort and explains that he coined the term hip hop generation to distinguish Black youth and their unique experiences from White youth who primarily comprise generation X.

As some hip hop critics (jamila 2002, 383–386; Kitwana 2002, 12–24) note, this generation of African Americans is the first to come of age in an era of globalization, increasing technology, and desegregation, while also experiencing de facto segregation "in an America that preaches democracy and inclusion" (Kitwana 2002, 13). However, regarding women hip hop generationers, their status as both Black and female distinguishes them, in different ways, from both Black men and White women.

With respect to White women and the largely undefined but developing third-wave feminism, many women hip hop generationers are reluctant to claim the third-wave label, not because they reject or fear feminism as an ideology, but because they are uncomfortable with its inattention to "historical context and community imperatives" (Springer 2002, 1060). According to Springer, although useful for internal critique, "the wave model perpetuates the exclusion of women of color from women's movement history and feminist theorizing" (p. 1063). For example, in Helene Shugart's (2001) analysis of the intersection of third-wave feminism and generation X, she argues that "the point at which Generation X and third-wave feminism clearly diverge—

dramatically, in fact—is on the issue of multiculturalism. One of the defining features of third-wave feminism is its explicit inclusion of members of various races and ethnicities" (p. 161). In fact, Shugart goes so far as to note the criticisms of various hip hop generationers who dismiss generation X culture based on its hypocrisy and empty claims of multiculturalism. However, when determining her sample of contemporary female popular culture personas who represent generation X, Shugart limits her selection to four White women— Alanis Morisette, Courtney Love, Winona Ryder, and Janeane Garafola. But what about Queen Latifah, Jada Pinkett, Lauryn Hill, Missy Elliott, Mary J. Blige, Lil' Kim, Eve, Brandy, and Venus and Serena Williams?

Although Shugart concludes that the third wave appears to be more of a feminist subculture of generation X, she maintains that "the fact that feminism is forging a niche in the mainstream at all is notable" (p. 165), a conclusion that, given the narrow focus of Shugart's analysis, with respect to race and culture, becomes untenable. Consequently, analyses such as this, which in no way represent an anomaly, underscore the need for a hip hop feminist epistemology—a way of investigating the subjugated thought and behavior of young Black women and girls that simultaneously addresses gender, race/ ethnicity, sexuality, class, culture, and historical context. Most popularized by journalists and activists such as Joan Morgan, dream hampton, and Eisa Davis, and later advanced by academics such as Gwendolyn Pough and Kimberly Springer,[7] these women and many more boldly identify as hip hop feminists (Pough 2002). Argues hip hop feminist/activist/educator shani jamila (2002), it is necessary to acknowledge the significant roots of Black feminism. However, she argues, in order for any social movement to realize its maximum potential, it must be "applicable to the times" and hip hop feminists must write their own culturally and historically specific stories. She continues,

> It seems obvious to me, however, that just as the shape of what we're fighting has changed, we need to examine how we as a community of activists have changed as well. Hip hop is the dominant influence on our generation. …Those of us who embrace feminism can't act like hip hop hasn't been an influence on our lives, or vice versa, simply because claiming them both might seem to pose a contradiction. They are two of the basic things that mold us. However, we must not confuse having love for either one with blind defense. We have to love them enough to critique both of them and challenge them to grow. (391–392)

Thus, the present framework employs a hip hop feminist epistemology by centering the voices of self-identified gangstresses among other members of the Black female interpretive community. Additionally, it grounds gangstress practice in the political, social, and economic realities for women and girls of the hip hop generation. Consequently, it extends Patricia Collins' (2000, 251–271) concept of a Black feminist epistemology because it makes feminism more inclusive of and accessible to women and girls beyond elite Black spaces, such as educational institutions, government, and the media.

With respect to the documentary *Gangstresses*, it is truly a valuable resource. However, because it heavily informed the present framework, it is important to acknowledge the inherent biases of the film that necessarily accompany any project or research endeavor. For example, no information is available regarding sample selection—why particular women were interviewed, or why others may have declined to participate. Nor is the viewer privy to information regarding the editing process. Moreover, the viewer can only ponder the ways in which the product might differ if the director was a woman. With this in mind, the documentary is necessarily supplemented with print media coverage of female rappers who self-identify as gangstresses. Additionally, I draw from criminology literature on girls and gangs, particularly the less traversed area of Black female gang participation, for comparison of these two cultures.

Therefore, based on these collective sources, I have defined gangstress as a self-descriptive label that some girls and women use to denote an unabashed ability to survive in a racist, classist, and (hetero)sexist world using any means at their disposal (Pitts and Davis 2000). The culture is particularly hedonistic and marked by violence, the latter of which necessarily accompanies participation in such illegal hustles as prostitution, boosting (shoplifting), credit fraud, drug trafficking, and armed robbery.

Additionally, this high volume of violence reflects their vulnerability as women and girls, which statistics about female victimization show. According to the Rape, Abuse and Incest National Network (n.d.), seven of eight victims are female, and although 65 percent of all victims are White (substantially less than their 83.3 percent racial proportion of the U.S. population), Blacks are more likely to be attacked—disproportionately comprising 30 percent of all victims, compared to their comprising 12.5 percent of the population (Rennison and Rand 2003). Moreover, people who earn less than $15,000 per year are 2–3 times more likely than higher income people to be sexually assaulted (U.S. Census Bureau 2006, table 311), urban residents are more vulnerable than suburban and rural residents (Rennison and Rand 2003), and homeless women are at greater risk than women who live in sheltered living spaces (Wenzel, Leake, and Gelberg 2001).

Regarding gangstresses specifically, women and girls who deal drugs on the street (as opposed to rock houses, which afford more security), are vulnerable to customers of varying mental states, as well as rival gangs who sometimes engage in hostile takeovers (Lauderback, Hansen, and Waldorf 1992). Even further, nonindependent female gang members often experience nondiscriminatory violence, such as drive-bys, because of their affiliation with a male gang (Laidler and Hunt 1997). Thus, similar to Springer's (2001) discussion of the albeit problematic utility of the Sapphire model for Black girls and women in general, criminologists Laidler and Hunt remark,

At one level, female gang members' "in your face" aggressive posturing is an attempt to "look bad", (as opposed to "being bad"), and is part of an overall protective strategy to the dangers of a highly masculinized street environment (Campbell 1984; Maher 1997). The girls' participation in violence is an expression of youth resistance as well as a power struggle among a group who are constrained by their race, class and gender (Messerschimdt 1997). (2001, 670–671)

Although these women and girls partake in various illegal activities, many of them also pursue dreams of attaining success in the fashion and entertainment industries—particularly, rapping, singing, and modeling (Pitts and Davis 2000). However, although they may actually lead a gangstress lifestyle, women who aspire to achieve mainstream success partake in illegal activities minimally, if at all, as full-fledged participation in such a lifestyle is incompatible with success in the entertainment industry. Regarding rap music, specifically, successful women rappers such as Lil' Kim, Mia X, and Queen Pen are testaments to this realization. For example, following a series of violent confrontations with her father, a much younger Lil' Kim stabbed her father (not fatally), and then survived on the streets by transporting drugs out-of-state and what she describes as "just doing what I had to do" (Gonzales 1997, 64). As a runaway, Kim also experienced a frighteningly close call when she was stopped and searched at an airport while transporting someone else's illegal proceeds (Siegmund-Cuda 2002). Similarly, Mia X admits that her drug stint began at age nineteen when, after observing a relative, she realized that she could cook rock cocaine "almost better than anybody who had been doin' that for years" (Alvarez 1998/1999, 126). Lastly, Queen Pen, on the other hand, who has been in the streets since the age of sixteen and a half, remains vague about her hustling strategies. She simply remarks that she has seen and done many things. However, more reflectively, and in a similar fashion as underground rapper BonnieClyde (Pitts and Davis 2000), Pen adds,

> I could sit at a roundtable with any female artist and pull out credentials and cards on the table and half of them ... it's just that a lot of times a lot of females allow the domination of hip-hop to get to us so much that you feel like this is what you gotta talk about but how could you talk about something that you don't know nothing about. (Thompson 2001, 45)

As scholar Cheryl Kirk-Duggan (1997) notes, the explosion of hip hop culture has afforded female gang members a much more public persona. This is partly attributable to the fact that hip hop, particularly rap, has demonstrated itself to be not only a viable alternative to poverty and danger on the streets, for those who possess the talent, but also an extremely visible and attractive option. Conversely, as Pen and BonnieClyde allude, gang culture and various hustling lifestyles have not only become more visible, but also extremely attractive. Consequently, many young women who are far removed from such environments romanticize them, and when given the opportunity to record music (similar to young men), are more likely to become studio gangstas.

Therefore, in light of the intertwinement of hip hop and gang culture, it is surprising that research on women and hip hop has not explored the bidirectional influence of these two worlds, particularly between music and film, and female gang or other criminal activity. Thus, to help bridge this gap in the literature, the present framework grounds performatory hip hop gangstressism in both working- and non-working-class subcultures that are specific to hip hop generation street gangstresses (who may or may not be affiliated with an organized network) and Black female "homegirls" (gang members). Because female rappers are often marginalized both in and beyond the rap music industry, this initial step allows for recognition of their social positioning as a factor that influences the nature of their protest in both the streets and the studio. I recognize that not all hip hop gangstressism emanates from experiences that are associated with socioeconomic disadvantage, and that similar to some male rappers, some women appropriate this image to boost their careers.

However, because the current framework names the hip hop music industry as a site for economic mobility, I argue that authenticity is irrelevant because agency, generally, is a struggle that cuts across class lines for women and girls in the male-dominated industry. Thus, a hip hop music gangstress may be either a woman or girl who actually lived such a lifestyle, such as Lil' Kim, or someone who has seized the opportunity to gain economic and social capital via a gangstress ethos. Lastly, regardless of one's reasons for practicing gangstressism, for better or worse, it frequently engenders success. Therefore, similar to socially disadvantaged women and girls who hustle drugs, their bodies, and/or "hot" (stolen) goods to survive, many female emcees recognize the rap profession as a legitimate hustle—a means of survival and success.

A Definition of Hustling

As several authors (Carmichael 1975; Shaw 1982; Valentine 1978; Wacquant 1998) note, hustling subsumes a wide range of activities that are generally disapproved of by law enforcement and the middle and upper classes. Many of these activities require "mastery of a particular type of symbolic capital" (Wacquant 1998, 3) such as the ability to manipulate others, chicanery, cajolement, and violence if necessary. Such activities range from the relatively innocuous, such as betting on games of chance, to felonious property crimes, such as stripping and stealing unoccupied cars. However, most people affiliate hustling with violent crime, such as carjacking, drug trafficking, racketeering, and pimping. Consequently, many people, including some scholars (Carmichael 1975; Wacquant 1998), gender hustling as a male activity.

Regarding women and hustling, research (Fishman 1999, 76–82; Laidler and Hunt 2001; Pitts and Davis 2000; Valentine 1978, 130–131) suggests that women are acutely aware of the gendered nature of the streets, and therefore, consider the risks of physical harm and arrest, as well as their own notions of femininity when determining their hustling strategies. Such strategies include targeting other women who are less likely to fight back, using sex to manipulate men, working with male accomplices, and engaging in "gender-appropriate" and less violent crime, such as prostitution, buying and selling stolen goods, hosting card parties, and selling marijuana (as opposed to harder drugs, such as cocaine).

However, regarding Black women and girls, specifically, several criminologists (as cited in Fishman 1999, 83–84 and Laidler and Hunt 2001) argue that "distinctive socialization" is a critical factor in determining the nature of their criminal and delinquent activity. According to this theory, both lower-class Black girls and boys, unlike their White counterparts, have been socialized to be more assertive, independent, and to take risks in order to effectively function within the constraints of limited resources and consequential increased risk of victimization. The reader should note that in low-income communities of color particularly, women and girls regularly face direct threats to their survival not only in the form of physical violence, but also indirectly via economic violence.

The term economic violence is frequently utilized to describe the economic consequences of Western imperialism in developing nations (Meyerstein 2003; Orogun 2004) and international women's human rights (Merry 2003), but generally refers to structural inequalities that function to strangle marginalized peoples and maintain the social hierarchy (Fullilove et al. 1998, 925). Thus, economic violence is not necessarily a violent means itself, but rather refers to political outcomes that indirectly lead to violent ends. For example, American feminist scholars and activists have argued that welfare reform is a type of economic violence, which often leaves battered women with no alternatives other than to return to abusive partners or try to survive on the streets. In this context, hustling, whether it involves drugs, theft, or sex-industry work, and despite the inherent dangers of such a lifestyle, offers some degree of agency and autonomy. As Laura Fishman notes, these

> hustling techniques are learned and shared as a way for gang girls to put a few dollars in their pockets. The need to hustle is accepted as legitimate, as necessary to survive. ...Whether or not they are on the streets or in their homes, black women and girls generally are not safe. To survive, they must be constantly alert to male assaultive behavior in such forms as rape, battering, physical assault, and robbery. In response to the unsafe environment, Brooks ... observes that the Black woman must be socialized to defend herself, her family, and her hard-earned property against aggression because she is not likely to receive protection from anyone, including the police. (1999, 68)

Thus, Black women and girls demonstrate greater role flexibility—such as partaking in traditionally "male" activities and crime—out of necessity because of their social positioning. Consider, for example, the differing philosophies and hustling strategies of three women from *Gangstresses*:

> It's funny, you know what I'm sayin', 'cause a lotta squares don't understand the real deal ... squares meanin', people outside of pimpin' and hoein'. Don't understand ... what this is all for. This is all to come up. This is all to stack your money to own your own businesses after everything is over. ... I don't plan on being a hoe all my life. But as soon as I stack all my money, you best believe I'm investin' it in somethin' that's gonna ... help me out and my kids—for when they are born and once they get older. By that time, I'll have everything situated. They won't have to look for ... no job. ... They can just go to school [and] get they education. Soon as they get out ... they got them a business sittin' right here 'cause momma own it. I'll sell my pussy! Sorry to say that if any young viewers [are listening] ... I will sell my pussy and get out on the block before I become homeless. (Pitts and Davis 2000, "Pumpkin")

Consistent with previous findings on female offenders, Pumpkin, who also sells drugs, is aware that prostitution will provide a steady income with little overhead costs. Additionally, the reader should note that like most women who prostitute, Pumpkin is not a nymphomaniac, but rather, views sex as a means to an economic end. Similarly, although Lil' Kim maintains that she was never a prostitute, she admits nevertheless that, "Sometimes, if I thought I could get more out of a guy, I'd sleep with him. And I got kinda caught in that mentality" (Marriott 2000, 130). These views, however, are in stark contrast to that of Mama Mayhem, who wishes to minimize her risk of injury and arrest by primarily enterprising in the sale of hot merchandise (indicated in testimony not shown here). Additionally, she seems vexed by the sexual exploitation of women on the streets. She exclaims,

> I don't want my kids out there wantin' and askin' nobody for nuthin'. Anytime they want it, you come and see Mom-dukes. Okay? I will get it fuh you. Fuck that nigga ... that pimp ... that crack dealer on the street. Mommy gotchu, straight like that. All o' that otha stuff that they be sayin' ... I don't wanna hear nuthin' about that, but if you comin' at me wit some straight legit way that we can make some money and we don't hafta shake our asses and I don't hafta give up no cuts [sex], then I'm rollin' witchu all day and all fuckin' night. Whateva you need to be done, we gon do it ... so that we can make this dough, straight like that, 'cause I love money and I know that money loves me 'cause when I got it, I shows it love, also ... When I eat, ev'rybody around me eat. You understand what I'm sayin'? That's what bein' a gangstress is all about. (Pitts and Davis 2000, "Mama Mayhem")

Unlike Mayhem who opts for more safety, Shaka Don, who made a cameo appearance in Kim's "No Time" (1996) video, and according to photographs appears to have been friendly with both Lil' Kim and Mary J. Blige (at least, earlier in their careers), seems unfazed by the danger of the gendered streets. True to her surname, the Don,[8] who dons a fur coat and matching fedora, reflects on being "setup" by insiders and brutally beaten by adversaries who wanted "the money" (indicated in testimony not included here) and vows revenge. While nursing a gun in her lap, to which she refers as "the Blickey," she avers,

> I'm independent. I'll do … what a nigga'll do to live and survive and make money out here on these streets. That's me. I don't depend on no man. But I don't depend on nobody. I don't ask nobody to do nuthin' for me. I do what I gotta do for myself. And I will continue to do that until I get where I wanna be in life. I got the Roley [watch] on … I got a lil' 8-carat ring on. It was a gift to myself. … For all muthafuckas that be frontin' on the Don, [I] keep the Blickey. (Pitts and Davis 2000, "Shaka-Don")

Similar to street gangstresses, gangstress rappers demonstrate role flexibility and frequently combine different hustling strategies in a single song. For example, in "Spend a Little Doe," Lil' Kim avenges her boyfriend's disloyalty to her by seducing, robbing, and then killing him. The song opens with a fictitious dialogue between the estranged couple following her release from prison. She blames him for her incarceration because, despite his own culpability, he reported her to the police and convinced her to serve jail time with a promise of love and wealth. When she asks why he severed contact with her during her imprisonment, he replies "I ain't wanna see my bird in no cage, but I'm ready to take care of you now" (K. Jones and Willis 1996, track 4). We hear a gun cock, Kim blows him away, and then she boasts of how she uses her sexuality to seduce and then rob men who, in her opinion, are deserving of such treatment (Beatty 2002).

Thus far, I have illustrated the intimate relationship between real life and rap music gangstressism by linking economic violence and hustling strategies as experienced and practiced by women of the hip hop generation. However, while I have explained why women and girls who actually practiced gangstressism on the streets and/or lived in extremely impoverished environments might reflect these experiences in their music when given the opportunity, it does not necessarily explain why women and girls, so-called "studio gangstas," who are far removed from such environments often appropriate this image in their music. Nor does it explain why successful women rappers who are fortunate enough to move beyond that lifestyle maintain a gangstress persona.

Thus, to answer these questions, it is necessary to apply a broader definition of hustling to rap music gangstressism, one with which I am particularly familiar as a function of having been reared in a working-class family. As writer Rufus Shaw notes in *Hustling: The Art of Black Financial Survival* (1982, 1), many people associate the word hustling with criminal behavior and they do so for good reason. Most if not all "successful" criminals have mastered the art of hustling to such a degree that the term hustler has become synonymous with a risk-taking and street-wise individual who has attained success under difficult and perilous circumstances. However, many people also use the term more generally to describe a hard work ethic and creativity. This may range from working both overtime and multiple legitimate jobs, to marketing one's own skills (i.e. styling hair) or homemade wares (i.e., clothing) either full- or part-time. Therefore, hustling may also be defined as

> (1) Making something positive happen under difficult circumstances by using a combination of common sense, an understanding of human nature, daring and hard work. (2) Making money where none appears. (3) Hustling is a state of mind. (4) Hustling is a 24 hour per day occupation. ... Hustling is an art. It is not taught in colleges or universities. It is not recommended by guidance counselors but damn near every successful black person has employed the art of hustling to achieve financial success. ... The regular channels of financial security were denied to black folks. But black folks developed an art that enabled them to succeed and make money in spite of racism and other obstacles. That art is hustling. (Shaw 1982, 1–2)

Evidence of the hip hop community's cognizance of both uses of this term is found in both the music of and public discourse about female and male rap artists. For example, in *Vibe*, Robert Marriott (2000) describes Lil' Kim as "perhaps, the greatest public purveyor of the female hustle this side of Madonna, parleying ghetto pain, pomp, and circumstances into mainstream fame and fortune" (126). Regarding music, rappers often use hustling as a double entendre to both glamorize illegal hustling and boast of their own success as entertainers. For example, in addition to boasting about her sexual talents and physical attributes, Trina rhymes, "Tourin' on the road getting stacks/ 20 grand karats for the show no tax" (K. Taylor, Seymour, and Jackson 2002, "Hustling").

As I have argued, even when rappers actually have a criminal past, success in a legitimate profession requires that they maintain a safe distance from elements of that environment. However, because gangsta authenticity mandates a particular level of street credibility (as determined by both fans and music executives), both female and male gangsta rappers often appropriate the criminal hustler persona, such as in Trina's "Hustling." Therefore, whether practiced in the streets, or in film and recording studios, gangstressism is about "coming up" and then maintaining a particular level of success.

At its simplest level, hip hop gangstressism reflects lived experiences of the street gangstress-turned-rapper, such as Lil' Kim, Queen Pen, and Mia

X. It is an articulation of her hopes, dreams, pain, fears, and fury. However, as numerous rap artists indicate, rap is just as much a business as it is an art form, and often the business side takes precedence when artists segue from underground to commercial spaces where they struggle to negotiate their craft, image, and consequently, their identities. From this perspective, rap music may be viewed as a type of hustle in which gangstressism functions as a strategy for success for both authentic and studio gangstresses, in a predominantly White-owned industry in which Black men predominate as artists and producers/executives. Consequently, this framework is useful for evaluating gangstress practice in hip hop because it positions the entertainment industry as a site for economic mobility, in addition to a site for artistic and political resistance and proliferation. Moreover, because this framework uses a hip hop feminist epistemology, it underscores historical context for women hip hop generationers. Particularly, criminologist Carl Taylor (1993) argues that

> Black women, while not identifying in the same way with white feminist "women's liberation," had grown up in the 1970s with the kind of strong black women symbolized by activist Angela Davis. In the 1980s, black females played a different role in gangs than in the 1970s. The 1980s brought about radical change for females in Detroit. … While females were not actually members of corporate gangs, they carried weapons, participated in transporting drugs, and learned the chemistry necessary to process dope. … Yet, none of these gangs proved unusual or outstanding. … In the 1990s, there is another dimension to females['] gangs besides that of commercial and corporate. Women's independence means taking power and territory and that means fighting over what is deemed important. (44–45, 47–48)

Some criminologists (Hagedorn and Devitt 1999, 261–262) charge Taylor with sensationalizing female gang participation and feeding a backlash against women's advancement in traditionally male occupations, and I concur that girls' experiences with gangs are much too complex to be framed as "breaking into a male world" (Chesney Lind 1999a, 309), especially given the overwhelming masculinist bias which contributed to the underreporting and misrepresentation of early female gang activity. However, it is important not to lose sight of historical context as a crucial variable in analyses of female delinquent and criminal behavior as some research on Black female gang activity indicates (Lauderback et al. 1992).

With respect to Taylor's contention that 1970s' Black women activists had an indelible effect on Black girls who were coming of age during that era (hip hop generationers), it is difficult to determine how much these figures directly impacted female adolescents. However, there is strong evidence that these women, at least indirectly, affected young girls. As political scientist Cedric Robinson (1998) and ethnic studies scholar Joy James (1999, 123–124) provocatively argue, near the end of the civil rights era, Hollywood commodified the images of radical Black women political figures and distorted them as sexualized "murderous mulattas" and divas. Maintains Robinson, following the widely televised footage of assaults on Black protesters by police hoses, dogs, and White mobs,

> Hollywood film makers recast the freedom movement as outlawry and, in a sub-genre of Blaxploitation, Black women were portrayed as vigilantes. ... One of the most effective and clever manoeuvres of the Blaxploitation genre was the appropriation and re-presentation of Angela Davis's public image. ... Davis's likeness and that of Kathleen Cleaver had become two of the most familiar and alternative gender significations of revolutionary America. Film, however, transported Davis's form from a representation of a revolutionist to that of an erotic Black nationalist, largely devoid of historical consciousness. ... The principal impersonations of Davis were performed by Pam Grier and Rosalind Cash, two young actresses who bore some physical resemblance to Davis. It was, however, a similarity with a difference: Grier's voluptuous figure licensed an eroticisation of Davis which consisted of sexualised violence (themes of rape, castration, and the broadest contraction of the gun and the penis). (3–4)

Therefore, given the reverence of women hip hop generationers and other hip hop community members for women blaxploitation icons, as indicated in female rap discourse and other hip hop artifact, the effects of real-life women revolutionaries on women hip hop generationers, while perhaps not delineable, is certainly undeniable. Regarding influences on female emcees, I contend that because of extreme marginalization, gangstress emcees identify with, respect, and admire other women whom they feel not only speak to their existence, but who also refuse to occupy a second-class position and have no qualms about resorting to unorthodox means to achieve their goals. These kinships, as I have demonstrated, are evinced as these artists immortalize both living and fictional legendary gangstresses in their music and nonfictitious artifact.

Conclusions

This chapter has examined the roles of agency, autonomy, and historical context in Black female rappers' practice of gangstressism, which is marked by discourse on violence, drug trafficking, and other crime. I have presented a framework of gangstressism, which grounds this practice in the political, social, and economic realities for female hip hop generationers. In doing so, I have utilized hip hop feminism as an epistemology. This framework extends previous research on Black women performers in four ways. Broadly, it situates the hip hop music gangstress as both producer of and conduit through which gangstress culture—from the streets, movies, and television—flows. In doing so, her relationship to both street culture and action/crime cinema, particularly to women characters, is explicitly outlined, rather than assumed via connections that have been made between male artists and these influences. Second, it identifies the entertainment industry as a site for economic mobility and identifies the pursuit and maintenance of a successful rap music career as a legitimate hustle, which explicitly links women's and girls' struggles for agency and autonomy on the streets with such struggles in the music and film studios. Third, this framework extends previous work by focusing on women's aggression and violence as resistance, rather than on sexual agency. Lastly, this work extends the budding body of hip hop feminist scholarship and considers the influence of historical context—in addition to race/ethnicity, gender, and class intersectionality—on gangstressism.

Notes

1. I make a distinction because hip hop refers to a culture in which rap is only one of four elements, including breakdance, turntabalism, and grafitti art. Additionally, fashion is a huge part of the culture. Regarding music, Sean "P. Diddy" Combs created the "hip hop soul" category and named singer Mary J. Blige, who identifies as a gangstress, "Queen of Hip Hop Soul" to market her music in 1992. Thus, rap, which is comprised of various subgenres, represents only one brand of hip hop music. However, because of gangsta rap's expansion, particularly, into mainstream culture, a fifth category called hip hop film, also know as New Jack or "homeboy" cinema, has emerged, in which gangstressism is also represented.
2. Although not specifically mentioned in the "Queen Mother" section of her chapter, Keyes recognizes Harmony's Afrocentric style in chapter 3 p. 88.
3. In response to protests from politicians and law enforcement officials, Time Warner recalled the original album and removed this song from later pressings.
4. The reader should note that there is no clear demarcation between these categories of female rappers. According to Keyes (2002, 189), female emcees may either shift between categories or simultaneously belong to more than one. Her remaining categories include "Fly Girl" and "Lesbian," the latter of which is problematic in that such artists are categorized as a function of their sexual identity rather than their style of rap.
5. In "Queen Bitch Pt. 2," Lil' Kim refers to herself as the "Teflon Bitch from the [Bed-]Stuy." However, as Pough (2004, 183–185) notes, this aggressive posturing is often at odds with the vulnerability that many gangstress rappers reveal during interviews.
6. These artists are not signed to a record label. They perform locally and sometimes nationally, and frequently market their wares at live shows, local markets, from the trunks of cars, and more recently via personal Web sites on the Internet.
7. Springer does not explicitly identify as a hip hop feminist in her article, "Third Wave Black Feminism" (2002). However, she acknowledges the importance of work by other hip hop feminists such as Joan Morgan.
8. This denotes a powerful Mafia leader.

References

Alvarez, G. 1998/1999. Mama knows best. *Vibe*, December/January, 126–127.

Beatty, A. C. 2002. Priming "bitch" schemas with violent and gender-oppositional female rap lyrics: A theoretical overview of effects on tolerance for aggression against women. *African American Research Perspectives* 8:131–141.

Binder, A. 1993. Constructing racial rhetoric: Media depictions of harm in heavy metal and rap music. *American Sociological Review* 58:753–767.

Bost, S. 2001. "Be deceived if ya wanna be foolish": (Re)constructing body, genre, and gender in feminist rap. *Postmodern Culture* 12(1).

Campbell, A. 1984. *The girls in the gang.* Oxford: Basil Blackwell.

Carmichael, B. G. 1975. Youth crime in urban communities: A descriptive analysis of street hustlers and their crimes. *Crime and Delinquency*, April, 139–148.

Chesney L. M. 1999. Girls, gangs, and violence: Reinventing the liberated female crook. In *Female gangs in America: Essays on girls, gangs, and gender*, ed. M. Chesney-Lind and J. M. Hagedorn, 295–310. Chicago: Lake View Press.

Collins, P. H. 2000. *Black feminist thought: Knowledge, consciousness, and the politics of empowerment.* 2nd ed. New York: Routledge.

Dodd, D. A. 2001. Power trippin'. *Honey* (August) 110–112, 114.

Emerson, R. A. 2002. "Where my girls at?": Negotiating Black womanhood in music videos. *Gender and Society* 16:115–135.

Fishman, L. T. 1999. Black female gang behavior: An historical and ethnographic perspective. In *Female gangs in America*, ed. M. Chesney-Lind and J. M. Hagedorn, 64–84. Chicago: Lake View Press.

Fried, C. B. 1996. Bad rap for rap: Bias in reactions to music lyrics. *Journal of Applied Social Psychology* 26:2135–2146.

Fullilove, M. T., V. Heon, W. Jimenez, C. Parsons, L. L. Green, and R. E. Fullilove. 1998. Injury and anomie: Effects of violence on an inner-city community. *American Journal of Public Health* 88:924–927.

George, N. 1998. *Hip hop America.* New York: Viking.

Gonzales, M. A. 1997. Mack divas. *The Source*, February, 62–64, 66–67.

Hagedorn, J. M. and M. L. Devitt. 1999. Fighting female: The social construction of female gangs. In *Female gangs in America: Essays on girls, gangs, and gender*, ed. M. Chesney-Lind and J. M. Hagedorn, 256–276. Chicago: Lake View Press.

Hall, S. 1996. What is this "black" in black popular culture? In D. Morley & K.-H. Chen (eds.), *Stuart Hall: Critical dialogues in cultural studies* (465–475). London and New York: Routledge.

James, J. 1999. *Shadowboxing: Representations of Black feminist politics.* 1st ed. New York: St. Martin's Press.

jamila, s. 2002. Can I get a witness? Testimony from a hip hop feminist. In *Colonize this! Young women of color on today's feminism*, ed. D. Hernandez and B. Rehman, 382–394. New York: Seal Press.

Jones, S. 2003. 'Scarface' echoes mightily with hip-hop artists: Two decades later, themes strike chord. *USA Today*, September 18, D.08.

Kelley, R. D. G. 1992, June 8. Straight from underground. *Nation*, 793–796.

Keyes, C. L. 1993. "We're more than a novelty boys": Strategies of female rappers in the rap music tradition. In. J. N. Radner (Ed.), *Feminist messages: coding in women's folk culture* (203–220). Urbana: University of Illinois Press.

Keyes, C. L. 2000. Empowering self, making choices, creating spaces: Black female identity via rap music performance. *Journal of American Folklore,* 113(449), 255.

Keyes, C. L. 2002. *Rap music and street consciousness.* Urbana: University of Illinois Press.

Kirk-Duggan, C. A. 1997. Kindred spirits: Sister mimetic societies and social responsibilities. *Journal of Gang Research* 4:23–36.

Kitwana, B. 2002. *The hip hop generation: Young Blacks and the crisis in African American culture.* 1st ed. New York: Basic Civitas.

Lacayo, R. 1995. America's cultural revulsion. *Time,* June 12, 24–30.

LaGrone, K. L. 2000. From minstrelsy to gangsta rap: The "nigger" as commodity for popular American entertainment. *Journal of African American Men* 5:117–131.

Laidler, K. A. J. and G. Hunt. 1997. Violence and social organization in female gangs. *Social Justice* 24:148.

Laidler, K. J. and G. Hunt. 2001. Accomplishing feminity among the girls in the gang. *British Journal of Criminology* 41:656–678.

Lauderback, D., J. Hansen, and D. Waldorf. 1992. "Sisters are doin' it for themselves": A Black female gang in San Francisco. *Journal of Gang Research* 1:57–72.

Lusane, C. 1993. Rhapsodic aspirations: Rap, race and power politics. *Black Scholar* 23:37–51.

Maher, L. 1997. *Sexed work: Gender, race, and resistance in a Brooklyn drug market.* New York: Oxford University Press.

Marriott, R. 2000. Blowin' up. *Vibe,* June/July, 124–130.

McLaren, P. 1995. Gangsta pedagogy and ghettoethnicity: The hip-hop nation as counterpublic sphere. *Socialist Review,* 25(2), 9–55.

Merry, S. E. 2003. Rights talk and the experience of law: Implementing women's human rights to protection from violence. *Human Rights Quarterly* 25:343.

Messerschimdt, J. 1987. *Capitalism, patriarchy, and crime toward a socialist feminist criminology.* Totowa, NJ: Rowman and Littlefield.

Meyerstein, A. 2003. On the advantage and disadvantage of truth commissions for life: Dreaming an Israeli-Palestinian truth commission. *Journal of Church and State* 45:457.

Morgan, J. 1997. The bad girls of hip-hop. *Essence,* March, 76.

Orogun, P. 2004. "Blood diamonds" and Africa's armed conflicts in the post-Cold War era. *World Affairs* 166:151.

Pinn, A. B. 1999. "How ya livin'?": Notes on rap music and social transformation. *Western Journal of Black Studies* 23:10.

Pitts, C. and H. Davis. (Producers), and H. Davis (Director). (2000). Gangstresses. Home Video. United States: Reel Deal Productions.

Pough, G. D. 2002. Love feminism but where's my hip hop? Shaping a Black feminist identity. In *Colonize this! Young women of color on today's feminism,* ed. D. Hernandez and B. Rehman, 85–95. New York: Seal Press.

_____. 2004. *Check it while I wreck it: Black womanhood, hip-hop culture, and the public sphere.* Boston: Northeastern University Press.

Quinn, M. 1996. "Never shoulda been let out the penitentiary": Gangsta rap and the struggle over racial identity. *Cultural Critique* 34:65–89.

Rape, Abuse, and Incest National Network. n.d. RAINN statistics. Retrieved December 3, 2003 from http://www.rainn.org/statistics.html

Rennison, C. M. and M. R. Rand. 2003. National crime victimization survey: Criminal victimization, 2002. Series NCJ 199994. Washington, DC: U.S. Department of Justice, Office of Justice Programs. Retrieved October 15, 2003, from http://www.ojp.usdoj.gov/bjs/pubalp2.htm#W

Ro, R. 1996. *Gangsta: Merchandizing the rhymes of violence.* 1st ed. New York: St. Martin's Press.

Roberts, R. 1991. Music videos, performance and resistance: Feminist rappers. *Journal of Popular Culture,* 25, 141–152.

Robinson, C. J. 1998. Blaxploitation and the misrepresentation of liberation. *Race and Class* 40:1–12.

Rose, T. 1994. *Black noise: Rap music and Black culture in contemporary America.* Hanover and London: Wesleyan University Press and University Press of New England.

Shaw, R. 1982. *Hustling: The art of Black financial survival.* Dallas: Rufus Shaw Publishing.

Shelton, M. L. 1997. Can't touch this! Representations of the African American female body in urban rap videos. *Popular Music and Society* 21:107–116.

Shugart, H. A. 2001. Isn't it ironic? The intersection of third-wave feminism and Generation X. *Women's Studies in Communication* 24:131.

Siegmund-Cuda, H. 2002. Breaking away. The Source: The Magazine of Hip-Hop Music, *Culture and Politics* 158 (November):144.

Skeggs, B. 1993. Two Minute Brother: Contestation through gender, 'race' and sexuality. *Innovation* 6:299–322.

Springer, K. 2001. Waiting to set it off. In *Reel knockouts: Violent women in the movies,* ed. M. McCaughey and N. King, 172–199. Austin: University of Texas.

————. 2002. Third wave Black feminism? *Signs* 27:1059–1082.

Taylor, C. S. 1993. *Girls, gangs, women, and drugs.* East Lansing: Michigan State University Press.

Thompson, B. 2001. 360 degrees: Queen Pen: 8 Ball. XXL, July, 45.

Trina. 2002. Hustling. *Diamond princess.* New York: Slip-N-Slide Records. CD.

U.S. Census Bureau. 2006. *Statistical Abstract of the United States 2007.* 126th ed. Washington, DC. http://www.censusgov/compendia/statab (Accessed August 7, 2007.)

Valentine, B. 1978. *Hustling and other hard work: Life styles in the ghetto.* New York: Free Press.

Wacquant, L. 1998. Inside the zone: The social art of the hustler in the Black American ghetto. *Theory, Culture, and Society* 15:1–36.

Wenzel, S. L., B. D. Leake, and L. Gelberg. 2001. Risk factors for major violence among homeless women. *Journal of Interpersonal Violence* 16:739–752.

2

TGG
Girls, Street Culture, and Identity

DOROTHY BOTTRELL

Introduction

Girls' participation in street culture has been problematized within discourses of "troubled" or "troublesome" girls. Such representations may be linked to or situated within a variety of other discourses and are related to reasons for girls being on the streets as well as their behaviors there. For example, homeless girls may be regarded as "troubled" and "at risk," in need of welfare intervention and support; but particular homeless girls who resort to illicit means of survival may be criminalized (Alder 1993; Davis, Hatty, and Burke 1995), and thus reconstructed as "troublesome" or "risky." In both cases, there may be additional or underpinning concerns about them being on the streets because they are girls. "Moral panics" (Cohen 1980) may surround the presence of youth on the streets because in groups, and particular kinds of groups, their appearance or behavior disrupts other dominant public or private interests. Concerning girls, moral panics may be as much about their transgressions of femininity as legal transgressions. Feminist subcultural studies have suggested that the mere presence of girls in street subcultures, including breakdancers, graffitists, and delinquent and "spectacular" groups and gangs, represents the contestation of behavioral norms for girls (McRobbie 1991; Campbell 1987; Carrington 1989, 1993).

Subcultural studies provide evidence of the diversity of young people's practices, on and off the streets, and foreground differences, both in the varieties of young people's focal interests and through analysis of the interconnectedness of subcultural and other social identities, especially class, race, and gender. Carrington's study of delinquent working-class girls, including joyriders, found that they "routinely invaded the masculinised space of the street and the local youth subculture" (Carrington 1993, 30). Within discourses of appropriate femininity and delinquency, the girls' nonconformity prompted measures for the regulation of, or intervention in, girls' participation. However, Carrington's finding that the joyriders were "ordinary girls from housing commission areas ... having fun ... or just hanging around in groups" (32) points to the importance of understanding constructions of gender, youth, identity, pleasure, and resistance in the specificity of local relations, including girls' own articulations of their participation. Carrington's girls did not set out to challenge feminine stereotypes, nor to express working-class resistance (key themes of early feminist and Marxist [Hall and Jefferson 1976] subcultural theory). Their street behavior was consistent with rebellious anti-authoritarianism in other domains, including family, school, and intervening authorities (welfare, police, courts) (Hall and Jefferson 1976).

Discrepancies between how girls understand their participation in street culture and how others understand them are constituted in a complexity of local and broader social relations, including discursive and regulatory practices in the governance of girls, and more broadly, youth. When girls are actively involved in street subcultures, they may be positioned as dangerous delinquents, in part because their behavior is "unfeminine," and they are not in their "rightful" place. However, changing definitions of what is appropriate and what is problematic, on and off the streets, both reflect and constitute changing social and cultural processes, constraining or facilitating diversity of girls' and youth behavior and practices.

Changes in popular culture, femininities, and gender roles underline the context-specific nature of behavioral expectations (Gilbert and Taylor 1991; Sweeting and West 2003). Recent studies have indicated a broadening of gendered self-expression through youth culture—from more liberating styles associated with popular music, dance parties, and raves of the 1990s (McRobbie 1994; Pini 2004), to the phenomenon of "girl power," celebrating girls' agency and choice in pursuit of self-invention (Paglia 1992; Bail 1996). However, attention to the social and ideological contexts of self-invention has reasserted the significance of socioeconomic position in accounting for the differential experiences of girls in both public and private domains (Walkerdine, Lucey, and Melody 2001). As neoliberal subjects, girls are offered the "can-do" ideal promising freedom, choice, and success but are also assigned individual responsibility for failure, within increased regulation of girls' behavior in education, work, and leisure, directed toward hegemonization of new norms (Harris 2004). When girls claim their space on the streets as workers and consumers, they may achieve adult "accreditation" (Sercombe et al. 2002, 14), though the success of certain types of girls, in reinforcing the ideal, simultaneously reinforces discursive assumptions about the failure of others and positions them as "at risk" (Bradley 2005; Harris 2004). Girls' public visibility in adult roles and domains may shift and legitimate conceptualizations of girls' "places" in society. However, the structuring of roles and sites within the varieties of often contradictory discourses place particular kinds of girls and practices within or outside dominant social norms and interests. For example, consumption is demanded in the ascendency of teenagers in consumer markets; but claiming social space as nonconsumers within domains

of consumption, such as shopping malls, is problematized and typically subject to strict surveillance and possible criminalization (Wyn and White 1997).
Dominant and marginal positions are evident in the structurings and restruc-
turings of specific sets of relations, practices, and sites; and always in relation
to broader social divisions and relations of power.

"Problem youth" has been a persistent motif in concerns about young
people's rebelliousness and resistances as threats to social order, particularly
through media depictions and the social regulation of youth (Wyn and White
1997). However, youthful rebellion has also been understood as a passing
phase of adolescence (Griffin 2004). Other dominant discourses are implicated in the production and meaning of "problem youth" and "problem girls."
Contemporary discourses of "law and order" and "risk," and government policies and governance practices that enshrine them, effectively position youth as
potential threat; other discourses about "youth at risk" may extend the governance of risk, for example in its application to crime prevention, or may have
very different implications for institutional practices (Armstrong 2004, 2006).
In broad terms, the interpretation of youthful behavior within these contrasting frameworks may determine whether a punitive or supportive, developmental approach is adopted. On and off the streets, it is marginalized youth
who are constructed as "other" than the ideal subject positions established
for youth and who are more vulnerable to social exclusion (MacDonald and
Marsh 2005) and punitive regulation (Muncie 2004).

How marginalized girls are positioned and inscribed as problematic is
explored in this chapter. How representations of girls and girls' own self-representations structure relations of subject positioning and subjectivity are
central issues. Street culture is a significant context for understanding not
only the diverse interests and cultural self-expression of girls, but for understanding marginalization both as social position and social processes. As
evident in the youth and cultural studies literature, the very public visibility
of street culture elicits powerful discursive and regulatory responses. However, girls' own understandings, contestations and discourses as constitutive
of street practices and engagement with discursive and cultural continuities
and differences they encounter, may reveal alternative configurations of the
problematics of girls' street culture.

The Study

This chapter is based on research completed in 2002. In 1999, I had started in
the position of coordinator of the youth service which became "home base"
for the study. Situated in the inner city (Sydney) suburb of Glebe, the youth
service provides a range of casework, recreational and educational programs
and services for 12- to 24-year-olds of the local public housing estate. In Glebe,
public housing is concentrated at one end of the suburb, traditionally a working-class area, and in sharp contrast with the expensive private housing and

affluence of the other end. Established in the 1980s, the estate is a combination of cottages, terraces, and newer low-rise apartment blocks, traversed by the main street of cafes, bookshops, gift and antique stores, and alternative lifestyle centers. It houses mostly families with complex support needs and is a focus for police and government agencies concerning child protection notifications, disturbance complaints, vandalism, and car break-ins. Specific problems for youth in the area include truancy, drug use, and involvement in street crime (Families First 2000). These youth issues and their interrelatedness constituted the substantive focus of the study.

Truancy and offending were key issues for the youth service. In 2000, 80 percent of the regular attenders at the youth service who had left school, typically at or below the legal school-leaving age, had not obtained the Year 10 School Certificate (obtained on completion of the fourth year of secondary school in New South Wales). Official figures indicated that only 57 percent of 15- to 18-year-olds from the estate end of Glebe were still in school, compared with 93.8 percent of their peers at the more affluent end (Families First 2000, 13). Although local police reports provided at community forums indicated the continuing decline of crime in the area, and that only a small number of young people were responsible for most juvenile crime in the area, in 2000, around one-third of regular attenders at the youth service were or had previously been involved in the juvenile justice system. Although this figure declined significantly during the period of the study (to 10 percent in 2002), this "tradition," discussed below, is an integral factor in how young people of the area are represented.

The aim of the study was to explore the links between young people's truancy, "hanging around," and offending. From my perspectives as a practitioner, previously as a high school teacher and in work with girls in a juvenile justice center and then at the youth service, the links were apparent. As a researcher, I wanted to understand more the perspectives of marginalized girls, how they understood what happened in and out of school and the interconnections between these.

Girls who came regularly to the youth service were invited to participate. Twelve 13- to 24-year-olds, mainly Aboriginal and Anglo-Australians, volunteered, following small group or one-to-one information sessions. All of the girls live or have lived in the estate and strongly identify with the area. At the time of interviewing, three were living independently, two with their own children; the others with family. The two with children relied on the government parenting allowance; three were unemployed and receiving the government youth allowance; six were enrolled in school and one had dropped out of school and had no income. Of the six girls who had left school, one had obtained the School Certificate. All of the girls have been involved in petty crime, such as shoplifting, other stealing, and illicit recreations. All have friends or family who have been convicted or incarcerated. Two of the girls have convictions; others have faced court or police intervention.

Interviews and other data collection took place in 2000 to 2001. The interview guide for semistructured interviews had been developed around key themes from everyday work at the youth service and which were key issues raised by girls, and boys, in conversations in and around youth service activities, among peers and with staff. In addition to these themes of schooling, recreation, being in trouble, achievements, and concepts of success, others were later identified from the interviews. The latter include sense of place, reputation, drug use, and crime. Participating in community forums and interagency networks was important for developing an understanding of local discourses about youth and youth issues. Field notes and documentary sources, such as local papers, minutes from community meetings, and government and nongovernment reports on educational, welfare, and youth justice issues about or pertinent to Glebe, were also important sources for the study.

Girls, Boys, and Street Culture

This chapter focuses on Glebe girls' participation in street culture and its place in their identity work (Hey 1997). "The process whereby a person takes her or himself up as a person [may be] understood as an ongoing process through which the individual is constituted and reconstituted" (Davies 1990, 322). Here, two assumptions are made about this process. First, the individual constitutes and reconstitutes herself within her own ongoing identity work. This work is always relational and always social and may include the influences of a variety of social identifications. The individual comes to know herself and to define who she is and who she wants to be within relations with others. Second, she is constituted and reconstituted by and within extended relations, locally and as socially positioned (Smith 1987). In identity terms, subcultures, friendship and peer groups, and youth neighborhood networks may all be "places" for identity development and self-expression, though individuals' positioning within broader categories of identifiable groups may be central to the construction of their social identities. In this sense, gender, class, and race may be understood as "immanent conditions" (Pini 1996, 413) of agency and structural constraint, discernible in the specificities of contexts as lived relations. However, the material conditions of people, place, and everyday practices may be seen in dialectical relationship to such immanent conditions; they are mutually constitutive. Ongoingly constituted and reconstituted, identity work engages knowledge of self and others in the multiple contexts encountered in everyday life. Experiences within and across different contexts ongoingly constitute and reconstitute identity as socially embedded subjectivity and belonging to identifiable groups. Understandings of patterns of similarity and difference are central to identity work, to placing oneself within the web of local conditions and relations.

The first section situates "TGG" as local identity and a territorial claim. Within local street culture, the girls identify as "TGG," "outsiders." TGG connotes local loyalties and demarcates "insiders" and "outsiders," The local youth network is an important context of girls' identity work. In the following section, this context is problematized because it is street based. In other suburbs, a group of friends may meet outside their homes unnoticed. In the Glebe estate, the proximity of homes to the commercial center produces a tension between residential and commercial interests. It also blurs boundaries between private and public, and makes what is ostensibly private behavior vulnerable to surveillance by businesses, security, police and the public.

In the girls' discussion of experiences on the streets, including fighting and drinking, the ways in which they and their peers understand street culture are very different to others' accounts. Local discourses about "problem youth" generalize the association of youth and crime, to the extent that the girls feel stereotyped and targeted. For the Glebe girls, growing up in an area associated with crime and social problems is a fundamental context for everyday experience. In the interviews, their discussion of Glebe focuses significantly on others' attitudes toward them. Their line of argument is that because they are young and because Glebe has a bad reputation, they are assumed to be "bad kids." They are adamant that they are "categorized" (Linda, Sarah) and "stereotyped" (Jodi).

Sarah: Everybody like knows it [Glebe]. Everyone's like, oh you live in Glebe, oh how can you live there? And like, call me names and stuff, like Glebe chat. They're just stereotypical about it.
Linda: Yeah, they categorize other …
Sarah: … put you into a category.
           There's two different ends of Glebe. Like, there's the good half and then there's what …
Jodi: The bad half.
Sarah: … everybody says is the bad half … I live down in the bad half.

Their accounts of street culture indicate a struggle to resist those stereotypes especially to protect their reputation. This is difficult, however, because fighting, drinking, and other illicit recreations are understood as simply "the done thing" and to not participate would mean missing out on fun with friends. Though articulating these competing concerns, the girls continue to participate in street culture at the risk of reinforcing the very stereotypes they resist.

The next section argues for the importance of situating the girls' participation in street culture in the context of the rest of their lives. Decontextualized, their illicit recreations provide a narrow and problematic representation of the girls. Less visible and more private experience, within friendships and neighborhood networks, indicates the sorority and solidarity of TGG loyalties. In ongoing difficult circumstances which are the lived experience of social problems, "hanging around" with friends may provide the emotional and practical support needed. However, such positive resources of the youth network remain invisible to public view; and thus do not serve to challenge the discourses that stereotype them. The girls' critique of social problems of the area indicates some understanding of the differential distribution of social resources. However, understanding social problems as everyday experience may also provide justification for illicit resourcefulness. The principle of "sticking together" underpins their lines of argument.

Everyday experience of problems and pleasures requires negotiation of center-marginal relations, norms, and expectations. In the final two sections, it is argued that the girls engage in a struggle about chosen and unchosen social identity. Despite the adversities common among the girls, their participation in licit activities, their achievements, mutual support, and strategies for managing are indicative of their resilience and the positive aspects of local culture.

TGG as Local Identity

On my first visit to the youth service I noticed that TGG and TGB (The Glebe Boys) were ubiquitous "tags" written on toilet doors, over posters, and etched into the old furniture at the office. They dominated the graffiti boards provided at the small hall where after-school "drop-in" was held. They were also evident around the neighborhood.

Not all local girls claim the title TGG. The titles TGG and TGB originated with previous groups of girls and boys, bonded in neighborhood friendships, whose common interests included joyriding in stolen cars, stealing, and other petty crime. The projected image of those who created the "tags" was all about toughness, daring, and defiance of authorities. TGG and TGB were titles passed on and proudly claimed, signifying status within the local youth network. Although the importance of TGG and TGB waxes and wanes, it is a strong identification within the girls' narratives.

For boys, TGB is "earned" through notoriety. TGG status may be similarly acquired, but its "criteria" are more open, about being around and known, being "one of the girls," and part of the youth network. There are close friendships between TGG and TGB, and girls' identity is attached to both. Loyalty to TGG and TGB involves a friendly rivalry: painting the two tags for a youth service art project, Tracey states, "Hey, TGG should come first, you know, 'cause us girls ..." "Eshay" ["Pig-Latin" for "yes"], says Nola. "We're the best," continues Tracey. They laugh at how "the boys would be pissed off."

Identifying as TGG connotes loyalty to neighborhood peers and serves a territorial function, in contradistinction to groups from other suburbs. Girls in other inner-city suburbs, such as Waterloo, Redfern, and Millers Point, also identify in this way. Over the years there have been animosities between TGG and The Waterloo Girls, The Redfern Girls, and Millers Point Girls. Persistent rivalries have grown out of fights or verbal confrontations concerning slurs on reputations or over relationships. An individual girl may be targeted in this way, and although she may be the instigator of retaliation, her TGG crew will be there to back her up. Having back up is understood, among the various groups of girls, as the way things are done and would be expected on both sides in a confrontation. Such confrontations and fights are episodic, however, and do not constitute a gang mentality. The practices of girl gangs may include similar confrontations, but other gang requirements and behaviors clearly distinguish them from groups like TGG. The strict initiations, rules and codes, and aggressive "default" street behaviors characteristic of girls' gangs (Campbell 1987, 1993; Chesney-Lind 1993) are not adopted by TGG.

TGG and Street Culture

Being on the street is commonplace for young people at the estate end of Glebe, for various reasons: there may be nowhere at home to gather; to escape into youth-only sociality; and because there are few other recreational options. The local youth service is a focal point during the day, but generally closed at night and, because of their limited financial resources, most young people cannot regularly access commercial recreations. The girls describe fighting, drinking, and getting into trouble as inevitable: "there's nothing else to do." However, there are significant differences in the girls' and others' understanding of what takes place on the streets. Discrepant perspectives are constructed out of conflicting meanings and interests associated with particular practices, heightened by the visibility of street culture.

Using Public Space

The location of the youth service on the main street is significant to local street culture. As a place where young people congregate, it is a highly visible site, and as the main street is predominantly commercial, it is a contentious site. As a youth space, it is known as an important community resource. Arguing the case for the establishment of the youth service, local residents and community leaders stressed the importance of providing for young people's needs and interests and somewhere other than the streets for young people to go. This view persists among many in the community, especially young people's families. However, "keeping youth off the streets" is also valued out of concern for public order and the area's reputation. This perspective is particularly important to commercial interests. The location is thus problematic in the public visibility of young people attending and within conflicting notions of legitimate uses of public space. However, it is not only location, but also the reputation of the youth service that also elicits diverse perspectives. That the service has always been accessed by young offenders has colored its perception by the local community. Some parents will not allow their children to attend the service because "it's only for kids in trouble" or "too many rougher types go there."

Despite offering a range of recreational and educational programs that attract a broad clientele, the service is primarily associated with "problem youth."

From some perspectives this association is daily reinforced by the congregating of youth and by their behavior. Around the youth service, mainly during late afternoons, the girls and boys take up space on the footpath and are highly visible as a group, including groups of Black young people who stand out in the predominantly White street population. The general (bad) impression is created in young people's conspicuousness and by their "antisocial" sociality. Many smoke cigarettes; the younger ones meander about on bikes; their talk and fun is typically noisy. Mucking around, having fun, at times progresses into antisocial behavior. Hassling or deriding passers-by, throwing stones or running onto the road between traffic, and very public altercations, are grounds for generalized fear and complaint.

Nighttime behavior is also problematic. Residents and businesses complain of girls and boys skylarking, yelling, fighting, and smashing bottles. Police are often called to disperse the small groups. Such incidents make ordinary daytime "hanging out" all the more contentious. Moreover, those participating in antisocial behavior are often blamed for more serious incidents of vandalism and break-ins.

Local papers and community forums regularly raise issues of vandalism, graffiti, and youth crime. At a local council committee (which met monthly during the research period), businesses attributed loss of customers to car break-ins, which for several years have been the highest reported crime type in the area. According to police, business clientele are "perceived as wealthy and therefore robbed" and their "cars are targeted." Some businesses say that "gangs" intimidate customers and operators. At one of the council committee meetings, a local park where young people drink was described by a nearby business owner as "an epicenter for gangs," where "a gang of around half a dozen youths are holding the area to ransom"—they are "out of control." Residents on the council committee suggested that strategies are needed to "discourage teenagers and young twenties gathering and loitering" in parks and vacant blocks. At such community forums, concern is expressed not solely about antisocial behavior and crime, but also that young people need support, that they are caught up in family and social problems. Attitudes toward local youth range from this to outright condemnation.

The committee acknowledges that a minority of young people are involved in crime, but the long-standing "youth problems," evidence of vandalism, and media reports of incidents and "youth crime waves" translate to dominant local discourses which generalize the association of youth and crime. All young people at "the bad end" are vulnerable to ideological criminalization and pathologizing.

Girls' street behavior may be problematized as transgression of appropriate femininity. Boys' "bad" behavior may be seen as consistent with traditional notions of masculinity; whereas girls' boisterousness and visible street presence may be interpreted as "the antithesis of appropriate female behavior" (Baines and Alder 1996, 28). Like boys, girls' behavior may be depicted as anti-social or in terms of legal events. However, in their "doubly deviant" (Baines and Alder 1996, 28) transgressions, girls may be removed from the streets on legal grounds which obfuscate disapproval of girls' "unfemininity." The girls' behavior is also problematized by the company they keep. Regardless of the extent of their involvement in illicit activities, they are perceived as implicated. They "hang out" with others in the local youth network, the subject of complaints about antisocial behavior and "youth crime waves." The girls describe their situation as being stereotyped and targeted.

Jodi: Just because you're sixteen, you must do what that sixteen year old did ... you know, bashed someone. Oh, you live in Glebe, you're a thug.

Sarah: Or ... you go round bashing people or you go round breaking into cars, or ...

Jodi: Cause everyone's heard that's what Glebe is.

Patsy: You're constantly watching your back ... even if you weren't in trouble. ... If you were in a group that wasn't, you'd get targeted anyway. So, and that makes it hard.

Fighting

Girls' fights may similarly be problematized as transgressive of both gendered and prosocial norms and within conflicts of interest over public space. However, the girls' discussion of fighting indicates its normalization within street culture and that it has important functions for their identity work. Being known as a fighter enhances reputation and accrues status within the youth network.

It is, in part, from the history of TGG confrontations with other groups, that certain girls have gained the reputation of being good fighters. But fighting is not restricted to defending relationship territory against outsiders. Despite their close friendships, there is much in-fighting among the girls, including verbal fights and punch-ups. Girls fight "over everything." Some fights are specifically about drug debts or "stupid things" like borrowed or stolen items unreturned.

Fighting is an acceptable way of settling disputes, especially concerning boyfriends and talk behind backs. Hearing that someone has named another girl as a "slut" or "bad cunt" (Nola, Carol, Rebecca), is cause for organizing a fight to sort it out.

Carol comments:

They just run off at their mouth. [Laughing] They do! And then it gets back to whoever they said it about and then that's it.

Fighting for relationship territory can settle a long-standing grudge or current infidelities in which the "other girl" is likely to be "sorted out" by fighting, while the boyfriend is either dropped or excused.

Protecting reputation is a central issue in the girls' perspectives on fights. In terms of understanding the contradictions of TGG friendships and in-fighting, however, other insights are important.

Jodi: Like, if a girl bashes another girl, and they're like, oh, don't muck around with her, she's tough, she, she, you know, won't stop if you fight with her. Heaps like that.

Rebecca: Like Natalie tryin to throw Tammy on the train track after a dance party. She had a go with Carol too, but Carol can fight like fuckin Tyson, mate. She throws head butts and just gets in and like *knocks* em! She's one angry little bitch.

Clearly, there is status attached to having a reputation as a good fighter. Nola says, "You don't go out to fuckin fight" but walking away would mean "you'd get paid out, you're shit, that's it." Despite her final comment, "But if you don't want to fight you don't have to," the expectation of fighting exerts a pressure to do so, for claiming or maintaining TGG status. Fighting is also deemed necessary because it is just the way conflicts are resolved and just the way it has always been in the area. In her interview, Jodi's first comments about what it is like in Glebe were:

It's good cause you got your friends around here and it's a pretty small area. … And even though people do fight, nearly everyone gets along. It's pretty good. You still, fight with someone, you've still got someone else. All people with all different attitudes.

All of the girls say fights are as integral a part of local relations as friend-ships. Ironically, it is through fights, as well as despite them, that some of the girls have developed enduring friendships. When Carol left school, she was living with Rebecca. She mentions that they met because of an intended fight.

Carol: I met Rebecca one New Year's Eve, down at [laughs] Darling Har-bour. Her and Tammy were gonna have a go. And then, yep, that's how I met her.

DB: And you became good mates?

Carol: Yeah.

Rebecca tells more of the story.

Carol was drunk and she goes, happy New Year and gave me a hug. And she goes, "Who are you?" And I say Rebecca, and she goes "Ooh, my sister has a fight for you", so … I wanna get this over and done with now. I walked up to Tammy and she's like a *little* girl. She was like fourteen then, and just a little girl … I'm like, you're the one who wants to fight me? You wanna fight—fight! And she's like, "You say we're bad cunts." Oh, this is *not* gonna happen. I said see ya, walked off. End of the night, she come up, she was, first time she'd ever got drunk ... and said, "You still wanna be friends?" I went, oh yeah, all right. And then gradually we become friends, started hangin' around with them ...

Although fights are not anticipated as pleasure, positive and pleasurable outcomes are subsequently enjoyed—the recounting of "legendary" events, the friendships formed, the positive reputation and status acquired. And given the apparent necessity of fighting, the girls continue the tradition. Their fighting is understood and accepted by peers and often parents and neighbors who themselves grew up with the same norms and may still at times settle their adult disputes with fights.

Fighting brings status but can also be problematic for a girl's reputation. Rebecca was "kicked out" of two schools "for having a punch-up":

I had a few fights because I was little and they used to pick on me and then I used to bash em and then they'd get upset and then like, the word gets around—ah, Rebecca, she's mad. ... And like, you go to a different suburb to see them and they're like, "You didn't come here to bash me?" And like it gets really boring ... like, reputations, they get out of hand. ... Everyone used to call us the little bitches. ... It's something, you gotta prove something.

To outsiders, with different behavioral norms, fighting may be regarded as always unacceptable. Apart from policing, the Glebe girls are inevitably caught up in the bad reputation of others' judgments; and this is the dominant view expressed in mainstream and media discourses.

Drinking

Drinking alcohol is a significant feature of youth street culture in Glebe. Although the girls say there is "nothing else to do," their discussion of "doing nothing" elaborates a range of their activities and how "ordinary" illicit recreations are structured into girls' identifications with TGG and the youth network. "Hanging out together," just walking or "cruising" around, or in the parks, drinking, are "something to do to have fun" (Rebecca).

DB: What else do girls do around here, for fun, for something to do?

Nola: Oh, go cruising round in cars. Um, what else? Well, if I go out with the girls or the guys, I go nightclubbing, that's better. But some people don't have i.d. yet, so ...

DB: The cruising around—are there many girls who've got cars or do they get their boyfriends to cruise?

Nola: No, we get one of the boys to drive us, our friends pick us up.

Dance clubs for the under-18s and, for the older girls, nightclubs are favored for nights out, though financial and age restrictions mean that these are only occasional. Patsy comments:

> There are certain spots where you'd go drinkin, smokin and ... And like, there's discos and stuff, you know, like in the city ... but most of the time we didn't go because a lot of people didn't have, you know, money or whatever, so we'd just throw in all the money and then get a drink and [laughs] smoke.

Being out with friends is "something to do" and when drinks in the park are on, there may be a gathering of anywhere between ten and forty young people, so "something might happen" (Sarah). Often that "something" is simply talk, romance, and skylarking.

DB:	So, give me a story of a typical Friday night.
Nola:	Go to the bottleo, [bottle shop or off-licence] get alcohol and go find somewhere to drink and—get blind! [Laughs]
DB:	And then what?
Nola:	Just talk to one another, muck around, that's it, then go.
Jodi:	It's a fun thing to do, get drunk in the park on the weekend. [Laughs] *Very* popular.
Linda:	Just go to the park or flats or something ...
Sarah:	If you don't have alcohol, you just sit around. [Laughs] There's nothing to do, just, like, oh it's real boring now, there's nothing to do.

There is unanimous enjoyment and light-heartedness about the tradition of park nights. However, some of the older girls are concerned that there is more aggression associated with the drinking than when they were regularly involved. Nancy comments that "kids do the same sorts of things ... but it's just getting worse." Now "they get drunk and bash ... people walking past in the street." This is seen as mainly a problem with the boys. Rebecca says the girls would get together to have a quiet drink but some of the boys "would throw bottles at White people who walked past."

Concerns are expressed, then explained away. "But everyone has episodes when they're drunk" (Rebecca). And there have always been incidents at the park gatherings. "Most of the Glebe boys used to fight in packs ... There's been heaps of mad riots and that" (Rebecca). Fighting and drinking inevitably get some young people into trouble; and the "mad riots" make good headlines. At the same time as the girls enjoy telling these stories, they are also aware of their impact on their reputation. Word quickly gets around when young people are arrested, and when reported in local and mainstream media, bad reputation is further entrenched.

The girls are critical of those involved in violent "episodes," but this is seen as the extreme behavior of a few "stupid boys" who cross the line from what are ordinary local recreations. "There's nothing else to do" is a continuing refrain from the girls regarding drinking, hanging out with friends, even fighting.

DB: ...Two things that girls often talk about round here are drinking and fighting.
Nola: [Laughing] Oh, it's funny. Um, I dunno. There's nothing else to do!
Nancy: In Glebe, it's just the thing to do.

"Problem youth" and "bad girls" may predominate in public discourses, but the girls' own discourses situate street culture as ordinary recreations and pleasures which provide access to empowerment and status that are unavailable or not readily accessible to them from other mainstream sources. Their participation conforms to local youth traditions, embraced by the girls even though they are aware of others' disapproval. On the one hand, they acknowledge the transgressive nature of street culture but rationalize it in terms of their location: "It's Glebe. It's a bad place" (Casey). On the other hand, they resist the stereotyping of their end of Glebe as a "bad" place. When Sarah notes that "there's two different ends of Glebe," her distinction is important: "what everybody says is the bad half" indicates awareness of local discourse and her place within it. It also suggests that "the bad half" may not be her characterization of the estate end of Glebe. According to Jodi, media and rumor networks contribute to the bad reputation. Girls from other areas who have visited school friends at the "good end" of Glebe say to her,

> "Oh, their house is nice, you must be rich, you must live in a house like that." And I'm like, no, I live in a housing commission flat, I'm not rich or anything ... and they're like, "Oh but ... isn't Glebe really good?" And then they hear the stories like on the news and stuff like that, or things in the newspaper, oh, Glebe's bad, Glebe's bad. And then they hear stories just through friends and stuff, rumors and things like that. 'Cause everyone's heard ... You can tell by people's reactions ... They stereotype you.

TGG: Girls' Sorority and Solidarity

The girls are far more than their participation in street culture. Stereotyping discourses and pejorative ascriptions derive from actual and perceived youth crime and antisocial behaviors and their visibility. But public and neighborhood critiques ignore or are unaware of other aspects of the girls' lives which are significant in their self-representations. This discrepancy is in part an effect of the interconnectedness of local and "distant" (media and governance authorities, for example) discourses as local street culture is contextualized within understandings of "problem youth" and stereotyping arising out of street behavior attaches to young people regardless of their behavior in other locations. Aisha protests that some shopkeepers and other adults who do not know them "don't give us a chance, just because it's Glebe ... bad things happen here. ... You don't get to even know them yet and so you've judged 'em wrong." All the girls vehemently express resistances to stereotypes as unjust and pejorative, but also because their knowledge of other ordinary cultural practices challenges the essentializing and totalizing identities through which others "fix" them into problematized street culture as well as categories.

Sticking Together

At the youth service, the girls may be observed as "ordinary" teenagers enjoying ordinary recreations. Catching up with friends is the primary interest, in and around the activities. The girls are active in all sports, sometimes cook for everyone at drop-in, make artworks, music, and videos. They use the computers, read magazines, and enjoy the movie nights. They sometimes organize activities for themselves and others. Their sorority is evident at the youth service, where girls generally arrive in pairs or small groups and often the girls all "hang out" together.

But being TGG means that "The ones that come around here like stick together" (Nola), and that is about more than hanging around with friends. The girls support each other in practical ways, for example, lending clothes, pooling funds for nights out or "a feed," giving or lending cash if they can, babysitting, places to stay when needed. Due to conflicts at home, evictions or simply a preference for staying with friends (or relatives), girls stay at each other's places for a few days or weeks at a time. They help each other to obtain assistance and resources through the youth service and other agencies. If someone is going to court or has been locked up, others are there to support or visit. Just "hanging around" together may also provide needed support through periods of hardship, loss, and ongoing difficult circumstances. Parents' alcohol or other drug use is problematic in most of the girls' families and four have had to deal with parents' mental illness. Some have had family members in jail, and all have had friends locked up. Their narratives tell of chaotic and traumatic periods. Between them they have experienced early loss of many relatives and friends, friends' suicide or overdose, assaults, transience, family violence, and all forms of abuse. They have managed personal experiences of accidents, problematic drug use, depression, abortion, miscarriage, homelessness, school exclusion, unemployment, solo parenting, and the daily difficulties from low or no income.

Despite and perhaps because of the personal and family experience of social problems, traditional ethics of care and loyalty are dominant social practices of their working-class and Indigenous neighborhoods. The principle of helping mates is still strong and the girls participate in the everyday practicalities of this support. These pragmatic "acts of community" reflect values of loyalty, pride in making ends meet and social responsibility, of ensuring that those who are alone or "doing it tough" are not forgotten or neglected. The girls' toughness and stoicism in the face of adversity are learned practices and responsibilities to "just get on with it" because there are "no quick fixes" (Rose).

Understanding the Way It Is

It is in the context of their belonging to their people, as insiders of marginal culture, that the girls articulate their understanding of the problems of the area. They variously foreground the interrelations of family, place, and troubles. At times their commentaries concur with outsiders' identification of social problems, but often with different meanings and very different conclusions. Youth crime is a case in point. The girls distinguish between their, and others', involvement in petty crime, especially illicit recreations, and more serious crimes involving violence. They also distinguish between those who occasionally cross this line, usually associated with alcohol or drug-related "episodes," and those who are caught up in a cycle of crime.

Jodi: In the end they go and do it, but in the end they regret it. They get into trouble for it, they get punished, they sit there and complain and say, oh God, why am I here, like if they're in the police station or whatever.

Sarah: But it's all their own fault.

Jodi: They like say, I won't do it again, I won't do it again and then it reoccurs and they think, oh why'd I do it again? Still happens. Like, becomes part of their nature.

With their understanding of how things are for people in difficult circumstances, the girls differentiate necessity as legitimate justification.

Jodi: Maybe sometimes they don't have a choice though, they don't have money so they go and steal. That's their only choice, the last resort. I'd say about, I dunno, twenty-five percent maybe, do it because they have to … the rest don't have to. Just … follow, a lot of followers … Maybe one of the … boys does, or another girl does, *has* to go and steal because they *have* to, but [others] just … want to … fit in …

Rose: There are some kids that aren't on drugs that haven't got enough money for clothes and stuff like that, so they need to do it. [My friend used to do] it to give his brothers and sisters a feed at night and buy some clothes for himself. That was about all …

Lack of funds makes them vulnerable to criminalization, whereas others who have the resources for the same illicit activities can "get away with it." On marijuana use, Rose says,

There's a lot of people who have money who are on drugs and they can just get it whenever they want. If they don't have money, they're gonna have to go out and steal it.

This recognition of double standards strengthens conviction that the activity itself is harmless and that the means are justified when only some people get targeted.

Other stresses and problems in individuals and families are also identified as causal factors in youth crime.

Jodi:	They might approach things differently. … It's just they might have been brought up different. … Maybe they had a broken family and um, I dunno, a lot of stress or something, might not have grown up with a father. If it's a boy, maybe they need a father figure, to sort of control them, something like that.
Sarah:	Abuse in the family or something. Maybe a violent childhood.
Jodi:	They might have a really big family, like, and they don't get all the attention put on them. Maybe it's a bit easier when you've got a smaller family 'cause you get more attention. Maybe they haven't got much money. … Maybe they've got very low self-esteem and they think, oh if we do this we'll be right, we'll have more friends, people will think, oh yeah, look at them, they're rebels.
Sarah:	They'll think people will look up to them.

But the girls do not see these as personal deficiencies or cause for condemnation. Their understandings lead to very different conclusions. Jodi comments:

I can't change my friends for, just because they do bad things. You gotta accept people like that you can't just put people down cause they might have a different background or something like that. They might do things differently in their life, approach things differently, you can't sort of run them down because of that.

Loyalty is warranted not only in resistance to outsider stereotyping, but also because it is just what you do. People are not "written off" because of their difficult circumstances and getting caught up in detrimental aspects of local culture.

It is not the "ordinary" illicit activities that are criticized, as much as the consequences of participating, not only in terms of "trouble" and "punishments," but in how it positions them. In Jodi's words:

Cause they can take risks and stuff and some people might be scared to … It's not something really that you should be looked up to for, but that's just the way it is. Some people look down on people for doing it as well.

The girls' perspectives indicate a double consciousness of their own and others' interpretation of street culture. The contexts of crime, drinking, and fighting indicate awareness of differential distributions of social resources and how difference is lived. Identifying as TGG, sticking together, and confronting adversities are all colored by awareness that how they are seen by others is not *their* definition of who they are.

TGG and Identity

Chosen and Unchosen Social Identity

The experiences of the Glebe girls suggest that there are two distinct forms of belonging to identifiable groups: that which is "chosen," claimed, and desired, as well as "unchosen" positioned and ascribed identity. The girls' struggles to be, and be seen as, who they are, may be read as struggles *for* chosen, and *against* unchosen, social identities.

It is difficult to separate the girls' perceptions of Glebe, and themselves, from their responses to others' perceptions of Glebe. Place and reputation are inextricably enmeshed. Awareness of how "people" see their end of Glebe clearly colors their own sense of place and their place in it. They do not want to be "put into a category" based on perceptions of their area which identify Glebe as "bad" and which "place" them at the "bad" end. Alongside this critique, the girls claim the margins (hooks 1990) and proudly belong to their people. This does not mean that the girls are uncritical of problems within their families but they maintain strong bonds and are quick to defend them. Nancy remarks:

> I needed a stable environment. But if you turned it back, I wouldn't want it different cause I am who I am today. … I had good parents, don't get me wrong and like, they might drink and that, but no drugs, they wouldn't swear in front of us, nothing … We had a strict home … that's one thing that probably saved me. …They taught me right from wrong, good from bad. They taught me respect, for myself and other people.

TGG "stick together" and "are always gonna hang round with the boys" (Nola) of the network because they are "mates" (Nancy); and because they have learned that respect is first and foremost to be attained where they are known.

The girls claim their positive identification with their people, in part, by differentiating the respectable community of those who hold to the ethics and practices of working-class and Indigenous traditions, from others at the "bad end" who are "no-hopers" (Rose). They distance themselves from those who are using heroin, dealing, and are involved in other serious crime, among whom "there's no respect," who are just "lookin' out for number one" (Nancy). They also distance themselves from the "snobs," "the ones that have the money" (Jodi). Reflecting on what "success" would mean for them, the girls prioritize personal and community qualities over material achievements. It might be argued that such priorities are pragmatic, given their lack of resources and structural barriers to mainstream success. However, the girls recognize that they desire the material benefits they see. What they reject is both conspicuous affluence and the values of that kind of "other" whose assumed superiority is integral to the denigration of their kind of people.

Articulating her position in broader social terms, Rebecca says,

> ... people look at us kids like scum. ... It's society too that when it puts people in classes, makes you feel like shit ... they're trying to downgrade you to the lowest.

She rejects this labeling, in part by rationalizing that "there's no set class for anyone":

> There's no upper class, middle class, down class, cause everyone sometimes is down, sometimes is middle, sometimes is up ... money doesn't make you nice, doesn't make you happy ...

But she is aware of other differentiating markers of social status:

> If I like won the lottery today, I wouldn't be looked at any different as I did the other day because I came into money.

Rebecca's status is determined by more than class. Her physicality on the streets carries other important identity markers: she is Aboriginal, young, and female. Dominant societal distinctions of race, class, and gender, and deep and both overt and subtle related prejudices, underpin local reinscriptions of differentiated identifiable groups. The girls refer to these in vernacular terms as "standards," "looks," and "categories," and the ways girls and youth are talked about in the area.

Chosen identity is never outside the unchosen, as both are constructed within the dominant paradigm of center-marginal relations. Those relations privilege being White, middle class, and male (Apple 1997; Fordham 1996). The experiences of the Glebe girls suggest that the more one's chosen identity deviates from that norm, the greater the "othering" effects of unchosen identity. The girls' use of public space, for example, is problematized within "moral panics" more because of who they are than what they do. Even when they are "doing nothing," just "hanging out" together, they may be judged as transgressing socially acceptable behavior.

Unchosen identities are difficult to counter, because they are structured in relations largely controlled by others. Rebecca's grappling with the complex layerings of reputation is an acknowledgment of this difficulty. On the one hand she acknowledges the value of a tough image; on the other, bad reputations make life difficult.

When you live in Glebe, there's heaps of emphasis on Glebe, you know what I mean, that's supposed to be like that's where all the hard cunts come from.

There is a reputation to live up to; but Rebecca's comment also challenges the presumption of Glebe's hardness as a stereotype. She attempts to pin down these issues, within an awareness of the scrutiny of the local community and of society's "standards." Her preferred social practices may result in further damage to reputation at the same time as they are established marginal norms and thus fit with her chosen cultural identity.

Identity work involves making sense of competing values and norms. Values that are privileged within their neighborhood culture underpin the girls' behaviors, which are "ordinary" in that context and "connect them with one another, their families, and their community" (Brown 1998, 128). In "outside" contexts, the same values and behaviors are unacceptable. Resistances are thus integral to maintaining chosen identity to counter its perceived denigration, being "downgraded to the lowest." When failure in "other" cultural contexts is simultaneous with success in one's home culture, girls "do seem to be in a position where everything they do reinforces somebody's negative attitudes towards them" (Stanley 1993, 40). In attempts to maintain or regain control or power, the girls take up and take on, as well as contest, aspects of negative ascriptions. Accentuating behaviors that fit the stereotypes may constitute resistance for personal empowerment. The girls' vehement repudiation of stereotypes may be seen as the defense of chosen identity but the difficulty of countering stereotypes becomes a factor in justifying illicit recreations.

Resistance, Resilience, and Identity

Resistance as Resilience

Limits of location, discursive and socioeconomic marginalization, and the specific difficulties of the girls' lives, are the context of their resistances. In this context, their resistances may be reframed as resilience, as positive adaptation despite adversity (Redl 1969; Werner 1989).

Resilience building has recently become a new touchstone for supporting marginalized young people. In education, welfare and community work, juvenile justice, and youth training programs, resilience building has become a key principle and outcome focus (see for example, Benard 1998). However, decontextualized and asocial definitions of resilience may be too narrow to identify some marginal forms. Defined from the center, resilience predominantly refers to behaviors that conform to center norms; all the more so when resilience is posited as counter to risk and deviance. Recognizing resilience in marginalized young people requires a shift in perspective, looking and understanding from alternative centers.

Participating in street culture and the support network of TGG, the girls claim "the margins" in ways that accrue different (marginal) cultural capital, the positive resources and esteem of their people. From this "center," they refuse to identify with images that denigrate them or their people; they buffer themselves from negative labeling and from failure that seems inevitable even when the effort to succeed is made. Such resistances indicate girls' strengths rather than deficiencies.

Resistance and Resilience in the Margins

Resistances may at times be expressions of deeper anger, an inevitable emotion in claiming social identity when it is simultaneously known to be denigrated by others. The girls' street resistances are indicative of their "failure to adjust well to subordination" (Lyman 1981, 59). This failure, this refusal, nonetheless is contained by concerns for reputation. They want to elude the bad image of their end of Glebe, to avoid it "sticking" on them. They claim their place in the margins, in the network, but want these affiliations on *their* terms, not as defined in delimiting ways by others. Their resistances may at times prohibit conventional options, but maintaining a strong sense of self and the loyalties of alliance as forms of solidarity and empowerment may be taken as indicators of resilience in their determination to be successful on their own terms.

The girls' resilience is acknowledged within their neighborhood communities. The girls, and their peers, are known and "owned" by their people. Individual achievements, for example in sport, in obtaining an education credential or a job, or having a baby are celebrated and admired. Within the local youth network, these achievements also accrue status, alongside that accorded to criminal and fighting prowess, involvement in "legendary" incidents, and street cheek which entertains, retaliates, or relieves boredom.

However, outside the context of being known and belonging, resistances are assigned notoriety that overshadows positive achievements. Moreover, their positive achievements may be unknown or unacknowledged. There is no accrual of "legitimate" cultural capital nor "official" validation of marginal achievement. The absence of "good news" from "the bad end" is a factor in the reinscription of negative stereotypes.

Even though young people thrive on recognition and status assigned within their peer groups and neighborhoods, it is evident that their awareness of the persistence of others' denigrating stereotypes diminishes their resilience: pride can readily transform to shame and anger in the face of outsider put-downs, as with Rebecca's resentment at "being looked down on" and Aisha's concern about being prejudged.

Pragmatic Resilience

Alongside their social critiques, the girls individualize responsibility. "It's their own fault" (Sarah) if young people do crime. "It's their choice" (Jodi) if they drink or take drugs. "If you don't want to fight you don't have to" (Nola). Fulfilling aspirations about education, work and other life goals is "down to me" (Nola); "you have to be able to help yourself" (Rose). Claiming "solutions" as depending on "yourself if you want to reach where you want to go" (Linda) is placed alongside experiential knowledge of difficulties and barriers. Desiring conventional rewards is tempered by a wariness of expecting too much, because, as Carol and Rebecca put it, they have "been told" they "are not going to amount to nothing … you come from Glebe, you go nowhere."

When girls give up on schooling or job seeking, these decisions may be necessary interruptions to protracted efforts. It is not that they completely give up their aspirations, rather that other demands take priority: for making ends meet, for having some fun, and looking after friends and family. At the "bad end," these priorities may require much more effort because individuals, and the social groups to which they belong, are underresourced and marginalized. When everyday life is difficult in fundamental ways, giving up may be simply a matter of "regrouping" to face the next period of struggle. Completing or returning to education features strongly in the girls' aspirations. Nola wants to "get my own license and go cruising with the girls! Get my own place. Yeah and finish, do some school, and get a full-time job." Patsy aims to "get some more … education. Once I feel more confident in myself, that's it, 'cause there's so much I want to do."

Rose sums up the girls' depiction of a struggle against the odds, but the individual might prevail.

I think you create your own success. I always thought … there'd be an easy way out, but there isn't. If you wanna do it, you gotta do it yourself. But, it is hard.

For Rebecca, success is about being happy in herself. Finding her own equilibrium is a milestone.

Like, happiness is good, yeah I'm happy—but you can always be happier, you know? But like, you don't want to get there and be so happy and then go back to so sad and, you know what really happy feels like, you can just get really sad? I dunno. It's just one day you're happy, one day you're shit, one day you're all right—up and down.

Pragmatic definitions of success also include being able to provide for their children, in ways that they were not always provided for. Patsy comments:

I'd like when my kids are teenagers, for them to be able to come to me and say I need money for this or whatever and be able to give it to them. That would make me feel real, knowing I've done my job, to be able to chuck them a sixteenth birthday party or eighteenth or whatever. That's why, you know, I wanna work. Also once my kids are grown up, you know, be able to have that money to go on holidays or be able to give presents for my kids and yeah. But I think of the future a lot, about grandkids and stuff like that, 'cause I want to be there for them and their kids. I think of it all the time, you know, I want to do things differently, everything, buying toys or food or, you know, just the whole thing. What in life I have they got the opposite, you know, a better world.

Nancy's definition of success is also about being happy, on her own terms:

The so-called thing is house, car, family, which is the beginning. That's just to keep you going, I reckon. A successful life is being happy, with yourself, and getting to the point where you know yourself. 'Cause you can have all them things and still be fucked, you know what I mean? The main part is you've gotta be happy with yourself and be true to yourself and don't do bad things to other people.

The girls' pragmatic philosophies reflect their agency, and its limits, within their specific social and cultural context. Being from the "bad end" does not necessarily mean you are a "bad kid" as others may define you.

Nancy: I've seen kids that have had bad lives but you see other kids up here they've had heaps bad lives and they're not the worst kids. They're not bad, bad kids. ... You've just gotta have a stable environment. All kids are born good, do you know what I mean? They're turned bad. They say that's a bad kid, that's a bad kid, but it wasn't born bad, it was a good kid. ... All the shit that's there is bad, bad on top, so it's hard to get to the under layer, you know what I mean? The good kid's still there. They can stay bad and then they go good, you know what I mean?

DB: Have you seen any people who are like that who then do come good? [Long pause]

Nancy: I was a bad kid. [Laughs]

DB: I can't imagine that!

Nancy: I was! I was a bad kid.

Outsiders may judge differently, and attempts to counter stereotypes may seem futile. But within their own neighborhood, where people understand what happens, how youngsters can "be turned bad," there is more hope for strengthening a different kind of "cultural capital" than that required for status by conventional standards. Conventional pathways are not readily accessible, but within local traditions, resources can be acquired, values can be asserted, and young people can be known as "good kids." The girls are counting on the potential of their agency and the support of their people for turning around their experiences into something better in adulthood, and something better for their children. The resilience of the girls is the flipside of their resistances, and chosen identity supports and strengthens that resilience.

Conclusions

Understandings of the girls' experiences are standpoint dependent. Within contested claims to public space, the problematizing of the streets can readily problematize the girls themselves. Similarly, the identification of social problems where they live can readily pathologize them, in their belonging to identifiable groups. Behaviors that are regarded by the girls as integral to "ordinary recreations" may be categorized by others as delinquent, deviant, or dysfunctional, as individual or social problems at the bad end. On legal grounds the same behaviors may be criminalized. Theories of cultural reproduction assume structural limits to agency but ultimately rely on ascriptions of false consciousness or inability to mobilize collective political action, indicative of deficiency rather than strengths. The alternative interpretation of resistance as resilience assumes the cultural relativity of behavioral norms and that marginal perspectives need to be better understood.

The value of "snapshot" research is the elucidation of girls' present cultural experience. However, the "long view" of change and continuity over time, and the "bigger picture" of multilayered and overlapping contexts, are also necessary for understanding how identity work develops and adapts to changing conditions. In the present research it is significant that both younger and older girls' perspectives are heard. Street culture is shared experience, including their recognition of the constraints of locality, material, and discursive difference. They also recognize barriers to mainstream success, while holding aspirations for some of the center's rewards, but simultaneously prioritizing their own people and values over the socially dominant which they reject. But the older girls' experiences, in particular, are a challenge to the snapshot which would have "fixed" them principally as resisters, rendering them vulnerable to further reinscription as oppositional, antisocial, and ineffectual in attempts to counter pejorative ascriptions. That they are able, over time, to exert their agency in positive directions, despite the grip of local stereotyping, is significant.

In the face of adversity, the practices and pragmatism of the girls may be interpreted as resilient. They are making the best they can out of living in conditions of struggle that are their everyday experiences of social positioning and social divisions. Their identity work, in terms of rejection of unchosen identities and embracing chosen social identity, is essential to their survival strategies and pragmatic philosophies. Drawing on the resources, support, and positive attributes of their people, they cope, often stoically, they speak their critiques, assert their rights, and maintain pride in belonging to their home community. Everyday problems are solved by marginal practices coconstructed within their sorority and their relations with friends and family.

Their capability in creating workable solutions suggests positive adaptation despite adversity.

References

Alder, C. 1993. Police, youth and violence. In *Juvenile justice: Debating the issues*, ed. F. Gale, N. Naffine, and J. Wundersitz, 78–87. St. Leonards, Australia: Allen & Unwin.

Apple, M. 1997. Consuming the other: Whiteness, education and cheap French fries. In *Off white: Readings on race, power and society*, ed M. Fine, L. Weis, L. Powell, L. Mun Wong, 121–128. New York: Routledge.

Armstrong, D. 2004. A risky business? Research, policy, governmentality and youth offending. *Youth Justice* 4:100–117.

Armstrong, D. 2006. Becoming criminal: The cultural politics of risk. *International Journal of Inclusive Education* 10 (2/3):265–278.

Bail, K., ed. 1996. *DIY feminism*. Sydney: Allen & Unwin.

Baines, M. and C. Alder. 1996. When she was bad she was horrid. In *... and when she was bad? Working with young women in juvenile justice and related areas*, ed. C. Alder and M. Baines, 25–32. Hobart: National Clearinghouse for Youth Studies.

Benard, B. 1998. *The Bonnie Benard Collection. Vol. 1. Resiliency research findings*. Launceston: Global Learning Communities.

Bradley, H. 2005. Winners and losers: Young people in the "new economy." In *Young people in Europe: Labour markets and citizenship*, ed. H. Bradley and J. van Hoof, 99–113. Bristol: Policy Press.

Brown, L. M. 1998. *Raising their voices: The politics of girls' anger*. Cambridge, MA: Harvard University Press.

Campbell, A. 1987. Self definition by rejection: The case of gang girls. *Social Problems* 34 (5) (December):451–466.

Campbell, A. 1993. *Out of control: Men, women and aggression*. London: HarperCollins.

Carrington, K. 1989. Girls and graffiti. *Cultural Studies* 1 (3):89–100.

Carrington, K. 1993. Cultural studies, youth culture and delinquency. In *Youth subcultures: Theory, history and the Australian experience*, ed. R. White, 27–32. Hobart: National Clearinghouse for Youth Studies.

Chesney-Lind, M. 1993. Girls, gangs and violence: Anatomy of a backlash. *Humanity and Society* 17:321–344.

Cohen, S. 1980. *Folk devils and moral panics: The creation of Mods and Rockers*. Oxford: Martin Robinson.

Davies, B. 1990. Lived and imaginary narratives and their place in taking oneself up as a gendered being. *Australian Psychologist* 25 (3):318–332.

Davis, N., S. Hatty, and S. Burke. 1995. Rough justice: Social control and resistance among homeless youth. In *Ways of Resistance: Social control and young people in Australia*, ed. Cheryl Simpson and Richard Hil, 93–114. Sydney: Hale & Iremonger.

Families First. 2000. *Glebe community building research project: Final Report*. (September). Sydney: Families First in the Inner West, NSW Department of Community Services.

Fordham, S. 1996. *Blacked out: Dilemmas of race, identity, and success at Capital High*. Chicago: University of Chicago Press.

Gilbert, P. and S. Taylor. 1991. *Fashioning the feminine: Girls, popular culture and schooling*. Sydney: Allen & Unwin.

Griffin, C. 2004. Representations of the young. In *Youth in Society,* ed. J. Roche, S. Tucker, R. Thomson, and R. Flynn, 10–18. London: Sage/Open University Press.

Hall, S. and T. Jefferson, eds. 1976. *Resistance through rituals: Youth subcultures in post-war Britain.* London: Hutchinson.

Harris, A. 2004. *Future girl: Young women in the twenty-first century.* New York: Routledge.

Hey, V. 1997. *The company she keeps: An ethnography of girls' friendship.* Buckingham: Open University Press.

hooks, b. 1990. *Yearning: Race, gender, and cultural politics.* Boston: South End Press.

Lyman, P. 1981. The politics of anger: On silence, ressentiment, and political speech. *Socialist Review* 11 (3) (May–June):55–74.

MacDonald, R. and J. Marsh. 2005. *Disconnected youth? Growing up in Britain's poor neighbourhoods.* New York: Palgrave Macmillan.

McRobbie, A. 1991. Settling accounts with subcultures: A feminist critique. In *Feminism and youth culture: From 'Jackie' to 'Just Seventeen',* 16–34. London: Macmillan.

McRobbie, A. 1994. *Postmodernism and popular culture.* London: Routledge.

Muncie, John. 2004. Youth justice: Responsibilisation and rights. In *Youth in Society,* ed. J. Roche, S. Tucker, R. Thomson, and R. Flynn, 131–144. London: Sage/Open University Press.

Paglia, C. 1992. *Sex, art and American culture: Essays.* New York: Vintage Books.

Pini, M. 1996. Dance classes: Dancing between classifications. *Feminism and Psychology* 6 (3):411–426.

Pini, M. 2004. Technologies of the self. In *Youth in Society,* ed. J. Roche, S. Tucker, R. Thomson, and R. Flynn, 160–167. London: Sage/Open University Press.

Redl, F. 1969. Adolescents: Just how do they react? In *Adolescence: Psychosocial perspectives,* ed. G. Caplan and S. Lebovici, 79–99. New York: Basic Books.

Sercombe, H., P. Omaji, N. Drew, T. Cooper, and T. Love. 2002. *Youth and the future: Effective youth services for the year 2015. A report to the National Youth Affairs Research Scheme.* Hobart: Australian Clearinghouse for Youth Studies.

Smith, D. 1987. *The everyday world as problematic: A feminist sociology.* Boston: Northeastern University Press.

Stanley, J. 1993. Sex and the quiet school girl. In *Gender and ethnicity in schools: Ethnographic accounts,* ed. P. Woods and M. Hammersley, 34–48. London: Routledge/The Open University.

Sweeting, H. and P. West. 2003. Young people's leisure and risk-taking behaviours: Changes in gender patterning in the west of Scotland during the 1990s. *Journal of Youth Studies* 6 (4):391–412.

Walkerdine, V., H. Lucey, and J. Melody. 2001. *Growing up girl: Psychosocial explorations of gender and class.* Houndmills, Hampshire: Palgrave.

Werner, E. 1989. High-risk children in young adulthood: A longitudinal study from birth to 32 years. *American Journal of Orthopsychiatry* 59 (1) (January):72–81.

Wyn, J. and R. White. 1997. *Re-thinking youth.* Sydney: Allen & Unwin.

3

Third-Wave Feminism, the Global Economy, and Women's Surfing

Sport as Stealth Feminism in Girls' Surf Culture

LESLIE HEYWOOD

Women's and girls' sport marks one arena where the contradictions between and reformulations of terms like modern and postmodern, second- and third-wave feminism, and subcultural and post-subcultural most reveal themselves. Girls who have grown up with the opportunity to play sport in the 1980s and 1990s—perhaps particularly "extreme" sports such as mountain climbing, snowboarding, and surfing that until very recently remained coded as "male"—have experienced gender and identities in very different ways from women of earlier generations. Instead of having to renounce femininity to prove themselves athletes, these women assume their athleticism and strength and therefore demonstrate less concern about issues of gender. However, the same commodification of athleticism in both traditional and nontraditional sports that helped gain wider acceptance for female athletes now limits the potential of sport as a politically transformative space. Taking the sport of surfing as a test case in its shift from a female-hostile, primarily "male" space to a sport whose iconography and industry is increasingly inclusive of women, the chapter asks why and to what extent female surfers are being utilized as a sign for the positive aspects of the global economy, and what effect that usage has on popular representations of women's surfing practice—especially as these relate to larger problems within feminist theory, such as the divide between conventionally "second-" and "third wave" approaches.

The chapter explores contemporary surf culture and young women's place in it as an example of what might be called a "stealth feminism" that is expressed through sport—a form of "third-wave" feminism set in dialog with its own historical circumstances. Pointing to the impossibility of a strict divide between dominant cultures and subcultures, female surfers serve as both signs of the ideal neoliberal subject and as cultural signifiers that occupy a "third-wave," signal-crossed space, complicit with the dominant values of the global economy but nonetheless involved in the renegotiation of gender and its relation to core cultural values such as independence, personal competency, and strength. The female surfer (and the female athlete more generally) reflects a representational nexus where the female body, instead of primarily signifying a dependent sexuality as in second-wave feminist analyses that spoke of "the objectification of women," has come to signify an independent sexuality that reflects women's potential as "self-determining" wage earners and consumers.

Formulations of Post-Subculture and the Tribe of Surf

Because of its historically "subcultural" status, any discussion of contemporary surfing necessarily enters into the categorical debates. According to most formulations of post-subculture, traditional emphasis on the resistant function of subculture has broken down as a result of the turn to individualism that accompanied the consumer lifestyles associated with advanced consumer capitalism. Due to these structural changes, "the sorts of cultural involvement once deemed to be characteristic of subcultures have become more general" (Chaney 2004, 43). Nowhere is this clearer than in the case of the sport of surfing, where residual connotations of opt-out hedonism mix with its now-dominant place in the cultural imaginary. As surfer and filmmaker Dana Brown notes in *Step Into Liquid*, "the rebellious subculture has become mainstream" (2004). In fact, increased girls' and women's participation and the "feminization" of surfing that has been underway since the mid-nineties is an integral part of that "mainstreaming." Yet Paul Sweetman's complication to this formula also applies: "[the notion of subcultural mainstreaming] can also be said to overlook the more affectual or experiential aspects of 'subcultural' involvement, including the way in which coming together as a group—however temporary and fragmented that group is—can provide individuals with a sense of belonging and identification *as well as* a sense of individual identity and style" (2004, 79). Surfers are a quintessential example of what social researchers call "neotribes," "an empathetic form of sociality where what is important is ... the feeling of togetherness engendered by one's direct involvement with the social group ... centered around feelings. ... 'affective warmth' that allows for that 'loss of self in the group' or 'ex-static attitude' ... 'immanent transcendence' (Sweetman 2004, 86). Surfers describe themselves as just this kind of affective tribe whose bond is based solely on the shared experience of surfing: "we are the surfing tribe ... surfing can bring us together no matter race, creed, or color ... sharing a common pursuit of happiness" (Brown 2004).

For many surfers, surfing is their primary identity. Dana Brown begins his documentary *Step Into Liquid* with the statement "I'm Dana Brown, and I'm a surfer. This film isn't about a lifestyle, it's about a life. ... many of us have nothing in common except this shared passion." Surf pioneer Gerry Lopez explains that "all it takes is just one wave—not even that, just one turn, one moment, it keeps pulling you back to another moment, it never ends." Recent surf champion Rob Machado describes surfers as "a tribe of people around the world who feed off that energy [waves]" (Brown 2004). But as much as there is a shared identity in this tribe, a mutual commitment to and love of surf, gender remains a sort of divide that complicates this powerful affective identification, and which most points to discrepancies between identity and representation. As in most cultural forms, there is a gap between mass cultural or even subcultural representation and practitioners' experiences and subjectivities, a gap that, in the case of women's surfing, sometimes looms large.

In order to begin to make sense of the particular meanings embodied in women's surfing today, and how those might be linked to the larger global economy and its ideologies of neoliberal subjectivity that have a particular valence in relation to women, it is important to briefly discuss the history of surfing's subcultural status and its exclusion of women. Although it traces its origins to ancient Polynesian cultures, surfing became highly visible as a subculture during the 1960s, particularly in the United States. The initial explosion of cultural production related to surfing—which many surf historians attribute to the success of Frederick Kohner's 1957 novel *Gidget*, based on his teenaged daughter's surfing experiences—had a particular effect on the subculture. The superficiality of the Hollywood beach movies such as *Beach Blanket Bingo* that followed in *Gidget*'s wake, combined with the explosion of surfing images in advertising, and the popularity of "surf music" like that of Dick Dale and the Beach Boys all had a galvanizing effect on the subculture, which objected to the "feminization" such mass cultural productions suggested. One subcultural reaction to this feminization was what surf historian Matt Warshaw terms "the surfer's ongoing shift from [the early twentieth century idea of the] noble sportsman to [the 1950s–1980s view of the] bleached-blonde rebel" (2003, xiv). To the hardcore surfer, mass representation robbed him of his unique oppositional character, "feminizing" him by making his image acceptable to the mainstream that embraced family, nation, and surfing as good clean fun, which made the subculture react even more vehemently against those values. Academic sport historian Douglas Booth notes that "the hedonistic and irreverent culture adopted by young surfers offended many of their elders, members of a generation whose life perspectives were forged in depression and world war. Social commentators in the 1950s and early 1960s condemned surfing as an indolent, wasteful, selfish, and institutionally unanchored pastime. The surfer style, the trademark of which was long bleached hair, surfers' argot, humor, and rituals, and their nomadic lifestyle rendered them socially irresponsible" (Booth 2004, 95). As I will develop later, within an IBM-style "father-provider" scheme of corporate organization, the one prevalent at the time, nomadism and an inability to "settle down" were indeed countercultural. However, in today's global economy of flexible specialization based on global flows of capital and workers, an economy that requires mobility and the ability to adapt quickly to changing circumstance, these seemingly "free-form" characteristics have begun to seem much more normalized and even required.

One related and underdocumented aspect of the "subcultural surfer" tendency that Booth articulates here is its gendered aspect, where part of surfers' "social irresponsibility" involved the rejection of long-term domestic relationships with women in favor of "riding the wild surf," and claiming surfing as a masculine preserve free of women. As Krista Comer explains in "Wanting to be Lisa," the first academic work to fully analyze the gendered dimensions of surfing: "when the subculture 'wrote back' after Gidget to say that mass culture had sugarcoated and, in effect, feminized surfing, it countered with images of surfers as rebelliously masculine, sensual, anti-materialist social drop-outs" (2004, 238–239). One remarkably effective mode of distancing women and femininity from surfing—a mode that persists to some extent to the present day—is the disproportionate amount of media coverage women's surfing competitions receive, which is on par with the disproportionate coverage of female athletes more generally (Duncan and Messner 2000). Warshaw (2003) shows one such distancing method when he writes that "*Surfer* magazine didn't even bother to publish the women's division results" when surfing's World Championships started in 1964 (xv). However, although female surfers were largely invisible through the 1980s, the advancement of the athletic image in corporate advertising in the 1990s had a paradoxical mainstreaming effect, which in turn had some effect on the sport itself (this was also the case in many other women's sports).[1]

One of the most prominent ways that one can say "surfing became mainstream" is in the way that the then-countercultural individualistic hedonism documented by Douglas Booth, so much a part of late fifties into the mid-seventies surf culture, has become normalized, part of the corporate pitch to the individual and the fulfillment of individual desires (2004). As will be elaborated more fully in the following section, a global economy reliant upon flexibility in terms of location as well as mode of production, an ever-narrowing specialization in terms of product (many different kinds of computers or cameras, meant for many different uses, for instance, instead of one-size fits all), and the cultivation of niche markets demands different workers than an economy based on mass production of the same good. "Individualist hedonism" has become a market mainstay, from ever-more-customizable iPods to the $400 production of jeans built to individual specification. The inclusion of women in the hedonist, "fulfill yourself" horizon, and their cultivation as a market for sporting goods, began largely in the nineties, when U.S. women outspent men on athletic footwear for the first time in 1994.[2] Doing what you want becomes buying the gear that will let you do what you want, and the DIY (do it yourself) values associated with extreme or "X" sports like surfing, skateboarding, snowboarding, and Motocross all became part of a marketing pitch so that even nonparticipants could lay claim to the "nonconformist" culture through the consumption of products associated with it. Therefore, surfing's increasingly mainstream status has developed in conjunction with its "feminization"—the development of a mass industry associated with the sport and the inclusion of women in its representational imaginary since women, as well as men, are now said to "do their own thing." That corporate embrace of surfing, and women, is double-edged, and carries a burden of signification linked to the dominant economic philosophies of our time.

The Female Surfer's Body: The Physiology of Neoliberal Capital

Post-Fordist economic analysis would seem an unlikely place to discuss female surfers, but I would like to make the case that both the somatic body type required for highly skilled surfing and contemporary body ideals for women share a metaphorical connection with the post-Fordist conception of "flexible specialization." Furthermore, the doctrine of neoliberal individualism is expressed by and through that body type, suggesting a flexible identity that is nonetheless said to be self-determining. In post-Fordist analysis, the economic sector is now characterized by the following: (1) the globalization of markets, (2) the proliferation of information technologies, (3) emphasis on niche markets or different types of consumers instead of social class, and (4) the "feminization" of the work force in the shift to a service economy. These changes were precipitated by changes in the global economy in the early 1970s, such as the oil shocks of 1973, the acceleration of competition from foreign markets (especially Japan), privatization, and the end of post–WWII prosperity which made mass production (the production of generic, cheap goods) no longer profitable (Amin 1994). Instead, the diversification of product lines targeted to "niche" markets—what might be called "subcultural" tastes and styles—required a "flexible" approach to production that could quickly respond to market trends instead of huge expenditures on the mass production of one identical product. Similarly, on the sector level the mode of production itself was fragmented and diversified so that a single company no longer presided over the entire process from raw materials to finished product. Production was outsourced to individual firms that specialize in particular areas of expertise.

This kind of flexibility and fragmentation in economic production is often taken as one of the hallmarks of globalization, and is furthermore connected to the management and production of the human subject, the expectations for the "productive" member of society, and contemporary definitions of "success." In social terms, the shift from production to consumption as a framework for identity is focused not on what one's job is, but rather what one buys and how one creates and manages one's image. In order to achieve "success," all one needs is to generate income and consume and display the right signifiers. This shift is concurrent with the shift from full-time, long-term employment with the same company to part-time, short-term contract labor, and the shift from the safety net of a welfare state or programs such as "social security" to the privatization of all social networks.

These shifts are accompanied by what social theorist Anita Harris terms "a new emphasis on the responsibilities of individuals" since "public policy often employs the language of individual responsibility and enterprise bargaining to fill the gap left by deregulation" (2004, 4). Young women, whom Harris terms "future girls," are symbolically constructed as "a vanguard of new subjectivity ... a focus for the construction of an ideal late modern subject who is self-making, resilient, and flexible" (2004, 1, 6). Because the concrete gains of feminism such as equal access to education have actually benefited some women, "the neoliberal discourse that has accompanied deregulation and deindustrialization merges well with a version of girlpower that emphasizes self-invention and individual economic empowerment" (Harris 2004, 10).

Widely changed in its terms from the countercultural, politicized "girlpower" first enacted by the DIY Riot Grrl bands in the early 1990s, "girlpower" has now come to primarily signify the "four versions of girlpower" documented by Jessica K. Taft: "girlpower as anti-feminism, girlpower as postfeminism, girlpower as individual power, and girlpower as consumer power" (Harris 2004, 70). Each form of girlpower shares a depoliticization of the original term, and each notion of girlpower interacts with markets to sell a vision of girls as capable and self-determining, no longer dependent on others for their identity or livelihood. And although this iconography may be said to represent some of the realizations of second-wave liberal feminist goals and therefore be seen as a positive development, it is also true that this version of "girlpower" masks the ways girls' and women's labor is often exploited, particularly in the "cheap labor" provided by women in the so-called economic "South."

There is no more visible, compelling version of "girlpower" than that embodied in the female athlete, whose very body is the concrete realization of a project of self-creation, the "future girl" who has "take[n] charge of her life, seiz[ed] chances, achieve[d] her goals" (Harris 2004, 1). Especially in the case of professional female athletes, her image enacts an ideological suture between the supposed world of economic possibility and its attainment. The image offers an "if she can do it, I can do it" sense of motivation for younger generations, and indicates that the structures pertaining to the global economy are truly "new"—supposedly providing girls and women the opportunity to overcome what are seen as previous structural limitations based on gender (this rhetoric will be used almost word for word in several athlete biographies produced by Fuel TV that I will discuss shortly). One function of the image is to mask the fact that not "just anyone" can achieve success, particularly in athletics, where there is always one winner for every plethora of "losers," and where professional earnings, particularly for female athletes, remain quite low for most. As previously mentioned, at least partially due to these suturing functions, there was a mainstreaming of the female athlete image in the 1990s. While female athletes were once seen as sexually suspect pariahs who embodied an "unnatural" masculinity, the pitch to the women's market in the nineties dovetailed with the discourse of "girlpower" to normalize and sexualize a more muscular ideal (Heywood 2000; Heywood and Dworkin 2003). I would argue, however, that the ideal image being marketed then—the mesomorphic (muscular) body type of women's soccer star Mia Hamm, or Olympic track champion Marion Jones—was of a qualitatively different kind than the female surfer body, which is ectomorphic: leaner, less muscular and more flexible. As I have argued in "Producing Girls: Empire, Sport, and the Neoliberal Body" (Heywood 2006), the new ideal, instead of emphasizing solidity, instead focuses on flexibility and strength (or, in effect, the particular kind of strength associated with flexibility).

According to popular representations, the surfer girl is everywhere, marking the new beauty norm and ideal. In her forthcoming book *Surfing the New World Order*, American Studies researcher Krista Comer documents what she terms the conversion of "images of surfer girls in American popular culture" from "occasional and exotic visual anomalies" to "mainstay figures of desirable, global twenty-first century womanhood" (forthcoming). This conversion is best demonstrated in the market realm. Roxy, the division of Quiksilver marketed exclusively to women and young girls, had $1 million in sales in 1991 but $87.8 million in the third quarter of 2005 alone. Overall, women's surf/skate apparel sold $489.6 million in 2004, according to the SIMA (Surf Industry Manufacturer's Association) Retail Distribution study. The number of ASP (Associated Surfing Professionals) women's competitors went from 91 in 1995 to 180 in 2005. A Vans Triple Crown market research study claims that nine million American women say they "want to learn to surf," and enthusiastic press makes claims like "paddle out at either Surf City—Santa Cruz or Huntington—and you just might see two girls hassling every boy for every wave." However, it is still true that, although the number of women who actually surf has increased exponentially since 1999, of the roughly two million surfers in the United States in 2004, only 33 percent were women (quote and all statistics from the *Wet Magazine* press kit, 2006). It is also true that, as in other women's sports, resources in surfing are still largely controlled by men. The proliferation of images and rhetoric about women's surfing disguises the fact that, as Comer notes, "while women and girls are architects of this takeover [of surfing], they are not its principal power players, and they reap but the most negligible fraction of its profits. Furthermore, the assertion that surfing as a sport and culture is somehow wide open to girls … belies not just surfing's unapologetically sexist history, but also its very steep learning curve" (Comer 2004, 240). There is a gap between the image and its cultural functions, and the reality of surfing experience, a gap that is only explicable through reference to the global economy and the ways body ideals are linked to its changes.

The "hardbody" ideal of the 1980s, perhaps best exemplified by the visibility of Sylvester Stallone as Rambo and Arnold Schwarzenegger as the Terminator, has been repeatedly analyzed in relation to political and social trends. Yvonne Tasker, for instance, writes that "coming at the particular point that it did, the success of these films and stars could be read in terms of a backlash against the feminism of the 1970s, as indicative of a new conservatism in both national and sexual politics ... a figure who represented the antithesis of the 'new man' ... and the feminist gains he supposedly represented" (1993, 1). Samantha King writes of the same period that, "as the 1980's proceeded and the Reaganite/Thatcherite ideologies of self-responsibility gained the status of hegemony, the body became the site of condensation for a whole range of social anxieties" (2005, 25). In a similar sense, the female surfer embodies the ideological junctures of her own time. Simply put, she is the visual embodiment of flexible capital and the global culture of consumption. She visually articulates the dream of successfully negotiating constantly shifting conditions, the fluid ideals and dreams of possibility and their fulfillment.

Such images, which grace ads for everything from hair products to surf gear to multiple kinds of sport and fashion apparel (the Roxy Web site is characteristic), demonstrate a lean-muscled femininity that is linked to the sport itself. The surfers look happy, healthy, and strong in a flexible way—the kind of balance they exhibit on the board requires both strength and flexiblity. Extreme sports, especially surfing, require a body that can adapt to constant changes in the waves, whose strength is not in its bulk but in its adaptability to changing circumstance, much as the global economic context requires adaptation to constantly shifting parameters. The image fits. A lean, downsized post-Fordist economy has a symbiotic relationship with contemporary images and narratives of female athleticism. In addition to the appeal to young women as an important consumer market, this ideal image of female athletes perfectly incorporates the ideal of the new, can-do, DIY, take responsibility-for-yourself subject. As Harris writes, "today [girls] are supposed to become unique, successful individuals making their own choices and plans to accomplish autonomy. ... To be girl-powered is to make good choices and to be empowered as an individual" (2004, 6). Girl-power images are a central part of an appeal to an ideology of uniqueness, strength, and autonomy, but that "strength" is often figured in nontraditional terms, and, as will be discussed later, is typically paired with an emphasis on "style." This body, which is between ectomorphic and mesomorphic in its somatotype (long and lean, with a high metabolism, with some muscle), fits the profile demonstrated to be characteristic of competitive surfers. That body, which is "almost identical to Olympic swimmers ... with powerful shoulder flexion and extension capabilities" (Ford and Brown 2006, 119) lends itself to high achievement in this particular sport. Surfers have furthermore been found to "have some of the best recovery heart rates of any group of athletes" (Ford and Brown 2006, 119). Ideally suited to the negotiation of constantly changing conditions within the waves, recovering quickly, flexible and able to bend and extend at will, the somatotype of the female surfer and her image has become ubiquitous at least partially because of the ways she literally embodies the ideologies and "possibilities" associated with neoliberal capital. In order to fully examine the terms of this ideal and its relation to the cultures of girls and the cultures of feminism, I will examine the ways this kind of "flexible subject" is narrativized in cultural productions related to women's surfing and to developments in girls' and women's sports more generally.

Power, Potential, and Containment in "Stealth Feminism": A Third-Wave Feminist Reading of Fuel TV's *Firsthand* and the 'N' Network's *Beyond the Break*

In an article written in the late nineties, I first used the term "stealth feminism" to describe three simultaneous social occurrences: the infamous "I'm not a feminist, but ..." formulation much attributed to young women at this time, the vastly increased numbers of girls participating in sport post-Title IX in the United States (from 1 in 30 high school-aged girls prior to 1972 to 1 in 2.5 in the late nineties), and the nearly universal support for women's sports throughout mass culture in the same period.[3] Given sport's function as a site where traditional gender formations are continually challenged, a space where girls and women are not only *supported* in demonstrating achievement, competence, and strength but are *required* to do so given the nature of the activity, I defined sport as a site where the bad press that feminism received during this decade was mitigated by "a kind of stealth feminism that draws attention to key feminist issues and goals without provoking the knee-jerk social stigmas attached to the word 'feminist'" (Heywood 2000, 114). That function in girls' and women's sport continues into the twenty-first century, and sports like women's surfing and their practitioners' negotiations with their attendant representations articulate a decidedly "third-wave" or "stealth feminist" perspective.

In "Wanting to be Lisa" (based on ASP pro surfer Lisa Andersen), Krista Comer builds on this work and describes what I call "third-wave stealth feminism" as "a post-Title IX female athletic subjectivity" (2004, 241). Comer charts a shift within the attitudes of generation X (born 1960 to 1980) to generation Y (born 1980 to 2000) female athletes, especially in terms of their methods for negotiating gender. Gen X takes a more standard "masculine" attitude—"'surf like a man, aggressive and fierce' ... keep going no matter what, tolerate trash talk about women in the water ... blast any girl who gets in the way ... a fairly standard mental and physical plan for young women of this particular generation who are turning themselves from 'just girls' into athletes" (2004, 250).[4] By contrast, Gen Y, in what has become a characteristically "third-wave" approach, implements a more blended strategy: "embracing and valuing 'girl-ness' at the same time as one aims to achieve at the highest level" (2004, 241). However, as Comer notes, both approaches overlap in the contemporary women's surfing scene, "and the X/Y blend (we could also call it 'third wave') will inform young women's sense of themselves as gendered subjects for some time to come" (2004, 241).

Contemporary women's surfing can only be understood from this "third-wave" perspective. For those unfamiliar with the term, "third-wave feminism" developed in the early nineties in response to what was seen as changed historical circumstances: globalization and the "information age" and the ways these shifts toward a downsized economy and temporary, part-time work affected women and men born after 1960 who had grown up with second-wave feminism as an ideal—the very kind of changes discussed earlier in relation to Harris's formulations of the "future girl." From the start "postmodern," fractured subjectivities (and often trained in this mode of thinking if they had attended college), third wavers saw the multiplicity of identity as foundational—that is, the intersection of gender with race, sexuality and other variables was primary rather than a shared identity as "women," which necessitated a commitment to work against all forms of oppression, not just those related to gender. Gender is seen in the third wave as fluid and performative, and the divide between men and women part of essentialist constructions of masculinity and femininity that actually exist on a continuum between genders, with each gender possessing both sets of characteristics to greater and lesser degrees. Therefore, the inclusion of men in the movement is seen to be necessary to its success.[5]

Although second-wave feminism was largely a historical formation in response to restrictive norms and possibilities for women that caused many feminists to reject the conventionally feminine identification with beauty culture and other "girlie" forms, third wave is in dialog with the range of possibilities now supposedly and actually open to some women, and thus tends to embrace beauty culture and other forms of "girlie" rather than seeing them as a threat. Third wave is the feminism of those women who had the opportunity, for instance, to grow up playing sports, and so tend to not experience gender in the same way as a woman who grew up with the expectation that her possibilities were limited to marriage and motherhood. In true postmodern form, third wavers tend to experience all possibilities in the modality of both/and rather than either/or, and typically see no contradiction between career and motherhood, playing sports and participating in beauty culture.[6] In contemporary cultural productions related to women's surfing, this kind of "both/and" third-wave perspective is everywhere evident. I will examine two such productions, Fuel TV's biographical documentary series *Firsthand*, and *Beyond the Break*, the N network's fictional drama devoted to female competitive surfers and directed toward a teen girl audience, in order to demonstrate the prevalence of a third-wave perspective in contemporary representations, especially those directed toward girls and young women. I furthermore suggest that this perspective is an ambivalent one in terms of "progress" related to gender norms since it shows a very different articulation of femininity, one that has achieved some of the goals of second-wave feminism, such as independent identity and material independence, but it is an articulation that is in alignment with the dominant economic ideology of the time, that associated with neoliberalism.

Fuel TV is a network devoted to "Action Sports on TV ... Surfing, Skateboarding, BMX, Snowboarding, Motocross and Wakeboarding." One of its regular programs, *Firsthand*, is a show devoted to biographies of extreme or action sport athletes. According to the program description, *Firsthand* caters to the now long-documented American fascination with personal narratives and "reality" television, and follows the "daily, inside lives of surfers, snowboarders and action sports legends as they comb the globe looking for the perfect wave or untracked powder." It features half-hour-long profiles of both male and female athletes, although roughly 75 percent of the shows are devoted to male athletes. Although somewhat formulaic and reproductive of sport culture clichés, the shows are fairly substantive, showing the athletes interacting with others and providing insight not just into the history of their achievements but also their everyday experiences. These biographies provide important data for analysis of girls' surf culture because, as Krista Comer so eloquently puts it, biography has "emerged as influential precisely because its generic conventions suit it to the task of suturing the gap between mass culture's commercial motives and what young women regard as meaningful everyday subcultural life ... surfergirls most often encounter themselves in organized, storied form" (2004, 246–247). Examining cultural productions that "suture the gap" between second- and third-wave feminism, and the subcultural and post-subcultural formations where the representation and experience differ, I will concentrate on three particular episodes of *Firsthand*, all of which aired in 2005: those devoted to four-time ASP (Association of Surfing Professionals) World Champion Lisa Andersen, 2004 ASP World Champion Sofia Mulanovich, and ASP tour member Megan Abubo.

Andersen, indisputably the most recognizable face in women's surfing, has reached this point of visibility both through her pioneering championship status (she was one of the first to surf "like a guy") and through her compelling (very "third wave") life story: Andersen didn't win any of her World titles until after she gave birth to her daughter.[7] Her male contemporary, eight-time World Champion Kelly Slater (known as "the Michael Jordan of surfing") highlights the characteristically third wave, both/and formulation central to her story when he says that "she was one of the first women to have people say she has a man's approach to surfing a wave, more like tearing the wave apart, but also feminine at the same time, kind of combining the two approaches" (*Firsthand* 2005). The "two approaches" Slater mentions refer to the distinction in surfing between the "soul" approach, which "goes with the flow" of the wave, and the competitive approach, which attacks the wave.[8] The former, of course, is seen as more "feminine." Slater seems to be repeating the currently more commonly voiced blended GenX/Y "strategy for managing sexism in athletics" identified by Comer when he says this rather than actually articulating something specific to Andersen herself. Andersen, who was born right in the middle of Gen X in 1969 and developed her athletic technique and persona much earlier than any of the other girls on the current World Tour, is actually known for surfing "like a man." In fact, the image most often associated with Andersen is the shot of her surfing on the cover of *Surfer* magazine (the main insider publication directed toward men), a photograph famously accompanied by the caption "Lisa Andersen surfs better than you." Andersen's *Firsthand* biography doesn't seem to be a "firsthand" account at all. Rather, it seems more about how other people, particularly younger girls, see her. A different generational frame, with its own particular assumptions about gender, is being used to structure her narrative than that which was used ten years ago, and might even be used by Andersen herself.

This typically "Gen Y" framework, which alternates between masculine and feminine, and between her surfing achievements and her home life as a mother, structures the entire biography. Significantly, at the episode's end, when Slater is asked "so why do you think Lisa's so popular?" he responds, "popular? I think she's popular because she's cute and she's blonde and she surfs well." (In an era of male beauty ideals that has seen the commodification of men, Slater's own huge visibility is similarly attributable to the fact that he is "cute" or even beautiful in addition to his stats as World Champion).[9] Although a viewer informed by second-wave feminism may interpret Slater as articulating the "feminine apologetic," struggling to normalize Andersen in terms of gender by insisting on her "feminine side," I would argue that he is voicing a more "Gen Y," third-wave" reading of Andersen that sees "cute blondeness" as a positive attribute that does not demean or detract from but rather adds to her championship status ("third wave" tends to blend the views of both X and Y, and is therefore sometimes inconsistent on the beauty question).[10] Instead of rejecting beauty and interpreting a comment like this as a sexist insult, the girls and women who follow her see Andersen as having achieved both conventionally masculine and feminine ideals, and therefore relate to her as an example of what they aspire to. An article in industry publication *Transworld Surf* describes Andersen as "four time world champ ... hot mom ... and the woman who began the female surfing revolution," and points to the visibility of her profile when the interviewer tells her that "anytime I talk to any of these other girls, they're like 'Lisa Andersen this, Lisa Andersen that'" (Cote 2004a). So whereas a second-wave feminist viewer might see both the biography and Andersen's popularity as an obvious example of the "feminine apologetic in sports" in which a woman's "masculine" athletic achievements are mitigated by an emphasis on her "femininity," a third-wave viewer would be more likely to read it as Andersen's successful achievement of "balance" and success in all spheres of her life.[11]

This embrace of beauty culture *and* achievement is characteristically third wave and runs throughout women's surf culture and other women's sports. It is linked to the acceleration of consumer culture and its place in the global economy. The achievement of beauty, always in dialog with her other achievements, are characteristic examples of all of the following: what Harris describes above as the DIY subjectivity of the "future girl," what Comer describes as "more rigorous visual beauty regimes" in the 1980s and 1990s, and the way Susan Bordo's *Unbearable Weight* analyzes body and beauty regimes as key features of late twentieth and early twenty-first century culture.[12] It is this "rigor" and proliferation of beauty culture, formulated as part of a global economy run by transnational corporations that need at all costs to "grow" markets, that informs a significant part of the generational differences attributable to second- and third-wave feminism. As previously mentioned, second wave tends to reject beauty practices as limiting regimes of femininity that enforced rigid gender roles and women's second-class status. In the third wave, where educational attainment, achievement in sports, and achievement in careers is a much more common occurrence, beauty is experienced as playful and pleasurable rather than limiting *at the same time* as it is experienced as yet another requirement for the achievement of "excellence." Furthermore, it is precisely this ideology of achievement, however, that masks what Harris terms the "more complex lives [girls have] than the dominant images of girls' freedom, power, and success. Unlike the fictional 'level playing field' implied by those images, class and race inequalities continue to shape opportunities and outcomes" (2004, 9).

Although all three biographies emphasize self-making, determination, and success as an integral part of each athlete's story, issues of race and economic distribution in the global economy in relation to surfing's core ideologies are developed most in the profile of the Peruvian surfer Sofia Mulanovich, the WCT 2004 World Champion. Speaking to the idea that one's life is a DIY project in self-making for which each individual is responsible, "a new brand of competitive individualism whereby people are expected to create their own chances and make the best of their lives" (Harris 2004, 4), Mulanovich begins her profile with a discussion of Peru: "Peru is a third world country, so you have to work your butt off to make it good." She argues that her ability to surf is her way of "creating chances," as if anyone could do so: "If you're really passionate about something and you really want the thing you will get it—you just have to want it enough." Much footage in this episode is devoted to the devastated countryside, and to racialized, exoticizing images like close-ups on parrots and street bands, and much time is spent idealizing the Peruvian people as "great supporters" (a "feminized" position). Mulanovich is figured as the "can-do" achiever who "breaks down barriers" in a macho culture by being "the first to receive a corporate sponsorship" in sports. Ostensibly because of her background, Mulanovich says "I think I wanted it the most." Mulanovich is represented as breaking more barriers than her contemporaries since she faces challenges related to gender, race and class, but it is her "wanting it more" that the episode presents as her DIY ability to overcome and win the World Championship. Mulanovich's episode highlights the extraordinary individual "overcoming limitation" through her sport, suggesting that the same opportunity is available to all and glossing over the fact that she comes from a surfing family, and her experience and talent are not, in fact available to all—or even to a significant number.

Although Mulanovich's *Firsthand* emphasizes one characteristic mode in the representation of contemporary femininity, the extraordinary individual overcoming obstacles, Megan Abubo's episode takes up a second dominant trope, seemingly at odds with the first, and emphasizes the "girl gang" mentality that Comer reads as structuring the blockbuster Hollywood surfergirl film *Blue Crush* (2002). Suppressing narratives of individuality, Abubo's *Firsthand* is focused on the friendships between the competitors traveling together on the World Tour. Comer interprets *Blue Crush* as a mainstream film that for the first time highlights female camaraderie rather than competition: "all roads lead to figuring out how girls can hang together tight and back each other fully" (2004, 252). A long segment in the middle of Abubo's episode specifically discusses competition between women, emphasizing the idea of respect:

> I am a very competitive person … it's always kind of weird to surf against your friends—it's kind of nice, though, because you guys always respect each other in the water. It's always weird though if you beat them or they beat you. … I think I handle competing against my friends pretty well—what happens, happens. If your friend beats you, then they beat you fair and square. Or if you beat them don't boast in their face. … It's all about respect I think, its really important … what happens in the water stays in the water and what happens on land happens on land but I have respect for everyone who competes in the water. For the most part I try to treat everyone how I want to be treated (*Firsthand* 2005).

Emphasizing a thread that shows the women backing each other and interacting as friends, the last frame of the episode shows the women holding hands and skipping together toward the ocean. In the popular literature focused on girls' psychology, the 2000's era of "mean girls," "queen bees," and "wannabes" replaces earlier 1990s' stereotypes of girls as innately more relational and empathetic,[13] but this episode explores both. Although its almost exclusive focus on female camaraderie threatens to reinforce older gender stereotypes regarding women as innately relationship oriented and cooperative, there is enough counterpoint that emphasizes Abubo's competitive nature to make her episode a corrective to more current stereotypes regarding "mean girls," as well as to those older stereotypes. Although it is markedly different from the emphasis on individuality in Mulanovich's episode, Abubo's episode provides an antidote to the idea that girls are either always cooperative and nice or aggressive and destructive toward each other. Instead, in her *Firsthand* the two tendencies exist in complicated relation, a much more realistic view.

In a trend that has a complicated relationship to the intermingling of reality and fiction, experience and representation, the use of female surfers as a subject for mass cultural productions that began with *Blue Crush* has shown some staying power. Although the two 2003 female surfer-based reality shows, MTV's *Surf Girls* and the WB's *Boarding House: North Shore* each only lasted for a single season, in June 2006 the N network debuted a fictional series devoted to female surfers called *Beyond the Break*. The N, which is directed to a teen audience, promises to offer programming that deals with "real life," even though its shows are dramas rather than reality programming. The show is sponsored by Tampax, suggesting it is also directed toward a female teen audience. The Web site claims that:

> The N on TV is different than any other network. Because all of the shows on The N are about the way life really is and the stuff that really matters. The N is REAL. Real doesn't mean just "reality" programs, documentaries, or the news. It means the shows on the N are about your real life and the things you're dealing with every day. The N isn't about the Hollywood or make-believe version of your life. It's about your life the way it really happens. The N is built out of stuff you can really use in your life. And not "someday." It's valuable now. The N: It's real, it's about your life, and it's relevant right now. (http://www.the-n.com)

It is telling that in its claims to air "what's real" and "what matters," two of the network's nineteen shows (three of which are *Degrassi* spin-offs) are devoted to "extreme" or "action" sports: *Beyond the Break* to surfing and *Whistler* to snowboarding. There are no shows devoted to traditional, mainstream sports, which points to the increasing irrelevance of the old marquee triumvirate of baseball, football, and basketball to a younger demographic. Since surfing and snowboarding are presented as part of the "stuff you can really use in your life," this testifies to the importance of these sports to the youth market and their increasing predominance in the global economy. Furthermore, initial ratings have been high. According to the Neilsen ratings report, "the June 2 series premiere of The N's *Beyond the Break* won a 1.62 million female-teen rating, making it the highest-rated show for that demographic in that time period among all broadcast and ad-supported cable networks. For some comparative perspective, the popular reality show *The Simple Life* featuring Paris Hilton and Nicole Richie had a 1.2 rating two nights later" (Moss 2006). Beyond revealing a particular demographic appeal, however, the show is important in bolstering claims about the "groundswell" and explosion of popularity in women's surfing and is notable for the ways it negotiates contemporary contradictions regarding gender, economic realities, and race.

Beyond the Break is the story of four young female surfers who are living on Hawaii's North Shore, sponsored by a company called "WaveSync" and coached and supervised by Justin Healy (David Chokachi), a former Pipeline Master's champion whose surfing prominence has been reduced to this particular mentorship role to female surfers. Kai (Sonya Balmores) is a local Hawaiian surfer made good, Dawn (Suzie Pollard) is a rich party girl who is ashamed of her wealth and tries to conceal it, Birdie (Tiffany Hines) is an African American surfer who has never actually competed before her sponsorship, and the show's main protagonist, Lacey Farmer (Natalie Ramsey), is a teen runaway struggling to make surfing her livelihood. Lacey's story seems loosely based on that of Lisa Andersen, who at 16 famously left her Florida home without telling her parents to go to the "surfing capital, USA" Huntington Beach, CA.

At the same time it produces images of ideally beautiful female surfers, the show critically (or is it cynically?) comments on what Comer calls the "superficiality and marketing impulse behind most mass cultural visual images of women and surfing" and the cultural valuation of female beauty over athletic achievement (2004, 246). In the episode called "The First Test," Birdie admits to Justin that she's never actually surfed in a contest before. When her performance is rocky and she is knocked out of the contest, Justin turns to apologize to the WaveSync representative, saying "she'll get it." The representative replies, with a grin, "oh, she's already got it." When Justin asks, "what's that mean?" he smirks and says, "so she's not the best surfer in the world—she'll look great in our catalog, dude." Justin protests: "so that's what we're doing here, selling bikinis?" The WaveSync rep. smirks again and says "No—hats, sunglasses, t-shirts ... ." Valuing female athletes for their looks rather than their achievements is presented here as an act of corporate bad faith. As in the scene in "Vin, Lose or Draw," where Lacey tells Kai "I came to surf, not find a boyfriend," the show's writers seem at pains to reflect the current understanding of female surfers and the social issues and stereotypes they face, and the sometimes contradictory both/and ways the athletes use to negotiate them even as the writers simultaneously reinforce those very notions.

What both the Fuel TV biographies and the *Beyond the Break* episodes demonstrate is a characteristically "third-wave" sense of fluidity regarding gender, the sense that gender characteristics are attributes one can choose between and act out at will. When asked by Justine Cote, an interviewer for *Transworld Surf* magazine, "any advice to the young girls out there?," Megan Abubo responds with what can be seen as a characteristic popular "third-wave" feminist approach to gender: "don't forget who you are. Go out there and get a wave in your bikini with your long hair, who cares? You're a girl, do it. Or if you want to be a little tomboy, who cares? Be whoever you are, whether it's a tomboy or a girly girl. Just go out there and surf and have fun" (2004b). Abubo articulates some of the most widespread values in girl culture today:

be active and achieve, but also be "who you are," even (or especially) if that combines "male" and "female," and at all times, have fun doing it.

Conclusions

As I hope discussions have shown, the female athlete is an important icono-graphic figure in the global economy today, embodying the ideas of self-determination, success, and drive. She is the representation of the "new," the democratic possibilities globalization, neoliberalism, and free market capital supposedly extend to all who "work hard enough." In the current moment, the image of the female surfer in particular is the carrier of the neoliberal ideologies of flexibility, do-it-yourself subjectivity, and possibil-ity for all, rewriting the earlier cultural scripts of the male surfer as opt-out, nonproductive rebel. Her flexible physiological morphology is the amalgam of flexible specialization in the global economy, and the image she contrib-utes to the ideas of successful self-making has been effective enough to fuel a $489.6 million a year industry in surfwear. While she is complicit with neoliberalism and marks the same erasures of structural inequality that other modalities of that discourse perform, at the same time she also serves as an example of what has come to be known as a "third-wave feminist" rearticulation of gender and femininity, one that is a hybrid of beauty ideals and action or individual achievement, and that does not claim to be free of complicity with the dominant culture.

One might recognize the facetiousness of the myth of "advancement through hard work," while at the same time appreciating a femininity that signifies more than domesticity or second-class status based on gender. As renowned economic sociologist Manuel Castells has written, unless there is a complete revolution in contemporary values, it is not possible to invent a novel form, of gender or anything else, that can exist outside the vast network associated with the global economy: "Within the value system of productiv-ism/consumerism, there is no individual alternative for countries, firms, or people. Barring a catastrophic meltdown of the financial market, or opting out by people following completely different values, the process of globaliza-tion is set, and it accelerates over time" (2004, 330). The female surfer is an example of just such an acceleration, and although she may not fulfill every feminist ideal, and she may even serve to confound some ideals, she does mark an altered incarnation of femininity in the developed world, a "stealth femi-nism" many would admire.

An example of both the dominant cultural ideals associated with neo-liberalism and what were previously countercultural ideals of independent femininity, female surfers occupy a signal-crossed space, and show just how far independent femininity has become absorbed into the dominant cultural ideal. In control of herself and the wave she rides, female surfers in the mass media present an image of confident, balanced beauty and individual achievement. Such "mastery" is always an illusion, however, and one paradox that arises is that, for the women observing her, this "independence" is experienced primarily through consumer choices. Yet the fact that increasingly these choices are backed by dollars earned by women themselves makes some kind of difference in how gender is both articulated and experienced, and the experiencee of surfing itself cannot fail to provide feelings of competence to those who have the means to experience it. The experience of surfing, like many sports, however, is not available to all. Like other arenas, the potential of sport as a politically transformative space in relation to gender is limited in multiple ways, but these limitations do not categorically rule out the changes that have necessarily accompanied the shift to a global economy and the complications of women's highly differing positions within it.

Notes

1. See Heywood and Dworkin (2003, especially the introduction and Chapter 1).
2. See Heywood (2000 especially p. 108).
3. Title IX was part of the Education Act of 1972, and mandated, among other things, that women's sports be funded at a level equal to men's, and that women have equal opportunity to play.
4. For a memoir that tells the story of exactly this kind of generational response to being the first generation of women widely given athletic opportunity, see my *Pretty Good for a Girl* (1999).
5. See Heywood (2005).
6. There is at this point an enormous amount of literature devoted to third-wave feminism. For general reference, see Heywood (2005). For a succinct take on "girlie," see Jennifer Baumgardner and Amy Richards (2004).
7. Krista Comer's "Wanting to Be Lisa: Generational Rifts, Girl Power, and the Globalization of Surf Culture" (2004) is a must-read, the first and last word not only on Lisa Andersen but the cultural function of women's surfing and women's surf narratives in the contemporary, globalized world. This article significantly influenced and helped me to develop my own readings here.
8. On these contrasting approaches in the history of surfing, see Booth (2004).
9. On the commodification of the male body and male beauty cultures as they developed throughout the 1990s, see Susan Bordo (1998).
10. I should disclose here that I am on the older side of "Gen X" myself, and, because I find Comer's categorization of generational strategies exactly right, very much have made use of its "strategies for managing sexism in athletics" in my own life. Therefore, I am sometimes very uncomfortable with the "Gen Y" strategy, but it is the predominant mechanism or point of view structuring narratives about women in sport today, whether those narratives come from the athletes themselves or from outside them.
11. On the "feminine apologetic" in women's sports, see Mary Jo Festle, *Playing Nice: Politics and Apologies in Women's Sports* (1996), especially pp. 265–282.
12. See Susan Bordo (2003).

13. For an effective analysis of these two opposing trends and the ways they are racially inflected to the detriment of economically disadvantaged, non-White girls, see Meda Chesney-Lind and Katherine Irwin, "From Badness to Meanness" (2004).

References

Amin, A., ed. 1994. *Post-Fordism: A reader.* London: Blackwell.

Baumgardner, J. and A. Richards. 2004. Feminism and femininity: Or how we learned to stop worrying and love the thong. In *All About the Girl,* ed. A. Harris, 59–67. London: Routledge.

Booth, D. 2004. Surfing: From one cultural extreme to another. In *Understanding lifestyle sports: Consumption, identity, and difference,* ed. B. Wheaton, 94–109. London: Routledge.

Bordo, S. 1998. *The male body.* New York: Farrar, Straus, and Giroux.

Bordo, S. 2003. *Unbearable weight: Feminism, Western culture, and the body.* Berkeley: University of California Press.

Brown, D. 2004. *Step Into Liquid.* Documentary film. Artisan Home Entertainment.

Castells, M. 2004. Global informational capitalism. In *The global transformations reader,* ed. D. Held and A. McGrew, 311–334. Cambridge, UK: Polity Press.

Chaney, D. 2004. Fragmented culture and subcultures. In *After subculture: Critical studies in contemporary youth culture,* ed. A. Bennett and K. Kahn-Harris, 36–48. Basingstoke: Palgrave Macmillan.

Chesney-Lind, M. and K. Irwin. 2004. From badness to meanness: Popular constructions of contemporary girlhood. In *All about the girl: Power, culture, and identity,* ed. Anita Harris, 45–56. London: Routledge.

Comer, K. 2004. Wanting to be Lisa: Generational rifts, girl power, and the globalization of surf culture. In *American youth cultures,* ed. N. Campbell, 237–265. New York: Routledge.

Comer, K. (forthcoming). *Surfing the New World Order: Generation, gender, counterculture.* Durham, NC: Duke University Press.

Cote, J. 2004a. Girls gone wild: Lisa Andersen. *Transworld Surf* 6, no. 10. http://www.transworldsurf.com/surf/features/article/0,19929,696366,00.html. Posted 9/13/04 (accessed July 9, 2006).

Cote, J. 2004b. Girls gone wild: Megan Abubo. *Transworld Surf* 6, no. 10. http://www.transworldsurf.com/surf/features/article/0,19929,97493,00.html. Posted 9/15/04 (accessed July 9, 2006).

Duncan, M. C. and M. Messner. 2000. *Gender and televised sports: 1989, 1993, 1999.* Los Angeles: Amateur Athletic Foundation of Los Angeles.

Festle, M. J. 1996. *Playing nice: Politics and apologies in women's sports.* New York: Columbia University Press.

Ford, N. and D. Brown. 2006. *Surfing and social theory: Experience, embodiment, and narrative of the dream glide.* London: Routledge.

Harris, A., ed. 2004. *All about the girl: Power, culture, and identity.* London: Routledge.

Heywood, L. 1999. *Pretty good for a girl: A memoir.* Minneapolis: University of Minnesota Press.

Heywood, L. 2000. The girls of summer: Social contexts for the "Year of the Woman" at the '96 Olympics. In *The Olympics at the millennium: Power and politics and the games,* ed. K. Schaffer and S. Smith, 99–116. New Brunswick: Rutgers University Press.

Heywood, L. 2005. Introduction. In *The women's movement today: An encyclopedia of third wave feminism,* ed. L. Heywood, xv–xxii. Westport, CT: Greenwood Reference Works.

Heywood, L. 2006. Producing girls: Empire, sport, and the neoliberal body. In *Physical culture, power, and the body,* ed. J. Hargreaves and P. Vertinsky, 101–120. London: Routledge.

Heywood, L. and S. Dworkin. 2003. *Built to win: The female athlete as cultural icon.* Minneapolis: University of Minnesota Press.

King, S. J. 2005. Methodological contingencies in sport studies. In *Qualitative methods in sport studies,* ed. D. Andrews, D. Mason, and M. Silk, 21–38. Oxford: Berg.

Moss, L. 2006. New shows stand tough against *The Sopranos.* News Multichannel: Variety, http://www.multichannel.com/article/CA6342679.html (accessed July 9, 2006).

Sweetman, P. 2004. Tourists and Travelers? "Subcultures", reflexive identities, and neo-tribal sociality. In *After subculture: Critical studies in contemporary youth culture,* ed. A. Bennett and K. Kahn-Harris, 79–93. Basingstoke: Palgrave Macmillan.

Taft, J. K. 2004. Girl power politics: Pop-culture barriers and organizational resistance. In *All about the girl: Power, culture, and identity,* ed. Anita Harris, 69–78. New York: Routledge.

Tasker, Y. 1993. *Spectacular bodies: Gender, genre, and the action cinema.* New York: Routledge.

Warshaw, M. 2003. *The encyclopedia of surfing.* New York: Harcourt.

Wet Magazine. 2006. Press kit. Available at www.wetmagazine.org in PDF format.

4

Rescuing a Theory of Adolescent Sexual Excess

Young Women and Wanting

SARA I. MCCLELLAND AND MICHELLE FINE

During World War II, we bought sealed plastic packets of white, uncolored margarine, with a tiny, intense pellet of yellow coloring perched like a topaz just inside the clear skin of the bag. We would leave the margarine out for a while to soften, and then we would pinch the little pellet to break it inside the bag, releasing the rich yellowness into the soft pale mass of margarine. Then taking it carefully between our fingers, we would knead it gently back and forth, over and over, until the color had spread throughout the whole pound bag of margarine, thoroughly coloring it. I find the erotic such a kernel within myself. When released from its intense and constrained pellet, it flows through and colors my life with a kind of energy that heightens and sensitizes and strengthens all my experience.

Audre Lorde (1984)

So, it's the same thing, right, like being wet and having an orgasm, right?

16-year-old high school student, Jacqui (2006)

The two women in the above quotes imagine their relationship to their own desire quite differently. Audre Lorde and 16-year-old Jacqui are situated at different points in their lives, however, each narrates her capacity to *want*. Each speaks about how she imagines her body responding to sexual and desired moments. And although these moments may be dissimilar and even divergent, they alert us to what it means to hear a woman talk about her body, her fluids, and her desires. The second quote, Jacqui's, also feels like a punch in the gut—a failure to properly educate this young woman about her capacity to have an orgasm. Her question tugs painfully at us; where does her confusion spring from? How many more young women would ask the same question—or one much worse? Or not ask at all? For decades, we have heard Jacqui's words emerge from so many young women's mouths that we have imagined and documented their access to discourses of desire as missing, absent, and silent. And yet listen again to Jacqui, asking—from her body—is this all there is? Is there more?

The documentation of the empty spaces where desire should be spoken by young women has been valuable work; it has established the landscape of adolescent sexuality as an important and uneven terrain—a space where resources, education, and communication can have enormous impacts (see Fine 1988; Rasmussen 2006; Rose 2003; Snitow, Stansell, and Thompson 1983; Thompson 1990; Tolman 1994, 2002, 2006). In this essay, we try to inch forward out of silent spaces, and instead, enter into the *hidden transcripts of desire* (borrowing from James Scott 1990), eavesdropping into the corners where young women wonder, speak about, try on, and reflect on questions of desire. We seek to understand the *release points* where snippets of young women's desire can be heard in the culture and to reveal that which is designed to limit and encase such talk within discourses of (im)morality, protection, or victimization.

Refusing to believe that every generation must perpetually rediscover the embodied details of women's sexuality, each time starting from scratch, we take a new look at the images and words that circulate among teen women and between teen and adult women. We try to track how, when, and where young women think about desire and experience feelings of wanting. We next wonder how these yearnings and questions do move and refuse to move through individuals, through feminist discourses, and through media representations of young women.

In a set of essays published recently in *Harvard Educational Review, Emory Law Journal,* and *Qualitative Inquiry,* we have written on the explicit and insidious ways in which the U.S. government and fundamental religious ideologies have influenced schools, courts, and science with hegemonic practices that seek to extinguish or punish young women's desire in classrooms (Fine and McClelland 2006), in law (Fine and McClelland 2007), and in what we call the "embedded science" of abstinence research (McClelland and Fine in press (a)).

In these previous writings, we document the deportation of pleasure (and even prevention) discourses out of classrooms and out of adolescent bodies and theorize what we are calling young women's *thick desire:* a deep, material yearning for a secured sense of tomorrow, which situates sexual and reproductive freedoms in a larger struggle for human rights. *Thick desire* includes intellectual and economic freedoms, protection from violence, and entitlement to healthy sexuality and living in a nation that supports the education, health, and well-being of its people (Fine and McClelland 2006). In their search for thick desire, we argue that young women seek lives of pleasure and responsibility, strength of mind and body, alone and with community. Denied the enabling conditions for thick desire, young women pay a heavy price for their sexual and reproductive lives, layered by racism, poverty, homophobia, and antidisability policies.

In addition to theorizing the framework of thick desire as a way to conceptualize sexuality as not merely a private act but, indeed, a highly moderated public activity, we have worked at mapping the disparate consequences of state-sponsored surveillance and punishment for teen sexuality (see Fine and McClelland 2006, 2007; McClelland and Fine in press (a)). With this work in mind, we see the importance of not simply noting what lacks and what is lost for young women and their sexual selves, but to think about what should be, what could be, and what we, in fact, desire for young women. In this essay, we move towards the relatively unexplored terrain of what female desire looks and sounds like. In this chapter, we attempt to rescue a discourse of *sexual excess* within young women and track its circulation in feminist discourses and cultural practices.

Within medical, psychological, and cultural spheres, there has been significant debate around the subject of female sexual excess. Images of female eroticism, enjoyment, or pursuit have historically been linked with pathological categories, such as "nymphomaniac" and "slut." These images have been countered by feminist critiques that challenged the narrow margins in which female sexuality was permitted to grow. Audre Lorde's description of the erotic inside her body that begins this essay is just one example of how feminists have pushed hard to create space for the erotic to exist within the female body and not be labeled pathological. Although adult women have been somewhat successful in resuscitating a discourse of sexual excess for them/ourselves, the sexuality of teen women has remained more securely locked within a judgmental box that treats female teenage sexuality as dangerous, risky, and excessive—or as victimization. It is this conflation that concerns us here. Is it possible to bring women into this erotic sphere? Must young women and sexual excess remain mutually exclusive?

Three Aims

In an attempt to craft a theoretical model of sexual excess for young women, we stretch toward three aims. First, we look at how female sexuality has been historically considered excessive. With *excess* as our guiding principle, we then consider how re-claiming this once pathologized description might allow young female sexuality a space to emerge into—before it hits the cold air of risk prevention and commodification.

Second, through an analysis of four focus groups we conducted with a total of 36 young people in the New York City area, we peek under the covers of the term "desire" in order to look to an early stage of desire: the stage of *wanting*. We start with this idea of wanting because it seems the ultimate form of being excessive. "I want" is a small but powerful statement that exists at multiple levels—physical, emotional, material. This narration of excess is used as a way of bringing nuance to the conversation about desire; what more can be known about the moment of wanting and the discourses within it?

Third, we describe examples of what we refer to as "release points." We define release points as cultural practices and research methodologies that have the potential to wedge open a space that is not-yet. Using examples of informational and community-building Web sites aimed at young women, we see the potential for these outlets to create new language that allows young women's descriptions of wanting to get air and breathe before becoming covered with a salve of abstinence, safe sex and prevention. Most important, we draw attention to the link between how young women individually come to embody wanting and then, socially, how these experiences and inquiries travel across the landmines of teen surveillance and disease/pregnancy prevention. It is in this move from individual experience to social representation that we see the greatest potential for loss and for opportunities to let wanting, desire, and female excess into the room.

Rescuing Excess

Definitions of "excess" are revealing: "a quantity that is much larger than needed," "beyond sufficient or permitted limits," "overindulgence," "more than is required." These descriptions remind us of that which is too much, excessive. But a closer look reveals that excess is actually a word that draws attention to the line between what is required and what is not required, but is there anyway. Female sexuality, and specifically female sexual pleasure, exists at this very line. As a result, female sexuality has historically been linked with excess and fears of what lurks over the border of what is required, necessary, and sufficient.

Fear of excessive female sexuality accelerated into a moral panic in the nineteenth century when large segments of the medical community believed that masturbation and sexual excess caused insanity and disease (Cameron and Kulick 2003; Hare 1962; Whorton 2001). Excessive sexuality in women was considered suspect because of its potential to undermine patriarchy—it revealed that women did not depend on men for sexual release and that procreative possibilities were not the only outcome of sexual activity. In fact, the term "heterosexual" was coined in 1869 as a way to denote a perversion—having sex with someone of the other gender for pleasure rather than to reproduce. The first "heterosexuals" were men who had sex with pregnant women or who engaged in oral sex rather than intercourse (Cameron and Kulick 2003). Although this aura of perversion did not cling to heterosexual men who engaged in sex for pleasure, it has always clung to women.

Rescuing pursuits of pleasure has occupied feminist writers for the much of the last thirty years (Hite 1987; Irigaray 1981; Koedt 1970; McElroy 1995; Rubin 1984; Willis 1992). This has meant consistently decoupling female pleasure from reproductive capacities and staking out women's rights to orgasms, contraception, reproductive choice, and relations with other women. Part of this project has meant imbuing women with an inherent eroticism. One thinks of Irigaray's image of the woman always in pleasurable contact with herself—"two lips which embrace continually"—as representing pleasure in the very act of being biologically female (Irigaray 1981, 100).

However, even with this attention from some, issues of pleasure have, to a large degree, been supplanted in political organizing by issues of sexual freedom—freedom from violence, coercion, homophobia, sterilization, abuse, etc. Feminists and reproductive rights activists have come to understand that women's sexuality and reproductive freedoms must be fundamentally integrated into human rights campaigns. Women's access to abortion, contraception, condoms, child care, employment, freedom from violence, etc. are increasingly recognized (if not enacted) as foundational to global social welfare.

Although freedom from negative sexual events has often overshadowed the right to positive sexual events, there are a few examples of where this has not been the case. In various campaigns for sexual rights, demands for sexual pleasure have recently made a showing (see Correa and Petchefsky 1994; Edwards and Coleman 2004; Misra and Chandiramani 2005). In other words, we are slowly seeing the right to sexual pleasure integrated into the larger conversations concerning women's rights to sexual freedom.

In fact, feminist international advocacy work has recently taken an interesting turn. Cesnabmihilo Dorothy Aken'ova, a sexual rights activist with the International Centre for Reproductive Health and Sexual Rights in Minna, Nigeria, spoke at the Population Council in 2006 about her work on women's sexual entitlement. In a simple sentence, she captured the room when she explained: "If a Nigerian woman dares to ask for an orgasm, who knows, maybe next, she'll demand clean water." Reversing the traditional logic of a socialist-feminist-postcolonial platform—give her good schools and economic possibilities and she'll reduce her fertility rates—Aken'ova argued (not instead, but alongside), *give her body a sense of entitlement to pleasure and her political demands will follow.* In other words, although the right to sexual pleasure has long been held as a potential outcome of women's rights, it may be more powerful and practical to place bodily pleasure at the center of a rights campaign. When someone is able to negotiate what they want within themselves (and perhaps with a partner), these skills start a ripple in the water that continues to travel outward.

Although the articulation of pleasure as a woman's right has occupied some quarters of feminist discourse (McElroy 1995; Queen 1996; Rubin 1984; Willis 1992), there have been some corners that have gathered dust and remain less well explored. For example, novelist Suri Hustvedt notes that, "Feminist discourse in America ... has never taken on the problem of arousal with much courage" (Hustvedt 2006, 49). So too Katherine Franke (2001) argues that feminist legal scholars have focused so tightly on girls'/women's right to say "no" and questions of consent, they have abandoned the territory of pleasure, the right to say "yes" and to invite pleasure, to queer theory:

Women's right to enjoy their own body is entirely absent ... it has been the gay and queer legal theorists who see these issues as about a "right to sex..." (200–201)

... it seems that legal [and other types of] feminists have ceded to queer theorists the job of imagining the female body as a site of pleasure, intimacy, and erotic possibility." (182)

In her essay "Theorizing Yes" (2001) Franke challenges Catharine MacKinnon's position that female sexuality is always already colonized by male power. Franke is troubled that female sexuality is presumably never without coercion or violence; that "no" is the only viable feminist answer to any heterosexual question (198). She writes, "In this domain of legal feminism, sexuality is accounted for not as reproduction and dependency, but as danger. Sexuality is something that threatens from without" (199). Franke's work is an important step towards framing female sexuality as not merely something to be protected; she highlights the need to release it from feminist legal frameworks that consistently and relentlessly theorize women and their sexualness as in danger.

In response to these limited views on the potential for sexuality, Franke and others argue that female pleasure be recast as a radical space for theorizing *sexual excess*. Within the open range of sexual excess, women's capacity for multiple orgasms, orgasms free of reproductive consequence and transmission of sexual disease, pleasure with no market value and, perhaps, no evolutionary value—there have been inklings of research suggesting there is much to learn from women's pleasures. Quoting Miranda Joseph (1998), Franke writes, "revolution must involve heterogeneous expression, *wasteful gift exchange* (pure expenditure rather than accumulation, final consumption rather than productive consumption), and non-procreative sex" (emphasis added, cited in Franke 2001, 187).

In critical legal studies, and more recently in biology, interesting debates about sexual excess and female pleasure have heated up around the "purpose" of the (adult) female orgasm. If women's orgasms do not serve a genetic or species survival purpose, then why do they happen (again and again)? Women get pregnant just as frequently without having an orgasm during copulation—there is no evidence that orgasm affects fertility or reproductive success. Biologist Elisabeth Lloyd in her book, *The Case of the Female Orgasm* (2005), makes a compelling case for divorcing female orgasms from evolution. She decouples female orgasms from reproduction, which entails distinguishing "evolutionary function" from "biologically useful" structures. In a liberatory move of science, Lloyd argues that women's orgasms are indeed important (i.e., biologically useful), but not necessarily evolutionarily functional (they do not necessarily increase the likelihood of offspring). Women are so accustomed to being categorized as functional beings, this move away from evolution may seem (and has been) disarming for a number of feminist researchers (Fausto-Sterling, Gowaty, and Zuk 1997; Hrdy 1981).

But instead of a loss, we see this description of the female orgasm as a moment of reprieve—where women are not biologically driven (or obligated) to procreate and yet our pleasure is allowed to live on its own. This allows for what we consider a *release point*. It allows us to imagine sex as fantasy or practice—with oneself or with a partner (female, trans, male)—as outside the boundaries of drive, nature, and babies. It is an intellectual opening that gives permission to reclaim sex and pleasure for women without genuflecting to heteronormativity and natural destiny. Decoupling pleasure from reproduction, Lloyd makes female orgasms the height of excess. This move to redefine female orgasms as excessive is not meant to diminish or demote them. Instead, this move has the potential to be liberatory in how it helps us rescue what it means to be excessive.

In the flush of women's desire being asserted at the center of global human rights struggles, legal rights, and evolutionary debates, we ask now about *young* women. Have we successfully campaigned for the rights of girls and young women to feel sexual desire and reproductive safety in the United States or globally? Or, have we continued to shelter their bodies in discourses of prevention and victimization as a means to secure their legal, health, and educational rights? It seems clear that young women inherently mark the radical possibilities and dangerous boundaries of sexual excess.

Young Women and Excess

Young women are fundamentally and inherently sexually excessive. Their sexuality captures cultural attention and collects cultural (and feminist) anxieties. Collectively, we seem to wonder, how much is enough? Their sexuality flaunts itself as "much larger than is needed," goes way "beyond sufficient or permitted limits," and is consistently cast as overindulgent. Although the sex they want and the sex they have are *typically* intended to be decoupled from reproduction, they are considered too young to reproduce (see Geronimus 1997 for an important critique of this position); too young to know enough about their bodies and their capacity; too young to be sexually pleasured and pleasurable (Greif 2006).

Under the best of circumstances, when they choose to be sexual, teen women are the litmus test for how much room we have given women to be sexually excessive. Those on the political Right and Left join in their fears for the sexually excessive young woman: both sides arguing for laws and policies aimed at restricting the harms that young women face. She is indeed vulnerable; we all want to protect her. But how, in the process, have we become suspicious of her displays of excessiveness, just as we have learned to embrace our own? It seems we have restricted her access to expressions of excess. We ask her simply not to *want*.

Wanting and Wetness

Moving past the presumably missing discourse of young women's desire, we inch toward an investigation of young women's experiences of wanting. Wanting is wide and deep; it does not require an object. A theory of wanting allows the focus on other people, activities, outcomes, risks, and dangers to fall away for a moment. Wanting does not linger on the object of desire, but on the feeling in the mind or the body; therefore, it allows identities and orientations to progress after the identification of want within the self.

Wanting lives beside other related words that have histories of their own: desire, arousal, pursuit, release, orgasm, satisfaction, just to name a few. The term "desire" has been used to describe the early part of this sequence, while "behaviors" (and consequences) have covered the latter half. Typically, the thinking goes, he has desires and she has consequences. Given this and given the feminist reclamation of sexual pleasure, it is necessary to consider the frame around the words we have come to associate with female sexuality and ask ourselves, have we invited excess into the room? Or have we invited in just enough to not seem greedy?

We look more closely throughout this essay at moments when we heard inklings of *want* emerge from young women's mouths. These utterances would not have been considered statements of desire in any way. They were earlier, less formed, more unsure than desire. They were often in the form of a question; a question about whether her body had more to offer; whether she was entitled to more; asking, at base, how to ask.

Sixteen-year-old Jacqui's question at the start of this essay, her inquiry about her own experience of "being wet" speaks of wanting. *So, it's the same thing, right, like being wet and having an orgasm, right*? That is, she wants both an answer and an orgasm. In the moment of asking, we noticed, in retrospect, that she was right at the border of excess—evident in the giggles that subsequently tumbled through our focus group. Being wet is sufficient; having an orgasm is excessive. Her question alerted us to how these early inklings of want are important material to consider when imaging how sexual desire and anticipation meet up with sexual activity and satisfaction.

The question also brings us to the reality of vaginal discharge and the production of a viscous fluid that, for Jacqui, had come to serve as the proof that she had achieved pleasure. While wanting, arousal, and vaginal fluid are not all the same thing, they exist near one another and share a space in which anticipation hangs in the air. Elizabeth Grosz, in her book *Volatile Bodies* (1994), explores the history of viscous fluids in discourses of social control in the feminist writings of Mary Douglas, Julia Kristeva, and Luce Irigaray. Borderline states, according to Douglas, are sites of possible danger and contamination (and, we would add, excess). Bodily fluids tend to be present in these borderline states:

Blood, vomit, saliva, phlegm, pus, sweat, tears, menstrual blood, seminal fluids, seep, flow, pass with different degrees of control, tracing the paths of entry or exit, the routes of interchange or traffic with the world, which must nevertheless be clear of these bodily "products" for an interchange to be possible. (Grosz 1994, 195)

If we were to theorize the experience of wanting as a borderline state, as in the above image, we would need to add vaginal lubrication to this list of borderline fluids. However, we find in Grosz's work a reminder that viscous fluids—those that are neither liquid nor solid—are imagined as the most dangerous type of fluids. Perhaps this is why we resist imagining the experience of wanting and the fluids that it sometimes produces—we don't need any more reasons to link wanting or female arousal as dangerous or unseemly. Maybe we back away from describing this borderline state because we resist these linkages with danger and dirt. In the name of protection, we have perhaps cut off the visceral for young women.

Grosz reminds us that "it is women, and what men consider to be their capacity for contagion, their draining, demanding bodily processes" (1994, 197) that figure so strongly in how female fluids are imagined and handled. In our own work, we heard these same sentiments about the dirt, danger, and taboo of young women's sexual bodies. In an all-male (except for us) focus group, when asked about sexuality, desire, and dangers, for a few minutes the young men focused on the troubles of girls'/women's "dirt." "Just because she looks clean and smells fresh doesn't mean she is." To which another added, "I make sure she uses Wet Wipes, cleans up before we get busy."

In their work, both Kristeva and Douglas wonder about the costs of women becoming a social body—one that is required to be clean, obedient, and law abiding. Bodies that fall outside of this definition are suspect as dirty, marginal, and problematic. Although adult women have made strides in refusing to be labeled as dirty or having problematic bodies, young women remain stuck with these words. The only alternative they have is to remain within or feign virginal status. Young women of color and queer teens are caught materially and discursively in ways that are most oppressive. Held responsible for bodies considered disobedient and problematic, they are punished for sexual desire and excess at every turn (see Fine and McClelland 2006, 2007). Desire for young women too quickly metastasizes into danger.

Excess and Danger

We presume that desire swims through young women's bodies but gets stalled in the circuitry of social, legal, and educational policies, drowning in discourses of protection, victimization, heteronormativity and abstinence, searching for a language of its own.

But the situation is even more complicated than a twenty-first–century Virgina Woolf search for a discourse of one's own. Indeed, the French twist of *desire* and *risk* is constitutive of young women's sexuality. Risk is sexy and desire is risky. Desire, for young women, materializes into risk the moment it is enacted. That is, once young women's desires are performed or named, they sour potentially into risk and danger. Once her desire hits the air, her cleavage is displayed, her caresses linger too long, or she enters his bedroom, her desire curdles into cultural shame, slut, rape, pregnancy, and disease. Like blue blood that turns red at the touch of oxygen, young women's desire turns rancid once visible and/or enacted. Luscious and confusing in her mind, her body, and her fantasies, once released, desire collects danger.

In conversations among feminists, lawyers, and activists working on reproductive rights, like in more obviously conservative conversations about abstinence, we have found that the question of *young* women's desires renders a room squeamish. *They* need condoms, contraception, health care, access to abortion, sexuality education, freedom from parental waivers—because they have perhaps been exploited by an older man, a father, uncle, brother. If a young woman is drained of responsibility or sexual curiosity, it often makes it much easier to protect her.

Young women's sexuality has a collective hold on the popular imagination, at once a trope for innocence and for abuse (Greif 2006). And although we, too, are susceptible to these concerns, we worry that we have collectively smothered the flames—in public discourse—of young women's capacity to want. Political expedience, perhaps, has encouraged us all to render her innocent of desire—as though desire outside of marriage and/or reproduction were inherently contaminated and contaminating. It is hard to defend or fight for young women's right to sexual excess. Not that *it* is missing, not at all; but that it has been banished, sent to the margins, rendered mute, but not absent, itchy, but not named (see Reich 2002; Snitow, Stansell, and Thompson 1983; Vance 1984; Willis 1992).

For young women, then, *wanting itself is excess.* Although young women desire, like we all do, once their desire is, as Lorde writes, "released from its intense and constrained pellet"—spoken, enacted with herself, a young man or another young woman—it gathers up cultural shame, risk, punishment, hypervisible performance, or quiet secrecy. Although White middle-class heterosexual teens hold the ideological space of sexual containment, girls of color, poor girls, violated girls, and lesbians hold the ideological space of sexual contamination. These young women are held, culturally, most responsible for their excessiveness. No longer pure, they are at once contaminated and contaminating (Douglas 1966). They smell like want.

Is Being Wet the Same as Having an Orgasm?

In 2006, we held a series of focus group conversations with young women and men in urban high schools (ages sixteen to eighteen) around the New York metropolitan area to try to understand how young women and men spoke about sexualities and desire. The young people ranged from solidly middle class, to working poor; their schools spanned from deeply deprived to well equipped, all within the confines of public urban education in America today. Their racial/ethnic biographies ranged through White, Latina, Caribbean-American, African American, Vietnamese-American, Indian-American, and varied combinations. Their sexual histories seem to vary as widely. Two of our four conversations were "co-ed," one all female, and one all male.

To open, we asked them how they would design a textbook on sexuality education: "What do young people need to know?" The conversations swirled around sexuality, desire, and bodies, but the youth, for the most part, held us with discursive brackets of heteronormativity, focused narrowly on prevention of disease and pregnancy. That is, until we could pry open the well-patrolled discursive membranes. It was the rare moment when kernels of pleasure would be released into the conversation, like the yellow of Audre Lorde's childhood margarine. We offer snippets of these conversations in order to analyze how young people talk with each other in the presence of adults about sexuality and bodies. Searching for sea shells of desire, we found ourselves treading water in a sea of prevention talk. But if you look hard enough, granules of *want* float by.

Scene One: In the most impoverished community high school we visited, our conversation about sexuality fixated on the dangers of sexuality in an era of HIV/AIDS and pregnancy. When asked about designing a sexuality textbook for teens, what it would look like, and what should be included in it, Tiffany opened the conversation:

> I don't know what should be in the book, but I know that the last chapter should be something like, "If all else fails, and bad things happen, know that we still love you." I just want teenagers to know that we are there for you, even if something bad happens and you get sick or have a baby.

And that's where the conversation remained—on condoms, HIV prevention, and boys not trusting girls who might "poke needle pin pricks in a condom." The whispers of pleasure were wholly male; those charged as prevention police were female. In this school, sanctioned sex talk happened under the skirts of prevention, STD testing, and condoms. Talk of abortion or lesbian/gay/bi teens was more risky; perhaps it was excessive. In a school "flooded," according to the teacher, with teen pregnancy and a community "infested" with HIV, prevention was the primary available discourse. Although prevention talk is normative here—and this is an enormous accomplishment given the restrictions of the abstinence-only-until-marriage movement in the United States—when prevention is the only discourse in the room, it can suck the air out of a complicated conversation. When protection from disease and pregnancy is only the goal, a young woman's desire can too quickly been seen as "gravy" (Burns and Torre 2005) or perhaps, simply excessive.

Scene Two: In a more "mixed" urban high school—heterogeneous by social class, race/ethnicity, and neighborhood—we convened three groups: one all female, one male, and one mixed group for a discussion on sexuality. In our all-female focus group we heard a variety of discourses about sexuality. In particular, we witnessed how a discourse of prevention or victimization can give permission for "lite" discussions of wanting.

As the session began, we asked the young women to generate a list of questions one might ask in a survey of young people's experiences of sexuality. We positioned the students as experts with bodies, biographies, and serious inquiries. We asked them to consult on a hypothetical project to design a national survey, to help us understand what needed to be asked of young people if we wanted to understand their experiences of sexuality more fully. In the wording of their projected or embodied concerns, the dominant discourses of victimization, prevention, waiting, secrecy, and shame speak.

Michelle: So what questions would you add to a national survey, what would you want to ask other young women about sexuality?

Tammy: I would want to ask other girls how having sex affects your mentality, your mind. I had it really young, and I just want to know how sex affects you mentally.

Susan: What do you know about STDs? I learn from the nurse practitioner in the clinic but I would like to know more, and what could happen if you don't use condoms.

Niqua: What do you think the Bush administration is trying to do? High school students aren't stupid—look at the media, magazines, books, movies. Sex is everywhere. They have to teach us about it!

Parma: I don't really need to ask anything or learn anything now, because I am definitely waiting until I am married.

Sara: And then where will you learn about sexuality?

Jacqui: Society gives a message that [teen sex] is horrible, so how do you know when you're ready or if the person is someone you can trust? Saying condoms don't work is so dangerous!

Susan: The classes should be a conversation like this. Take them to a clinic so they know what they can expect. Have boys and girls in the same class.

Parma: Actually I would like to ask, what happens after high school, when you're married? It's not like the knowledge just comes to you.

Niqua: They should treat it seriously but not preachy. It has to be a conversation not a lecture!

Wedillo: Someone has to be listening and responding, not judging.

Jacqui: Teaching abstinence, and only the dangers of sex, is more dangerous than not teaching it at all.

Susan: In Catholic school we learned that even if you're raped you can't get an abortion.

Niqua: I need a place to talk about this. My parents know, but they don't want to see it.

Lin: My parents are immigrants; I can't talk to my parents because of the shame. I don't want to put them through that but I need someone to speak with.

We hear, across this ten-minute segment, traces of the discourse of *victimization* ("I had it when I was young … what does it do to you mentally?"); *morality* and *waiting* ("I am definitely waiting until I am married"); and *prevention/dangers* ("Saying condoms don't work is dangerous!"). And then, as if reenacting the orgasm cycle of Masters and Johnson, the group gained some momentum, reached a plateau, and spun into desire talk. First Parma asked the only legitimate and authorized question about women's pleasure: Where will I learn about sexual pleasure *after* I am married? Others expressed a deep desire for conversation about sexuality, a space for inquiry, and safety. And, then questions about sexual desire—outside of marriage and disconnected from reproduction—leaked into the room.

Michelle: So, if you could ask other young women any question about sexuality or desire, or whatever, what would you want to ask them?

Jacqui: So, it's the same thing, right, like being wet and having an orgasm, right?

Many respond: What do you mean?

Jacqui: Sometimes I don't get wet, and it hurts. But when I'm wet, that's an orgasm, right?

Another young woman, Khari, jumps in: "It's really important to be wet— you know, if you're not wet, or lubricated, you know the condom can break and then it's possible you can catch an infection or get pregnant. You need to buy some lube!"

We took this opening to explore with the group the politics and practices of wetness, lubrication, and orgasm. As outsiders, we suggested to the young women that they think about and explore their bodies, at home, to find sources of pleasure. But we note a recurrent dynamic—only after disease prevention and victimization discourses had been dutifully narrated by the group, could pleasure poke its head into the room. We see this both in Parma's delicate question about "after marriage" and then in Jacqui's more courageous question about "being wet." Immediately thereafter, as if in an act of discursive chivalry, worries about disease prevention swooped in: "If you're not wet … the condom can break … and you can catch an infection! You need to buy some lube!" Khari saved us from desire and returned us to (the safety of) prevention talk. Protection/prevention became a discursive cocoon for young women's talk of wanting/desire, a way to enter (and exit) the zone of pleasure.

Jacqui insisted that she was not about to purchase lubrication for protection or pleasure: "I'm not spending money on lubrication." And then in a shocking last minute victory for a hybrid discourse of protection-and-pleasure, Khari opened her purse, removed a sample packet of lubrication and handed it over to a much embarrassed, much delighted, laughing hysterically Jacqui as we all watched a conversation rarely had.

Additional stories about how long it takes for women to have an orgasm floated into the room, pushing their way into the conversation until one woman wondered aloud if women were ever meant to experience pleasure: "Why would our bodies be made so that it was so hard for us to have pleasure? Maybe we were just meant to have babies. Maybe we're not meant to enjoy sex." Her voice, while filled with disappointment, also disclosed that she was questioning her "fate" as simply not "naturally" able to experience pleasure. In her question, hope and disappointment slept together.

Studying the Unspoken

Anyway one cuts "positive," at least thus far in this body of research, [desire] crops up only sporadically, infrequent but extraordinary interstices that are portals to the positive.

Tolman (2006, 73)

Through our focus groups and readings, we have come to distance ourselves a bit from the earlier notion that a discourse of desire is missing (Fine 1998). We've gotten intrigued, instead, by the search for methodological release points that allow teen women's experience of wanting and desire to be heard and perhaps, languaged and made into words to be shared. Interested in articulating potential methods to accommodate emerging—and perhaps disguised—discourses of wanting in young women, we bump into issues of epistemology, theory, and method. That is, trying to capture the hidden transcripts of wanting and desire challenges us to rethink how sexual knowledge is constructed within and how it circulates among teen women (and researchers). This leads us to reconsider a number of other questions: where wanting/desire lives and how it moves in the body and in the body politic; what we ask and where we look; how embodied knowledge develops, speaks, and acts at the border between the body and the social membrane; how such knowledge circulates, scabs over in shame and prevention language, and is traded among peers and with adults; and, finally, how knowledge is cauterized by sexualized commodification and surveillance.

Like the young woman we heard earlier who worried that she couldn't have orgasms because her body was deficient or unworthy, we now believe that the missing discourse of desire hasn't been missing at all. Perhaps, just perhaps, researchers (at minimum) haven't figured out how to mobilize cultural practices (including critical research methods) that would allow utterances of young women's desire to breathe. Perhaps we haven't figured out how to move slowly enough towards understanding, how to neutralize the cultural brakes that shut it down in public, in research, and in the body.

As feminist researchers, we have focused with a keen eye on what was not there and what was missing when we listened to young women speak about their desires. This silence has been heart-breaking to hear. And we have simultaneously been committed to teaching young women to protect themselves from violence, viruses, and victimhood. These parallel discourses in adolescent sexuality research have created a chasm within our research methodologies. It is not that we have not listened carefully enough or that we have used the wrong methods to ask our questions. It is that there is simply not enough language and what language we have specifies danger, shame, and judgment. Our language of desire is insufficient, especially for young woman, to be able to describe adequately what it feels like to want.

Feminist researchers are on the cusp of creating new language for women to imagine and describe themselves and their erotic inner and outer lives. New words need to be made up, old words need to be reclaimed, and new ways of understanding sexuality need to be designed. This process will not stop until we have more than enough words to describe the nuances of sexual experience. *The missing discourse needs to be filled in.* We resurrected the idea of excess earlier in this essay because we believe it may hold some potential for imagining sexual feelings that grow bigger than they "need" to be. We think there is something important in thinking more carefully about the zone of sexual development pre-desire: the zone of simply wanting.

Release points are imagined as ways of making potential openings in the "assumed" and the "common sense"—even that of feminist research. We have been focused in this essay on creating a theoretical space for wanting and sexual excess to emerge. In other writing, we further elaborate potential release points—within methodological practices—that allow researchers to keep wanting and desire from being extinguished before being swallowed up by prevention and safety discourses (McClelland and Fine in press [b]). Below, we reflect on a *cultural* release point. We introduce this example of a cultural release point because we hope that it offers future researchers entry points into asking new questions, imagining new relationships with young people, and new language for filling in the gaps in our vocabulary and bodies.

Release Points: Youth Media

One important feminist project is to understand how the hidden or buried transcripts of young women's desire move through the capillaries of media culture. To examine this circulation more carefully, we turned to teen magazines and to Web sites created for girls and young women in order to see what languages were being used in these settings. Although the teen magazines continue to describe young women's sexuality as somewhat passive and problematic, in the Web sites we reviewed, we saw a different trend. We saw desire emerging as a fruitful and alive discourse and even the language of what it means to want showing up in new and unexpected ways. This shift in language represents an opening—a moment of interruption where we see new language developing to describe various aspects of female sexual want, desire, arousal, satisfaction, etc., as they circulate both in individual bodies and in the social body. These examples of youth media articulate young women's desires at the complicated intersections of race, ethnicity, class, sexuality, and (dis)ability. They use a variety of languages to speak out loud what wanting and desire might look and sound like for a young woman.

We reviewed thirty magazines aimed at teen women from the years 2005 and 2006, with the majority of the sources from *Teen People*, *Elle Girl*, and *Seventeen*. In addition, we also analyzed four Web sites aimed at educating young people about their sexuality: Scarleteen.com ("Sex Positive Sex Education"); SexEtc.com ("a web site by teens for teens"); MySistahs.org ("by and for young women of color"); and gURL.com ("an online community and content site for teenage girls").

Pleasure narratives were found with a staccato presence in teen magazines, typically with an authoritative voice-over that represented young women as fundamentally desired but not-really-very-desiring (see Isaacson 2006; McRobbie 1996). In a 2005 issue of the magazine *Teen People*, for instance, the ten most asked questions about sex were answered by the editors and two physicians. One read:

Why do guys seem to think about sex more than girls?

Guys' brains seem to have a whole section dedicated to sex, possibly because guys have more testosterone—a hormone that makes them have a higher sex drive—than girls do (yes, we have some). Guys are also more apt to be visually stimulated while girls tend to be more focused on the relationship and their emotions. "Guys probably feel more social pressure to have sex, says [a gynecologist]. "When guys see a beautiful girl, they want to have sex!" adds [an ob-gyn]. (Grumman 2005, 101)

Young women here are clearly imaged as having inadequate levels of desire (when compared to men). No danger of embodied excess here, only excessive provocation by young women. There were, however, plenty of examples of proclamations of being "in love," but the link to sexual expression was evident in only one example seen below and in this example, we only hear a whisper of desire in the often used phrase, "it just felt right."

Once we said we loved each other, though, we decided that if the right time came, we would be ready. So the night before Halloween last year, we were alone in my house, lying on my living-room floor, and things just felt right. (Wilson 2005, 100)

In contrast, however, there are remarkable Web sites run by and for teens, directly addressing questions and concerns generated by young people. The ethics of researching on online material still need to be articulated critically and collaboratively with participants in these Web sites. In the public sections of these sites, however, you can watch as young women's questions about their desire swim in their own bodies, between groups of young people, across sexualities, histories of sex and abuse, continents and zip codes, sexualities, racial and ethnic lines, bumping into risk as a necessary caution (but not stop sign) for how to proceed with embodied sexual subjectivities.

For instance, the Web site Scarleteen.com defines sexual desire as the following:

> We must experience desire to feel sexually aroused. People sometimes describe sexual desire as being "hungry" or "horny." We may feel sexual desire towards a particular person, or we may feel it simply in and of itself, a kind of free-floating feeling of wanting to be sexual. (Scarlateen 2006)

Definitions like this move us towards excess. Defining desire simply "wanting to be sexual" expands its boundaries by focusing less on objects or experiences; desire is allowed to be "free-floating" and, as a result, perhaps, given room to breathe before being attached to someone or something.

The Web site gURL.com echoed this same expansive sentiment when their advice columnist responded to a young woman who was "confused about what to call [herself]" when she "noticed that [she] was attracted to boys and, maybe, girls." When the young woman wrote to the "Dear Heather" section of gURL.com for advice "on trying to figure it out," the columnist responded:

> I think you should just relax about finding a name for your emotions and spend some time around both girls and boys observing what you feel. I believe it is very natural to have feelings for both boys and girls and that often it is the person and not the gender that really matters. … But I think for right now it is important for you to really enjoy the luxury of not giving all your feelings a name. (gURL.com 2006)

By advising this young woman (and all the young women who read the advice column) to "observe what you feel" and "enjoy the luxury" of feelings that bleed past the boundaries of identities and labels, Web sites like gURL.com offer young (lesbian, bi, and straight) women language with which to color in their experiences of want and desire.

In addition to expanding definitions and offering identities that have luxurious space for attraction and desire to develop, zines and virtual communities have been highlighted by other researchers for their opportunities to offer "covert models of both self-expression and networked activism" (Harris 2004, 170). As young women are faced with limited opportunities for full citizenship in certain areas (due to age and gender, race, ethnicity, citizenship status, class, disability, etc.), they may find opportunities to create "a new girl citizen" who does not just consume commercial culture and is not just consumed by commercial culture, but produces and critiques what she learns through the venues of girl-produced zines and Web sites. For example, MySistahs.org features articles written by young women of color on subjects such as "colorism" in the African American community, critical media skills, and women's sexual exploitation in hip hop culture. These cultural spaces are essential for social and sexual development because they exist outside of the market and provide opportunities for information and expression without relying on the marketplace to provide the circuitry (Harris 2004).

Conclusions

We write this piece with a sense that young women are now struggling at the nexus of embodiment and politics. They want to speak and act above ground about desire, wanting, and risk. Dutifully trying to squeeze their feelings of wanting and desire into discourses of abstinence, heteronormativity, or prevention, they seek a much wider platform for conversation, questions, and talk in which to think through their bodies, relationships, and their futures as both profoundly political and embodied. We want to help imagine, with them, a political, theoretical, and cultural plane—in youth movements and human rights campaigns; in zines, Web sites and movies; in health care settings and schools; in science; and in bedrooms—where young women's desire, upon "release," wouldn't be eaten by commercials, predators, or shame, but could loiter, a bit, in talk and body, among teens and even with adults. We would hope, that in these spaces, they be allowed to be *excessive in their expectations and demands for a fully embodied sexual present and future.*

We use this essay to imagine embodied desire, floating through bodies and also to track how young women's enactments and relations of sexuality move in conversation, Web sites, magazines, youth community settings, and in classrooms. These moments are stitched together from whispers and gasps—both heard in person and through cultural products that inspired us to speculate how a language of young women's wanting and desire can begin to enter public discourse, feminist research, and organizing. This requires that researchers, young women, educators, and the many other adults who shape young adult worlds, enable the lines of vision, the bodies, and the ambivalences of young women to emerge from the closet of abstinence, prevention, and hetero normativity. We must, for even a moment, hold the sex police at bay, turn away from our surveillance, and allow excess to emerge.

Acknowledgments

The authors would like to thank Carole Saltz and the Leslie Glass Foundation for its generous support.

References

Burns, A. and M.E. Torre. 2005. Revolutionary sexualities. *Feminism and Psychology* 15 (10):21–26.

Cameron, D. and D. Kulick. 2003. *Language and sexuality.* Cambridge: Cambridge University Press.

Correa, S. and R. Petchesky. 1994. Reproductive and sexual rights: A feminist perspective. In *Population policy reconsidered: Health, empowerment and rights,* ed. G. Sen, A. Germain, and L. Chen, 107–12. Harvard series on population and international health. Cambridge, MA: Harvard University Press.

Douglas, M. 1966. *Purity and danger: An analysis of the concepts of pollution and taboo.* New York: Routledge.

Edwards, W. M. and E. Coleman. 2004. Defining sexual health: A descriptive overview. *Archives of Sexual Behavior* 33 (3):189–195.

Fausto-Sterling, A., P. Gowaty, and M. Zuk. 1997. Evolutionary psychology and Darwinism feminism. *Feminist Studies* 23 (2):403–417.

Fine, M. 1988. Sexuality, schooling, and adolescent females: The missing discourse of desire. *Harvard Educational Review* 58 (1):29–51.

Fine, M. and S. I. McClelland. 2006. Sexuality education and desire: Still missing after all these years. *Harvard Educational Review* 76 (3):297–338.

Fine, M. and S. I. McClelland. 2007. The politics of teen women's desire: Public policy and the adolescent female body. *Emory Law Journal*, 56(4).

Fine, M. and S. I. McClelland. In press (b). Writing *on* cellophane: Trying to theorize girls' and women's sexual desires wrapped in culture of commodification and dangers. In *The methodological dilemma: Critical and creative approaches to qualitative research,* ed. K. Gallagher. Toronto: University of Toronto Press.

Franke, K. M. 2001. Theorizing yes: An essay on feminism, law and desire. *Columbia Law Review* 101:181–208.

Geronimus, A. T. 1997. Teen childbearing and personal responsibility: An alternative view. *Political Science Quarterly* 112 (3):405–430.

Greif, M. 2006. Children of the revolution. *Harper's Magazine,* November, 13–16.

Grosz, E. 1994. *Volatile bodies: Toward a corporeal feminism.* Bloomington: Indiana University Press.

Grumman, R. 2005. Your 10 most-asked sex questions. *Teen People,* October, 101.

gURL.com. 2006. *Help me Heather: Dating.* http://www.gurl.com/findout/hmh/qa/0,,626759,00.html (accessed November 28, 2006).

Hare, E.H. 1962. Masturbatory insanity: The history of an idea. *Journal of Mental Science* 108:2–25.

Harris, A., ed. 2004. *All about the girl: Power, culture, and identity.* New York: Routledge.

Hite, S. 1987. *The Hite report: Women and love: A cultural revolution in progress.* London: Penguin.

Hrdy, S. B. 1981. *The woman that never evolved.* Cambridge, MA: Harvard University Press.

Hustvedt, S. 2006. *A Plea For Eros.* Picador/Hentry Holt & Company.

Irigaray, L. 1981. This sex which is not one. In *New French feminisms,* ed. E. Marks and I. de Courtivron. 91–106. New York: Schocken Books.

Isaacson, N. 2006. An overview of the role of sexual health organizations, corporations, and government in determining content and access to online sexuality education for adolescents. *Sexuality Research and Social Policy* 3 (2):24–36.

Koedt, A. 1970. The myth of vaginal orgasm. In Turner, L. B. (ed.) *Voices from women's liberation*. New York: Signet, pp. 158–166.

Lloyd, E. A. 2005. *The case of the female orgasm: Bias in the science of evolution*. Cambridge: Harvard University Press.

McClelland, S. I. and M. Fine. In press (a). Embedded science: The production of consensus in evaluation of abstinence-only curricula. *Qualitative Inquiry*.

McElroy, W. 1995. *XXX: A woman's right to pornography*. New York: St. Martin's Press.

McClelland, S. I. and Fine, M. In press (b). Writing *on* cellophane: Studying teen women's sexual desires; Inventing methodological release points. In *The methodological dilemma: Critical and creative approaches to qualitative research*, ed. K. Gallagher. Toronto: University of Toronto Press.

McRobbie, A. 1996. More! New sexualities in girls' and women's magazines. In *Cultural studies and communications*, ed. J. Curran, D. Morley, and V. Walkerdine. London: Arnold.

Misra, G. and R. Chandiramani, eds. 2005. *Sexuality, gender and rights: Exploring theory and practice in South and Southeast Asia*. New Delhi, India: Sage Publications.

Queen, C. 1996. *Real live nude girl: Chronicles of sex-positive culture*. Pittsburgh: Cleis Press.

Rasmussen, M. L. 2006. *Becoming subjects: Sexualities and secondary schooling*. New York: Routledge.

Reich, R.B. 2002. *I'll be short: Essentials for a decent working society*. Boston: Beacon Press.

Rose, T. 2003. *Longing to tell*. New York: Farrar, Straus, and Giroux.

Rubin, G. 1984. Thinking sex: Notes for a radical theory of the politics of sexuality. In *Pleasure and danger: Exploring female sexuality*, ed. C. S. Vance, 267–319. Boston: Routledge and Kegan Paul.

Scarlateen.com. 2006. *The science of sexual response*. http://www.scarleteen.com/sexuality/response_2.html (accessed November 28, 2006).

Scott, J. 1990. *Domination and the arts of resistance: Hidden transcripts*. New Haven, CT: Yale University Press.

Snitow, A., C. Stansell, and S. Thompson. 1983. *Powers of desire: The politics of sexuality*. New York: Monthly Review Press.

Thompson, S. 1990. Putting A Big Thing Into a Little Hole: Teenage Girls' Accounts of Sexual Initiation. *Journal of Sex Research*, 27(3).

Tolman, D. L. 1994. Doing desire: Adolescent girls' struggles for/with sexuality. *Gender and Society* 8 (3):324–342.

Tolman, D. L. 2002. *Dilemmas of desire*. Cambridge, MA: Harvard University Press.

Tolman, D. L. 2006. In a different position: Conceptualizing female adolescent sexuality development within compulsory heterosexuality. *New Directions for Child and Adolescent Development* 112:71–89.

Vance, C. S., ed. 1984. *Pleasure and danger: Exploring female sexuality*. Boston: Routledge and Kegan Paul.

Whorton, J. 2001. Looking back: The solitary vice. *Western Journal of Medicine* 175 (1):66–68.

Willis, E. 1992. Lust horizons: Is the women's movement pro-sex? In *No more nice girls: Countercultural essays*, ed. E. Willis, 3–14. Middletown, CT: Wesleyan University Press.

Wilson, W. L. 2005. I have no regrets about losing my virginity. *Teen People*, October, 100.

Part II
Creating Spaces

5

The Empowered Fe Fes
A Group for Girls with Disabilities

SUSAN NUSSBAUM

The Empowered Fe Fes is a group of young women who have to go through life learning how to deal with disabilities, so the Fe Fes are like a support group.

Nikki[1]

Every now and then something happens in the Fe Fes that reminds me of the depth and reach of the paternalism endured by disabled people.

Last week, I was in downtown Chicago with a couple of the newer girls in one of the Fe Fe groups, both high school seniors. To my surprise, they mentioned they'd never been in downtown Chicago before, although they'd both grown up in the city. As the afternoon wound down, one of the girls asked me to go with her across the street to the paratransit van that was there to pick her up. I said, "Well, is there a reason you can't go by yourself?"

"I'm afraid," she said.

"Really?" I asked. "What are you afraid of?"

"I've never crossed the street by myself."

By now, I'd had plenty of practice in stifling my initial reaction to some of the things the girls would tell me. Nevertheless, I heard the exact wrong thing come out of my mouth. "You've *never* crossed the street by yourself!?"

We wheeled over to the intersection, and I explained the basics. The light changed. She crossed. I yelled across the street to her, "Now you've crossed a street by yourself!"

Half an hour later, the other Fe Fe asked me to show her how to cross, too.

I've always worked with high school girls. In 1971, I joined the Chicago Women's Liberation Union, a socialist feminist organization. My baptism into girl organizing was to explore the vast, uncharted territory of Catholic girls' high schools of Chicago's Northwest Side. The nuns of Alvernia and Mother Guerin read our feminist newspaper and gave me access to roam the classes and lunchrooms, slowly building my group of budding feminists. I was nineteen. I liked the work, and stuck with it for a couple of years, but faded from active political duty around 1974. Nixon had finally resigned, the Viet Nam war had ended, abortion was legalized, and I figured maybe I should go to college. Just before graduating from a local acting school, I was hit by a car and became a full-time wheelchair user. It was 1978.

Access Living

It wasn't long before my focus shifted from antiwar and women's work, to disability rights. Access Living, the city's first disability rights organization that was actually run by disabled people, opened up in 1980. It was never just a paycheck, but a place I came into my new disabled identity fully and proudly. It was this transformation, from the deepest shame, isolation, and sexual confusion to a newfound sense of belonging—not only to a community, but in this new body—that I knew must be shared with as many women as possible. I was a much older and more seasoned activist when I acted on that early commitment.

I have no formal training to work with youth, no degrees of any sort. But one characteristic of the emerging disability rights movement was the feeling that we were reinventing ourselves and our purpose in the world, and those of us working in disability rights agencies began making ourselves into experts on disability—high school dropouts became housing rights advocates, people with cognitive disabilities became peer counselors. We knew no one else could do the work we did as well as we did, because we were the real thing, the authentic article, we had been there, and after centuries of bearing our oppression in silence, we were demanding change—in the legislatures, the streets, and in social relations. I worked on and off at Access Living, in a few different jobs, but always as an organizer.

Smells like High School

The Empowered Fe Fe group grew out of Access Living's outreach effort into the Chicago public high schools. In 1998, I came back to AL after some years away to organize that outreach. My job was to get into a few schools that had large numbers of kids with disabilities and lead workshops on issues like disability rights, self-advocacy, and strategies toward a more independent life after high school. Getting into the schools was tedious, requiring endless phone calling and plenty of strategic booty kissing. When after weeks or months of trying, I would actually succeed in getting a meeting with a special education teacher, I was sometimes able to persuade them to let me in for a trial session.

Once in, I realized my skills as an organizer did not always extend to keeping a room full of teenagers engaged and wanting more. I had imagined that my message of challenging the ableist culture and fighting discrimination would so electrify these clueless disabled students that I'd have swarms of teenage crips on fire to become activists. Instead, they tuned me out as they would any droning adult. Those of them who were wheelchair-users seemed ashamed by my presence, as if my disability called attention to theirs, and those students with nonapparent disabilities refused to acknowledge their own disabled identities, furious at having been outed by virtue of my presence in their class. (Such are the intricacies of adolescent disability self-loathing.) I found myself compensating for their misery by getting peppier and more upbeat. I barely recognized the sound of my own voice squeaking in my ears. Also, I was entirely unprepared to work with students who had disabilities that affected the way they learned. I was constantly struggling to find ways of making the sessions accessible and interactive, but I was making it all up as I went. I suddenly realized I knew nothing about learning or cognitive disabilities, nothing about deafness—in fact, the only disability I knew much about was my own. From time to time, however, in spite of my ham-handed approach and gaps in education, the class was great and I rose to the occasion, and I left the school feeling high. But for the most part, I flailed without focus, and the work plodded along.

Spalding

In 1999, the Director of the Girl's Best Friend Foundation (GBF), asked me why no disabled activists were applying to them for money to work with girls with disabilities. She said GBF wanted to fund something for disabled girls, and that Access Living was remiss for not recognizing the needs of our own young women.

Not that there weren't great programs for girls all over the place. The city was overflowing with talented women organizers, working with girls of every culture, race, sexual orientation, and economic class. But none of them included disabled girls. The exclusion of disabled youth from these progressive programs, which otherwise emphasized diversity, mirrored the segregation of disabled people from all of society.

We arranged to meet with a group of girls at Spalding High School, the largest of Chicago's disabled-only schools. With us was another youth worker named Carolyn Gordon, from the Illinois Caucus for Adolescent Health, a health rights center for youth.

Since 1955, Spalding was where the majority of high school students with most kinds of disabilities—cognitive, physical, sensory, behavioral—were sent. It was finally shut down in 2004, over thirty years after the segregation of students with disabilities became illegal. The vast majority of students were people of color, a reflection of both the migration of Whites to the surrounding suburbs, and the ability of White parents to find private alternatives for their disabled children. It's a harsh fact that in 2005, 42 percent of disabled youth in Chicago public high schools failed to graduate.[2]

The theory behind places like Spalding was simple: the total segregation of disabled kids from their nondisabled peers. Beyond that perverse logic, there was no way of understanding why hundreds of children with every imaginable kind of disability were lumped together in this old, peeling, dimly lit building. The lack of services, the one-size-fits-all classes, and the oppressive atmosphere affected Spalding students the same as students at other harsh, underfunded schools—the place was rife with bullying and gangs, only these gangsters were smashing each other's faces in with crutches and wheelchair footrests.

About fifteen or twenty girls were pulled out of class to come to our meeting. A few were a bit shut down, others attentive, but puzzled. We asked the girls a series of questions about what kinds of after-school activities they participated in. One by one, they answered that after school, the bus took them home. They insisted that there simply were no programs. We asked them about sports activities during the school day, and they told us that they didn't get to participate in physical education, but were instead taken into a room to play computer solitaire. (Spalding actually had a swimming pool, complete with lifts to lower kids into the water, but it had been in disrepair for twenty-five years or so.) We asked them what programs they wished they could have, but they were unable to suggest any.

They think that they can't teach us anything, we can't learn, so why waste their time teaching us?[3] (See Figure 5.1.)

Dawn

Figure 5.1 Dawn conducting an interview for *Beyond Disability: The Fe Fe Stories.*

There was one straggler who came in the door late. She was more outspoken than the others, and wholly unintimidated. As the straggler broke the ice by being more critical of the school, the other girls became more forthcoming and animated as well. They explained that the school's buses, adapted to be accessible, took them home immediately after school, on a rigidly observed schedule. They were either at home or at school, watching nondisabled siblings come and go, busy with one thing or another.

The period ended and the girls filed out. I caught up with the straggler and asked her what had interested her in coming to our discussion. "I got to break outta class," she said. Her name was Taina Rodriguez.

Taina

After the meeting, I felt directed and motivated about the possibilities of youth organizing for the first time in years. Girl's Best Friend gave Access Living some funding so I could hire an intern, and I immediately called Taina. It was her first job.

I decided my own disability gave me the moral authority to come into these girls lives. I understood disability—the questions one dared not ask about one's sexuality, the unending struggle to fit in somehow, the invisibility of it. I understood how easy it might be to believe the lies all around when no truthful alternative was there to supplant them. I understood paternalism as a woman and as a person with a disability. That was what I brought to the table, and I figured it was enough for starters.

My new intern was my best teacher. Taina was eighteen years old, Puerto Rican, had grown up in a tough, rundown neighborhood on Chicago's North Side, raised by her Spanish-speaking grandparents. She had beautiful, long black hair, which she arranged with two long, heavily moussed strands that hung down over her face, as was the style. Her lips were outlined in black. She favored low-cut tops, which showed off her scar from heart surgery. Early on in her employment at AL, our executive director called me in to ask me to urge Taina to wear clothes that covered her cleavage, but I could never bring myself to float the suggestion out there. Taina had an innate pride in her body and her disability that transcended every attempt from external forces to squelch it.

She was also one of the best natural organizers I ever met. Dominique, who attended the first Fe Fe meeting and stayed in the group until 2003, remembers Taina talking her into coming to her first meeting:

> She just said, 'You know what? I'm just gonna put you in it cuz you ain't doin' nothin'.
>
> **Dominique**[4]

Carolyn, Taina, and I began piecing together our first series of workshops, which would include sexuality and disability, disability culture, and transitioning into life after high school (Figure 5.2).

Figure 5.2 Keesha works on posters for the 2004 Disability Pride Parade.

Getting girls to actually show up was the hard part. On the phone, many of them seemed vague or wary about coming to a meeting. There were physical barriers as well as psychological barriers. For example, none of the girls knew how to use public transportation. They had never received any kind of travel training from the school system, and their parents or guardians were either stiflingly overprotective, indifferent, or unaware. Some of the wheelchair-users lived up a flight or two of stairs, shedding their chairs in the building entrance after being dropped off from school so they could be carried up. They spent the rest of the afternoon and evening wheelchair-less, stuck in bed, or for those who could, crawling from here to there around the apartment.

Ironically, the first wave of disability rights activists had fought a militant and protracted struggle to win access to public transit systems all over the United States. It ended in a series of legislative victories starting in the mid-1980s. By 2000, when the Fe Fes first took real shape, Chicago was swarming with accessible buses, and the subway system was moving towards full access. But it was as if this incredible advance had never occurred, so deep was most of the disabled community's fear of taking a mainline bus. We began hooking the girls up with a paratransit system, which was a door-to-door service run by the city. The rides were hard to set up, inflexible, and dependably late, but the girls preferred all the inconvenience to the stares or open hostility they imagined would greet them out in the real world. Taina scammed a way for a few girls to take turns setting up paratransit rides for everybody, so each person didn't have to get up at 6:00 a.m. to call and schedule. There were a couple of girls who still fell through the cracks, and we ended up paying the city for "gold tickets," which were outrageously priced rides in accessible vans that could be used like taxis. One way or another, we got a good turnout at our meeting about sexuality.

"How to Take Care of Yo'Self!"—Becoming the Empowered Fe Fes

My mama, I didn't even tell her. I just said, we talk about stuff and she said what stuff. I just said stuff. I didn't elaborate.

Dominique[5]

There were about ten girls at our first meeting. I was worried they wouldn't feel comfortable really getting into the discussion, though. I reminded myself that it was only a first meeting and not to stress out too much if things didn't cut loose. The speaker, Judy Panko-Reis, from the Health Resource Center for Women with Disabilities, had been telling the group about how she met her husband after she became disabled. One of the girls, a terribly bright young woman named Sharday, who couldn't speak and could barely move, but was able to write with one hand, slid a note over to Judy. The note said, "What positions do you and your husband use in bed?" I guess it was at that moment that I knew that we were doing something right.

Soon after the first few meetings, it became clear we had a group. I suggested the girls think up a name to describe themselves, and Taina blurted out "The Empowered Fe Fes!" The group explained to me that "fe fe" was slang for female. The name stuck.

I liked being able to open up with no holds barred. That it was confidential.

Taina[6]

Every new Fe Fe group usually starts with the same series of workshops: developing a list of group agreements and discussing the meaning of safe space, learning the names and purposes of the female and male reproductive systems, learning about the sexuality bill of rights and the health rights of minors in Illinois. We discuss a variety of birth control methods, with an emphasis on barrier methods. Woven throughout these lessons are discussions about dating, romance, caregiver abuse and dating violence, body image, decision making, sexism, and heterosexism.

We sent out meeting reminders, usually made by the girls, with titles like "How to Take Care of Yo'Self!," "Body Parts—OOH!," "Peer Pressure How Deep," "Dating! Now That's What I'm Talking About!" with the further explanation "Hey gals, ever dated someone who comes from a different race or culture? Have you dated someone who doesn't have a disability? Ever been kicked to the curb? Do you want to share with us about your dating experience? Well, don't just sit there like a bump on a log, get off your Fe Fe tails and start yappin'!"

The girls did start yapping, and out came a whole world of contradictions. They longed to be viewed as the most deserving and desirable of girls, but refused to ever date a disabled boy. They shunned promiscuity and bragged about their own (sometimes invented) sexual conquests. They judged Lesbian, Gay, Bisexual, Transgender, and Queer (LGBTQ) people as unnatural, while confessing their own indignation about discrimination, and dread of the bully's invective. They were proud to be women of color and ashamed of their disabilities. They dreamed of independence, but would not venture onto a public bus. They worried about what their peers would think, what their parents would think, what their pastors or priests might think, what God would think. More than anything, they longed for love, but feared the possibility that it might never come into their lives.

> At first, I wasn't really sure if I was gonna come back. I remember the time we got deeper on the relationship part. Saying you can get hurt but you can move on. I thought, "Easier said than done." But I read the scenarios. I thought, hmm, maybe I should just think some more about this.
>
> **Dominique**[7]

Toward an Inclusive Curriculum

Carolyn, Taina, and I responded to all these issues one by one, meeting after meeting. Our curriculum was haphazard, conceived to address the need of the moment, a work in progress. We'd plan a workshop on family conflict, followed by one with performers from an LGBTQ theatre company, or a series of meetings about violence, then veer into a session about how to make a resume. The results were predictably uneven. It took several years to learn how to create a curriculum that expanded the group's understanding of the interconnection of multiple identities and achieved a coherent blending of the building of mundane skills with more complex perspectives on oppression. For example, how to find, finance, and be a good employer to a personal attendant is connected to the philosophy of the independent living movement and a pride in disability identity. The very notion that having assistance getting out of bed in the morning is connected to how we feel about ourselves, and how all of that is part of a larger movement for disability rights (which is part of the overall *human* rights movement), is a giant leap toward self-awareness and self-determination. So we no longer address LGBTQ issues in one or two meetings, but in *many* meetings. When the topic is violence, we bring in speakers who talk about how violence affects various communities of people, not only girls and women with disabilities. We discuss practical strategies and solutions, but move into a larger political discussion that sheds light on our commonality of experience with other oppressed people. This approach breaks down the tendency to compartmentalize ourselves by our various identity groups. Perhaps a Fe Fe who is also Latina and a lesbian can begin to feel less like a collection of minority identities and more like an integrated whole.

Our Bodies, Our Ambivalence

> We're viewed as not having sex, so even by knowing about our bodies, or carrying a condom in our purse, whether you had a boyfriend or not, it made us feel power—pussy power.
>
> **Taina, in a conversation with the author[8]**

> You can discuss things here that you cannot discuss with your parents. They would be, like, 'Why are you thinking about that?' My parents treat me like I'm a little girl, and I'm not.
>
> **Dawn[9]**

> I remember the sex part. The condom on the cucumber. I didn't get a chance to go to the sex store and I wanted to do that.
>
> **Dominique[10]**

> I remember when I was trying to put a condom on (a zucchini) with my mouth. They were all cheering me on!
>
> **Taina[1]**

Fostering a belief in the Fe Fe's inherent sexuality and sexual rights has always been a primary focus. Disabled people have endured centuries of infantilization, continuing up to this day—think of Jerry Lewis and his "kids" on the yearly telethon. The Fe Fe group is the first chance many of the girls have had to really talk and learn about sex and to break down the misconceptions we've all internalized about sexuality and disability.

> It made me realize that it was not just me and my situation and there were other people like that too, which made me feel better. It made me more out there about the situation about sexuality, because I used to not want to talk about it because no one took me seriously, so that was a good experience.
>
> **Anonymous[12]**

The Fe Fes are always in ecstasy when they learn how to put condoms on zucchinis and how dental dams are used. But despite the time spent learning the how-to's, there were many times when one or another of the girls would come to me with a pregnancy scare or a sexually transmitted infection (STI). Once I went into Access Living's tiny bathroom to find a Fe Fe anxiously trying to decipher a pregnancy test.

> One reason (disabled girls don't use condoms) is cuz they go by what the guy says. The girl is thinking cuz I'm disabled this is one of the rare opportunities I might be able to have sex so I better do what the guy says.
>
> **Taina**[13]

We had practice sessions on how to talk to a boy about why he should use a condom. The girls were always insistent to their role play partner that "No glove, No love!" before exploding into laughter. We even went to a sexual aids store where everyone picked out flavored condoms and debated where best to hide them from the prying eyes of family members.

The question of sexual responsibility to oneself, and even of what constitutes sexual pleasure, remains contradictory for the Fe Fes. They're sometimes willing to take risks with their health, and their futures, in order to affirm their sexuality or perhaps even for love, and yet they shun the one sexual outlet that is always pleasurable and utterly free of risk.

The Masturbation Dilemma

> When I was in the Fe Fes it was like we were the cocoons and you were trying to crash us out of those cocoons.
>
> **Taina**[14]

Every now and then, I dare to bring up the subject of masturbation. The suggestion is always rejected immediately and unanimously. So I try to find ways to sneak it in when they aren't looking, like when we play the Body Parts game, I always spend as much time as possible explaining the clitoris. When I suggest that touching one's own clitoris can be fun (and educational!), I'm shut down by a chorus of "eeuuws!" Clearly there were cultural and religious beliefs in place that forbade the actual practice, or at least, the discussion, of female sexual pleasure. Some of the girls said they felt it was disgusting to touch their genitals, except to wash themselves. Some of the girls most likely did masturbate, but were uncomfortable admitting it.

> It's embarrassing, it's private. You don't want your peers to think you're a freak. I remember [when I did it] I used to think I was really nasty and dirty cuz God's watching me.
>
> **Taina**[15]

From an early age, all girls are taught to be alienated from their bodies. So little of what we learn about how our bodies work, and what they're capable of, has to do with any kind of actual pleasure, much less pride. It's common knowledge that girls begin punishing their bodies at younger ages all the time, by dieting, starving, vomiting, straightening, douching, cutting, etc. In addition to the usual menu of sexist, racist, homophobic stereotypes held up as shining examples to us all, disabled girls often experience an even larger helping of cultural objectification. Many girls with physical or psychiatric disabilities undergo long hospitalizations in their youth, enduring what under any other circumstances would be viewed as torture. As patients, some disabled girls are continually made to strip naked, often in front of doctors, students, and whoever else may be passing through, to be probed and discussed for "educational" purposes. These episodes are frequent, sanctioned by parents who sit passively in a doctor's presence. A girl's body is at times a source of physical pain or mental anguish. Although Title IX (landmark legislation enacted in 1972 prohibiting sex discrimination in schools, including in sports programs) has given nondisabled girls a new way to experience their bodies and their power, sports for disabled girls remains unexplored territory. (Disabled boys tend to have greater access to sports, such as wheelchair basketball, rugby, etc.) At home, nondisabled parents, more often than not unaware of their disabled daughter's potential, teach her to expect little in the way of romance, sex, children, family—future.

> She (mom) isn't a disabled person. She didn't think I could be sexy, romantic. It was only from coming to this group that I got the message about my sexuality.
>
> **Anonymous**[16]

One day, one of the Fe Fe groups that had been together for over a year visited a small shop that was dedicated to the sexuality of women, with an emphasis on masturbation. We arranged for the shop's owner, a young woman not much older than the girls, to make a special presentation for us. At one point, she picked up a vibrator (it looked like a pastel-colored dildo) and turned it on. She handed it over to the group, and all of them started screaming at once. I doubt she's ever had a more enthusiastic and appreciative audience.

Beyondmedia

> I feel much more confident than when I started with Beyondmedia. I am smart. I can do stuff. I can help people more than I think I can. (See Figure 5.3.)
>
> **Alysha**[17]

In 2004, Access Living received a grant from the Department of Labor to contract with some community-based groups on education and job

Figure 5.3 Alysha at the 2004 Disability Pride Parade.

training projects, all aimed at youth. I had heard of the remarkable work of Beyondmedia Education, a small outfit of progressive women whose mission was to teach women and girls video skills so they could make movies about their lives. They had worked with incarcerated mothers, LGBTQ students in Chicago high schools, and many more such groups. I called Salome Chasnoff, the founder and director of Beyondmedia, and we quickly made a deal.

The batch of '04 Fe Fes was particularly strong and very bonded with each other. They'd already spent many months as a group, talking about sexuality, family issues, disability rights, etc., so when Salome and her small staff came to their first Fe Fe meeting, the girls were relaxed and excited, and everyone hit it off immediately. It was this mutuality of respect, fun, and desire to learn (on the parts of both the Fe Fes and Beyondmedia staff) that was the backdrop for the long and amazingly fruitful collaboration that was to come.

All the Fe Fes were coming out of special education programs in the Chicago public schools. None of them had ever enjoyed any access to extracurricular activities and had been consigned to a school lifetime of drilling the basics. Yet at that first meeting Salome put professional video cameras in the girls' hands and taught them how to use them. Other girls had still cameras, and they were shown how to use those, and from that day on, there were always a bunch of Fe Fes taking turns taping meetings, each other, skits or interviews.

Figure 5.4 Chaka gets ready to conduct interviews for *Beyond Disability: The Fe Fe Stories.*

They helped me see my disability differently. Like I felt negative about my disability but now it doesn't matter to me what other people think.

Anonymous[18]

The act of putting the technology in the hands of the girls gave them a kind of power and authority they'd never experienced. Salome understood this from the start, but even she was stunned by the ease with which the girls took up the skill. She'd never worked with disabled people before and had expected the barriers to be more significant.

I learned how to approach a camera in a professional way. I learned how to be me, it made me stronger. It's a lie that people with disabilities can't be on TV. It made me feel bold.

Anonymous[19]

Salome introduced the girls to new ways of seeing things. Two of the girls had visual impairments, so one of them did more interview work, the other focused on the sound equipment. The wheelchair-users who had trouble holding the camera had a camera attached to their armrests with a piece specifically designed for that purpose, which gave them the freedom to take footage while gliding through space in their power wheelchairs. We learned what "media literacy" was, and saw examples of how the media oppresses women and disabled people (Figure 5.4).

The Fe Fes went everywhere with their cameras, interviewing strangers on the streets of the city, and disabled activists at the first ever Disability Pride Parade. Most important, they interviewed each other, and everyone told their own stories of despair and renewal.

It made me have more confidence. Yeah, I can accomplish anything. Made me feel really proud.

Anonymous[20]

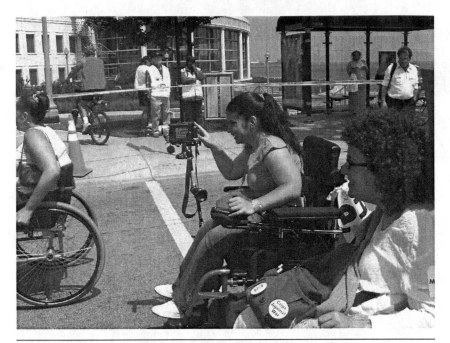

Figure 5.5 Veronica and the author at the Disability Pride Parade.

None of the Fe Fes was prepared for the premiere of their movie, which they named *Beyond Disability: The Fe Fe Stories*. The movie was shown on a large screen to a standing room only crowd of over 200 people. When it was over, the crowd rose to its feet (those who could, anyway) and cheered for what seemed like five minutes. The Fe Fes trooped onto the stage, barely able to believe that this was all happening to them. For young women who had been invisible all their lives, suddenly they were *known*, and respected, and the center of everyone's attention. When they were finally all assembled on stage, the crowd started roaring again. The girls responded to the questions from the audience with the kind of giddy excitement that comes rarely in anyone's life.

> [The Fe Fes] changed everybody so they knew who they are and who they should be are two different worlds. I'm the same way—you've got to keep going and we're there. (See Figure 5.5.)

Anonymous[21]

There were requests for screenings, interviews by newspapers, magazines, and the local public radio affiliate. Girl's Best Friend paid for two of the Fe Fes to go to Berkeley, California, to accept two awards from an important international disability film festival. In the years since that night, their public speaking skills have acquired a confidence and depth I could never have imagined.

I learned lots of new things. It gave me higher self-esteem.

Anonymous[22]

Making the movie, representing it to the public, and telling their stories was a transformative experience. It gave the Fe Fes the opportunity to actively fight stereotypes and defend their humanity. In an evaluation of the program that was conducted by outside facilitators in 2005, the girls said that being in the Fe Fe group made them feel special, but in a good way, as opposed to a stigmatizing way, which is what they were accustomed to.

I learned a lot about advocacy, about being aware that I have rights, that I shouldn't be walked over. People shouldn't treat me like I'm not human. I feel I learned to speak up for myself, to let people know I'm not stupid, that I have feelings like everyone else. I also learned how to control my own life.

Anonymous[23]

They still struggle with all the old external demons—unemployment, extreme economic deprivation, discrimination, violence, health issues—but their self-esteem survives more or less intact. A source of great shame—their disabilities—has become a source of tremendous pride.

If anybody says a visually impaired person can't do a video, I just showed them the proof!

Nico[24]

Race and Disability

I think I deal with the same amount of crap being Latina as being disabled. They cancel each other out. I deal with crap being a woman, too.

Taina, from a conversation with the author

Over the years, the racial breakdown of the Fe Fes has been something like this: 85 percent Black, 10 percent to 15 percent Latina, 5 percent White. In a 2005 article for *New Mobility* magazine about the Empowered Fe Fe's first movie, journalist Joelle Brouner, herself disabled, wrote:

Nearly all the young women featured in the film are young women of color, but they never explore how being a person of color affects their experience of disability or vice versa. Perhaps it is unrealistic to expect these young women to have all the conversations that the rest of the disability community seems to avoid.[25]

The disability rights movement (DRM) is perhaps more deeply integrated racially, by sexual orientation, class background, and in every other way than other movements for civil rights. Yet the DRM's leadership appears to be largely straight, disabled white people. Some activists believe that because the DRM's reason for being is *disability* rights, it's not necessarily urgent to look closely at how different identities intersect. They argue that the experience of disability oppression is so powerful, that commonality alone bridges other gaps in background and culture.

They don't see me for my race. They see me for my disability first.

Koko[26]

Women with disabilities won't get picked for jobs, mostly because of their disability. I was discriminated against cuz of my disability.

Shonda[27]

The DRM's hesitancy to take up the issue of racism is an ongoing dilemma. There's also been a disturbing absence of discussion about heterosexism. However, there has been some important discourse in certain parts of the movement. The Society for Disability Studies, a group of mostly academic disabled activists, dedicated its 2005 conference to the intersection of race and disability. But a really searching discussion of the issue has not found a way to trickle down to the masses of activists working day to day in the ranks of the disability movement.

I think we should address it more [racism] and talk about how we really feel. A lot of us are really sensitive and quiet about it. Discrimination happens and you don't know how to share it or deal with it.

Nikki[28]

We need to have a meeting to discuss it [racism]. Some Fe Fes might not be comfortable with it. That's a whole 'nother meeting.

Shonda[29]

The Empowered Fe Fe curriculum changes and adapts as it attempts to address the complex confluence of identities that disabled girls embody. We try to build confidence, independence, and sisterhood in the context of an understanding of how the dominant culture often works against those aims. We try to provide the safety and support that all girls need to get strong.

Reality These Days

In spite of the Fe Fe's occasional difficulty uniting theory with practice, they do retain a good deal of what we talk about in meetings, and over time, many of them feel more confident about integrating it into their lives. When one of the Fe Fes called late one night to ask if chlamydia was fatal, I assured her it was not. When she wanted to know more, I asked her if she still had the book

I'd given to everyone in her group, loaded with great information on female sexuality. She was able to find the answers to her questions on her own. She suddenly knew why the book she took home once and threw aside was an important survival tool.

The first Empowered Fe Fes are adults now, and I've lost track of quite a few. Some went on to college. Some are working and living on their own. There are seven babies I know of and two deaths. Some are still living in inaccessible apartments, trapped indefinitely like prisoners on house arrest. One is being battered by her husband, but is afraid to get any real help. One is a lesbian with one foot still in the closet. One is homeless. Many are searching—for jobs, apartments, love. One group of Fe Fes continues to meet on its own, and some have become disability rights activists. All are struggling day to day to hold on to their belief in themselves. They know that belief in oneself is fragile, and the realities of our complicated, difficult lives can sometimes shake us to the core.

Having a safe place to talk with our friends and sisters helps us remember how valuable we are.

Notes

1. Jennifer Roche, *Beyond Disability: The Fe Fe Stories* (Chicago: Community Arts Network, 2004).
2. 2005 Illinois District Report Card, City of Chicago District 299.
3. Beyondmedia Education, *Beyond Disability: The Fe Fe Stories* (Chicago: Beyondmedia, 2004) video recording.
4. Dominique G., phone interview with author, April 9, 2006.
5. Ibid.
6. Taina Rodriguez, interview with author, May 2, 2006.
7. Dominique G., phone interview with author, April 9, 2006.
8. Taina Rodriguez, interview with author, May 2, 2006.
9. Barbara Brotman, "Interview with Dawn, member of the Empowered Fe Fes," *Chicago Tribune*, August 22, 2001, Woman News section.
10. Dominique G., phone interview with author, April 9, 2006.
11. Taina Rodriguez, interview with author, May 2, 2006.
12. Anonymous, "A program evaluation masking identities of Empowered Fe Fe members," 2005.
13. Taina Rodriguez, interview with author, May 2, 2006.
14. Ibid.
15. Ibid.
16. Anonymous, "A program evaluation."
17. Beyondmedia Education, *Beyond Disability*.
18. Anonymous, "A program evaluation."
19. Ibid.
20. Ibid.
21. Ibid.
22. Ibid.
23. Ibid.

24. Beyondmedia Education, *Beyond Disability*.
25. Joelle Brouner, "The Empowered Fe Fe Story," *New Mobility*, November 2005, 50–54.
26. Koko E., interview with Fe Fe co-coordinator Ana Mercado, March 19, 2006.
27. Shonda P., interview with Fe Fe co-coordinator Ana Mercado, March 19, 2006.
28. Nikki S., interview with Fe Fe co-coordinator Ana Mercado, March 19, 2006.
29. Shonda P., interview with Fe Fe co-coordinator Ana Mercado, March 19, 2006.

6

Femininities as Commodities
Cam Girl Culture

AMY SHIELDS DOBSON

Introduction

The cam girl phenomenon could not have happened before this moment in history. It's the result of a combination of specific ingredients: inexpensive yet powerful technology to send and receive video images over the Net; a culture that places a higher value on fame than on the skills and talent that make people famous; teen celebrities who happily flaunt their bodies on the covers of national magazines; and the timeless rite of passage that is a teenage girl's search for identity and blossoming awareness of her own sexual power.

Frauenfelder (2002, 3)

Cam girl sites are a type of personal, amateur Web site focused on a Web cam that allows viewers to see live, moving images of the site owner. Although anyone who has a personal Web site that displays Web cam images and/or live footage of themselves could be considered a "cam girl" (or boy: there are a growing number of "cam boys"), a kind of online subculture has grown around the notion of this particular kind of Web site, the vast majority of which are owned and maintained by teenage girls and young women from approximately thirteen to twenty-five years of age. The intention of this chapter is to examine some pertinent aspects of the social and cultural climate that help us to understand the emergence of the cam girl phenomenon, as well as to examine some of the archetypes of femininity prevalent in cam girl culture.

Besides the Web cam, most cam girl sites typically have a blog and a wish list. The purposes of cam girl blogs vary wildly. They may contain anything from one-line entries about how the girl is feeling that day, simple advertisements such as informing the viewer when she will be performing a live member's show, or when she will be online to chat (often conducted via a tagboard—an instant message board—on her site), to detailed and comprehensive accounts of personal life, relationships, dreams, ambitions, and so on. The wish list is perhaps the defining feature of cam girl sites. Usually done in the form of a link to an online gift registry such as *Amazon.com* or *eBay* where fans can purchase the girl a gift and have it delivered to her home, these lists range from simple requests for online-store vouchers or money orders, to long lists with comments about each product and why she wants it.

As many cam girls themselves have noted, how much an individual cam girl receives is dependent on her looks and the type of images she displays. There are various other ways cam girls can earn money from their sites. Some sites contain their own "shop," where you can purchase cam girl-related merchandise, or even objects or products the girls have used. As Susan Hopkins tells us in a feature article on cam girls for the *Sydney Morning Herald*, pioneer cam girl Ana Voog receives $6.23 for her toothbrushes, and $45.55 for a hand-written letter (Hopkins 2002a, 4). Also, as cam girl sites grow in popularity, more girls are creating "members only" sections, which require payment to view and offer such advantages as more pictures in better quality resolutions, "raunchier images," or simply live, streaming cam footage—sexually explicit or not.[1]

The growing number of cam sites and fans has led to the opening of a growing number of cam girl portal sites, which offer lists and pictures of hundreds of cam girls whose sites you can view via a link, or, alternatively, you can pay to become a member of the portal and gain access to the archived photo and video images of each girl's site in high quality resolution, as well as access to members-only regular "live" shows by the girls (still broadcast via her personal Web cam). *Camgirldirectory.com*, or *CGD*, is the largest of these portals. At the time of writing, it contains links to over two thousand cam girls from around the world.

In the first part of this chapter, I contextualize the cam girl phenomenon by discussing first the values signified by "girl power" narratives in popular culture and culture for girls—visibility, celebrity, and consumerism. I then discuss notions of surveillance, confession, and display in popular culture, in which visibility and self-disclosure are encouraged as the path to success and empowerment. Third, I discuss the notion of girls as traditionally located in the bedroom, in order to draw attention to the tension between this new context of young female visibility and girl culture as historically private and invisible. I argue that this public exposure of girl "bedroom culture" does not necessarily signify a change in the nature of girl culture as traditionally private, personal, and domestically located, but further blurs the boundaries between public and private space and life for girls. Although the cam girl scenario may have turned teenage-girl bedroom culture into a public, productive, and commodified cultural space, the phenomenon seems to be still dependent on a reproduction and exploitation of more traditional notions of girl culture (as private and domestic) and well-established representations of young femininity.

In the second part of the chapter, I provide an analysis of three different archetypes I have observed in cam girl culture: I have categorized cam girls into

Cam *Girls*, Cam *Whores,* and Cam *Artists.* Their production of images has seen a return to "traditional" young feminine roles and identification with styles such as the "good girl"/girl-next-door (Cam Girl), the sexually insatiable/saturated "whore" (Cam Whore) and the aggressive, creative, sexual "dominatrix" (Cam Artist). I elaborate on the performance of identity within these three basic archetypes in cam girl culture with regard to: the general persona projected through text, graphics, Web cam, and still-photo images; the performative repertoires of each type; the common personal/political concerns and intentions expressed by each; representations of sexuality; and the audience relationship produced within each different scenario. Cam girl sites are an example of the way that many girls see their feminine image as a tool to be used towards the goals of economic and social success, power and self-actualization. It is not my intention here to provide commentary on this state of affairs, or analyze the effects of this situation on girls. This section examines the cam girl scenario from the perspective of analyzing the various performative methods and repertoires employed by cam girls towards these ends, as a way of making a place for themselves in the highly gendered, highly sexual, and highly commodified global, cultural landscape. I argue that the materialist feminist struggle against gender stereotypes and objectification no longer seems as relevant in this contemporary context. Instead, the concern expressed by the emergence of the cam girl scene seems to be how to make the concept of female-body-as-commodity and the dominant images of femininity, with which we are constantly bombarded, materially and socially valuable to girls themselves.

Contextualization of the Cam Girl Phenomenon

Girl Power

Perhaps one of the most culturally and generationally specific elements of cam girl culture is the desire to be seen, the invitation of constant surveillance, and willing exposure of private space. As the cam "girl" phenomenon demonstrates, this welcomed visibility is in many contexts gender specific. In her *Sydney Morning Herald* article on cam girls, Susan Hopkins writes:

> For this rising millennial generation, constant surveillance can be a dream come true—an affirmation of identity. Today, it seems you're nobody if you're not on camera. ... Cam girls make manifest the postmodern desire for omnipresence through communication technologies. If you have a life that is constantly recorded, you are culturally inscribed as someone worth watching. In today's media culture, to be "mere" image is to be empowered. (Hopkins 2002a, 4)

This leads to the question of how surveillance becomes desirable for girls, as is the case in cam girl culture. Narratives of "girl power" (a phrase made famous by the Spice Girls) have been extremely successful in popular culture and marketing over the past ten years and have had a huge effect on popular girl culture as well as feminist and academic discourses on girls and what it means to be "empowered." I will here examine the interconnected values signified in girl power narratives—namely consumerism, visibility/image circulation, and "celebrity"—in order to understand why constant surveillance is for many cam girls, as Hopkins says, a dream come true.

Anita Harris tells us that, although it was popularized by the Spice Girls, the phrase "grrrl power" was originally used in punk and indie music scenes by girls who intended a rejection of patronizing attitudes towards them. As Harris says, "the grrr stood for growling" and was meant to communicate anger (Harris 2004, 17). However, it is the Spice Girls' more upbeat and sexy interpretation of this phrase that lends itself so well to marketing and has led to a revolution in the advertising of girl culture products, and also a revolution in some strands of feminist and academic discourse. As Hopkins says, "Culture industries have accepted feminism as a fresh strategy for stimulating consumption," and slogans of girl power now abound in a wide range of consumer products (Hopkins 2002b, 23). Feminist discourses of empowerment and strong, assertive femininity are now sold to girls as consumable products, and identity transformation through consumption has been inscribed as the primary form of female power (Taft 2004, 75). The message being promoted in girl-powered icons and advertisements is that young women can and should "have it all." As girls, we should aim for the highest and not let anything stand in our way. High professional, social, and material ambition is promoted as the norm for empowered "can do" girls (Harris 2004). Many girl-culture academics and writers have analyzed recent advertisements for products aimed at girls and found that selling young femininity as weakness, submissiveness, and dominated by the search for a husband no longer works, and it is not the way youthful femininity is presented anymore (Driscoll 2002; Harris 2004; Hopkins 2002b; Levy 2005; McRobbie 2000, 2004). As Harris writes, "Empowerment and consumption are thus closely linked through associations made between products for young women and being confident, strong, assertive, a leader, a role model and in charge. Consumption is a shortcut to power" (Harris 2004, 90). In an article on the commercial viability of girl power in *Fortune Magazine*, Nina Munk observes, "If you want to sell anything to the Girl Power crowd, you have to pretend that they're running things" (1997, 134).

Surveillance, Confession, and Display

This new discourse of power for young women is a rejection of traditional patronizing attitudes to young women, but it is also a promotion of very specific types of power and values for girls. As Hopkins says, female power is tied, through girl power narratives, not only to power-through-consumption, but to "youth, beauty, speed, energy and sexuality" (Hopkins 2002b, 7), and to what Hopkins calls "celebrity power"—the power to control and constantly update one's image (Hopkins 2002b, 4). Hopkins asserts that this power over one's image has overtaken other powers in value because celebrityhood and fame allow "a visibility and a voice above all others" (Hopkins 2002b, 4) in contemporary society (not to mention the wealth required to consume endlessly). In late modernity, people become celebrities not through a particular talent or virtue, but through mere image exposure and visibility. The only skill required is the skill of image control and manipulation. According to Hopkins, in girl-powered culture, where girls are told they can and should be anything they want, and also have and buy anything they desire, fame and visibility have become "the most potent of young female fantasies" (Hopkins 2002b, 18), and have "replaced marriage as the imagined means to realizing feminine dreams" (Hopkins 2002b, 4). Visibility is demonstrated as a virtue in our culture that carries with it wealth, power, and success. Celebrities are admired because they have attained image domination. Cam girl culture demonstrates the importance of this postmodern value of constant visibility, even in the form of surveillance, for girls. In commodified, "celebrified" girl power culture, being a product in "high circulation" is the ultimate achievement. The fantasy that cam culture allows and propagates is that someone is always watching—presumably the highest compliment being that one is worthy of being constantly watched. If one's image is not in circulation, and not updated constantly, it has no value as a commodity or otherwise. For girls today surveillance, then, has become a validation of worth.

It is not only surveillance and exposure of image but of personal life, interiority, and "true, authentic" self that seems to be idealized in contemporary girl culture and the cam scene. Along with the values of girl power, the "regulation of interiority through the culture of display and confession" (Harris 2004, 125) is an important aspect of contemporary girl culture that helps to contextualize the cam girl phenomenon. A connection is made in popular culture, and reality TV in particular, between self-disclosure/exposure of one's "true" self, and success and fulfilment of one's dreams. As Harris says, "Visibility and display are both the medium and the message of young women's cultural and leisure products such as magazines, TV shows and popular music" (Harris 2004, 127). The most obvious example of this is reality television of all kinds. Reality TV is an obvious influence in Web cam culture. The message illustrated is one of confession, display, and exposure of private and "true" self, and the narrative constructed is of stardom attained "simply" through adhering to these guidelines. There are those shows that promote/facilitate success and wish-fulfillment through "discovering" talent, such as *Idol*, *Pop Stars*, and *Search for a Supermodel*; those that document the private lives of "ordinary" people, such as *Big Brother*, *Temptation Island*, and *Paradise Hotel*; and those that inflict physical and lifestyle changes in order to document the transformative process from "bad" (fat, ugly, invisible, nonconsumer) to "good" (thin, beautiful, celebratory, sophisticated consumer), such as *Queer*

Eye for the Straight Guy, Extreme Makeover, and *The Biggest Loser.* All of these varieties, as Harris writes, "indicate how ordinariness can be overcome and a celebrity life attained" (2004, 127). Harris also suggests that the process of transformation itself becomes the performance. The somehow dysfunctional person of "before" is no longer hidden, but is displayed and personally interrogated in order to reinforce the notion that they were "just like us" until the arrival of cameras into their lives. In this way, exposure of one's private self is constructed as the path to self-actualization and success.

While confession of the dysfunctional and undesirable is called for in reality TV, so too is exposure of one's "true" self, personality, and feelings. Particularly on *Big Brother* and other shows that document private life and turn the ordinary person into a celebrity worthy of our gaze, honesty and authenticity are valued above all else. In the 2006 Australian *Big Brother* series this was demonstrated in the way that the terms "playing the game" and "flying under the radar" were incorporated into the lexicon of the show. Both phrases were used to indicate that someone was not being their "real" self because they were either "playing the game" (as opposed to *pretending not* to be on a televised game) or "flying under the radar" by staying quiet and uncontroversial (as opposed to making their true feelings known in every situation). Big Brother allowed nomination of other housemates on either of these grounds if the housemates could justify how their nominee was "not being themselves." Big Brother also asked them whether they themselves were doing either of these things in a lie detector test given on the show. The housemates regularly incorporated these terms into their own conversations and judgments about each other (a model of regulatory power well documented by Foucault [1976]). On shows of this nature, the degree to which contestants can "be" and "show" their "true" selves is constantly scrutinized by both participants and audience.

In cam girl culture too, honesty, authenticity, and disclosure are of high value. Many cam girls feel the need to discuss the authenticity of their sites and state that they are as honest as possible in their presentation of self. Maximum disclosure of self and personal life are stated goals for some girls. Like the stars of reality TV who claim to be "being themselves," which they place in binary opposition to "playing the game" of which they are a part, many cam girls also claim that their focus is on "being themselves" rather than on their cam image. Further, although some girls are explicit about using their cam sites as vehicles for celebrityhood and "discovery," many girls also claim that their site is created for their own personal fulfillment, rather than for an audience. The question becomes then, why cam girls choose such highly visible, public mediums as vehicles for personal fulfillment and fun? If, as so many cam girls say, their sites are just for their own pleasure, why do they center on the projection of Web cam footage of themselves? Harris argues that "The normalization of the insertion of the public gaze into the private regulates young women by demanding a constant display of self. Young women become ever-available and ever-monitored. Ironically, this situation is held up as desirable, as the celebrity life is the exemplar of the can-do experience" (Harris 2004, 130). As both Hopkins and Harris suggest, perhaps for girls today visibility contains a pleasure in itself because of the connotations and fantasies of celebrityhood held within it.

Bedroom Culture

There is however, a tension in contemporary girl culture between the extreme visibility of girls and girl culture as traditionally private, hidden, and invisible. Girl cultures are still understood and represented as "private" (or rather, personal), interior, secret, and domestic, while girls are also, as Driscoll says, "seen as exemplary objects of 'being watched'" (Driscoll 2002, 240). Laura Mulvey too has examined the way that the female body itself in our culture connotes "to-be-looked-at-ness" (1989, 19). As discussed above, girls are now subject to an intense public gaze, both in objectification and surveillance; girls are choosing to disclose their own private lives, bodies, and selves; and in popular culture, the boundary between what has traditionally been considered public and private information is becoming ever more blurred. Cam girls provide a concise metaphor for late modern girlhood for this reason—the cam girl scenario combines the intensely public with the intensely private, further blurring these lines. Cam girls demonstrate notions of contemporary female visibility, surveillance, and "fame" while also representing young femininity as private, personal and, importantly in the historical context of girl culture studies, confined to interior spaces.

In their seminal essay *Girls and Subcultures* Angela McRobbie and Jenny Garber (2000) asked why girls were absent from the subcultural youth studies emerging from the Birmingham School in Britain in the early 1970s. They were among the first to apply the concept of female subjugation, repression, and domesticity in society and culture in general to the specific field of youth studies and examine important social and historical factors contributing to the absence of girls from street-based subcultures, as well as their general invisibility and marginalization in youth and subcultural studies. McRobbie and Garber assert that historically speaking, girls have had more domestic obligations and pressures than boys, have had to deal with issues of personal safety when it comes to being on the street, and have also had more general social pressure to remain indoors (2000, 14–16). They suggest that because of domestic and social pressures, as well as the broader marginalization of women in culture, girls' cultures have traditionally operated in the home, specifically, in the girls' bedrooms. Youth "subculture," defined primarily by the Birmingham school as being "alternative" and "resistant" to the mainstream in its styles, activities, and beliefs, and as being located primarily outside the home and on the streets, was a male-dominated phenomenon (McRobbie and Garber 2000). Publicly, as Driscoll writes, girls are "understood as marginal participants in youth as spectacle, and proper to more enclosed spaces—houses, bedrooms, and shopping centres. As central participants in activities that are not spectacular, or even invisible, girls thus do not conform to many of the defining characteristics of youth culture" (Driscoll 2002, 258).

As a recent phenomenon in girls' activities, the personal Web site and cam girl phenomenon is noteworthy because it both reinforces and broadens the parameters of a traditional "girl culture." In their essay on homepages by young girls, Jacqueline Reid-Walsh and Claudia Mitchell propose that Internet culture for girls functions as "virtual bedroom culture." They write, "Thus analogous to their physical rooms, we consider these Web sites to be semiprivate places of creativity and sociality, and sites of 'virtual bedroom culture'" (Reid-Walsh and Mitchell 2004, 174). If insular and interior spaces such as houses, bedrooms and shopping centers[2] are the central locations of girl culture, then perhaps the embrace of personal Web site technology by girls is an unsurprising progression into an even more "interior," "personal" space. Reid-Walsh and Mitchell consider the homepages of young girls as "private rooms or domains open to the public under certain conditions stipulated by the owners" (2004, 179). They note that the sites of many young girls appear as "virtual representations of their bedrooms," with patterns, colors, and images selected by the girl typical of the aesthetics associated with young girl "bedroom culture"—cartoon animals, hearts and stars, pictures of popular culture idols, and music lists or tracks playing that the girl might play in her real room (Reid-Walsh and Mitchell 2004, 180). However, they argue that, although "an onlooker receives the impression of being invited to see private aspects of a girl's life … her interests, her hopes" (2004, 180), the viewer does not necessarily receive a personal experience, and access to these private spaces is a carefully constructed illusion (2004, 181). Cam girl sites are often more intimate spaces because of the inclusion of the camera, which shows not just an aesthetic representation of a bedroom, but an actual bedroom space, and the invitation to view is often more explicit. However, as Reid-Walsh and Mitchell note, in reality, "The Web site creator remains apart and untouched by the viewer" (2004, 180), and it is the girl who controls the amount and type of communication she has with viewers. Reid-Walsh and Mitchell write, "A girl's homepage appears to be a kind of contradictory space—a *private* space that exists openly in a *public* domain" (2004, 181). The paradox expressed here remains the same in cam girl sites: their "virtual bedroom culture" is very publicly located and easily accessible.

The Internet can be a vehicle for *public display* of one's private space and private life, with the sense of security that comes from being in one's own room, in a private space. In their use of the Internet, cam girls are making their own invisible spaces and activities very visible. They are exposing private and insular cultures without necessarily changing the nature of this culture to fit a public context. I am by no means suggesting that behavior displayed on cam girl sites is "natural" and is not modified in any way, but as my examination of cam sites shows, the activities and images displayed by many cam girls are often quite personal, private, and even taboo, as opposed to subcultures that exist more in exterior, public contexts. The viewer of cam girl sites is often allowed access to the private lives, personal relationships, and solitary activities of the girl via the cam, and I would suggest that these revelations and activities would be quite different to those the girl may choose to display in a more public context, such as at school or social gatherings. Girls often use their sites like a diary, explicitly detailing friendships, crushes, sexual encounters, and explicit images of themselves: aspects of one's life that would usually be considered private. In other words, cam girls' use of the Internet does not signify a change in the traditional nature of girl culture as private, personal, close, and insular, rather it makes these previously invisible aspects of girls' cultures visible, in line with the wider social context of "confession and display."

The cam girl shows herself in the environment in which she has traditionally been placed and often doing the things she has traditionally been seen to do. McRobbie writes, "Boys are thought to occupy the public world for their leisure and subcultural activities, while girls are thought to resort to the private sanctuary of the bedroom where they read teeny bopper magazines and indulge in fantasies with their girlfriends about rock stars and Jackie pin-ups" (McRobbie 1991, 72). In the cam girl scenario, girls often show themselves doing exactly these activities, along with posing for the camera, chatting to friends online or in their bedrooms, listening to music, and putting on make-up. On one hand, the visibility of this culture serves to naturalize, or at least reinforce assumptions made about girls belonging to the domestic sphere and the consumption-based activities that dominate bedroom culture and girl culture in general. McRobbie and Garber suggest that girls' bedroom activities center around consumption of magazines, make-up, music, and pop idols (McRobbie and Garber 2000, 16) and that even within subcultures and their representation "women have always been located nearer to the point of consumerism that to the 'ritual of resistance'" (2000, 18-19). Cam girl culture then takes feminine consumerism and consumption to another level, by actively seeking to trade the feminine image for consumable products. As well as displaying traditional "girl" activities, cam girl sites contain never-ending, constantly updated wish lists of products desired by the girl. By choosing to make visible their private spaces and lives and ask for material gifts in return, the cam girl turns traditional notions of girls and girl culture as a personal, private, passive, and *consumer* culture into a valuable *commodity*. In other words, she exploits notions of girlhood and femininity for her own personal and material gain, very much in line with the values expressed in wider "girl power" culture. On the other hand then, the cam girl does disrupt traditional notions and analyses of girl culture to the extent that she makes it not only highly visible, but also proactive and *productive*. Reid-Walsh and Mitchell assert that the Internet is "a cultural space that blurs the boundaries between production and consumption" (2004, 174) because of the system of easy access to and consumption of popular culture, as well as the cheap and accessible production it facilitates. Cam girls have made a place for themselves as producers in the image market but, ironically, only through their mastery and reinforcement of rather traditional representations and notions of girl culture and young femininity.

Three Archetypal Cam Girls

In my observation of cam girl sites, their commodification of both girl "bedroom culture" and self seems to have led to a resurgence of traditional roles which have in the past been seen as oppressive stereotypes for women and girls. Like the Spice Girls, who chanted "Girl Power!" while constructing themselves as five flavors of feminine sex objects, it is the traditionally feminine nature of cam girl imagery that seems to make it popular and profitable for girls themselves. In my experience of viewing cam girl sites from a performance theory perspective, three roles or archetypes seem to emerge as dominant in the culture, re-occurring in various ways. I have named them Cam Girls, Cam Whores, and Cam Artists, to describe the persona of the "average/good" girl-next-door, the sexually insatiable/saturated girl-"whore," and the creative/alternative, often aggressive, often dominatrix-styled girl-artist. In the following section I analyze cam girl sites as a type of performance, because it is the public context, the *choice* to make visible that defines cam girls and makes them of interest as a postfeminist girl culture phenomenon. They are sites of self-expression, self-construction, and experimentation, and as many cam girls state, done for reasons of self-fulfilment and personal enjoyment, but always—we must remember—for an audience.

These "archetypes" were originally formulated by myself, and the other members of our theatre company, FireEngineBlue, Kim Swalwell and Kristy Barnes-Cullen, after each of us conducted our own dramaturgical research into cam culture. After discussing and sharing our findings, we started to formulate ideas about the re-occurring characters we observed in cam girl culture and the common features of different types of sites that lead to our categorizations. We agreed that different cam girl sites could be broadly categorized into three genres, defined and aligned by commonalities such as age group, aesthetics, stated purpose/intention, politics, and relationship with the viewer. Below I outline the three categories and discuss their defining features. U.S. academic Terri Senft completed her Ph.D. on cam girls, in which she posits that there are "at least five overlapping genres of camgirls: the life camgirl, the art camgirl, the porn camgirl, the house camgirl, and the community camgirl" (Senft 2004). At least two of these genres—the porn camgirl and the art camgirl—contain similarities to the categories of Cam Whores and Cam Artists as defined here, whereas the other three genres may be more detailed categorizations of the general category Cam Girl. Obviously with so many sites there are many unique personalities, and whereas some sites fit very neatly into the categories I have here named, others overlap and of course, many variations occur.[3]

It cannot go without saying that there are apparent links between cam girls and the pornography industry, as well as cam girls and sex trading practices. It is not my purpose here to analyze the complexities involved in these choices of feminine representation for the girls themselves, or to make judgments about whether or not their practices are "empowering." However, it is my intention to analyze these categories in terms of performance repertoires, and in doing so, to draw attention to the way that complex links to porn culture and aesthetics are often taken for granted in cam culture, and, particularly in the Cam Whore scenario, politically and socially complex repertoires of sexual performance are drawn upon by girls very easily, unproblematically and unquestioningly. It is my contention that despite this new context in which the girls themselves are seen to be in control of, and making choices about their own representation and objectification (we must, however, also be conscious of the possibility that male site owners or pornographers could be behind any of these sites), and despite the ways in which some of these sites can be seen as subversive of traditional notions of femininity, the representations that appear on cam sites are essentially reproductive of quite specific, and often heavily problematic, performative repertoires of femininity.

Cam Girls, or "the Girl Next Door": Young Teenage, 13–25

The typical Cam Girl projects a young, "nice," and "girlish" image. She defines herself through cultural icons, such as bands and music that she likes, and through her social group(s). Comparatively, her content is based more on text and graphics than Web cam images or photos. She is friendly and invites communication through chat, e-mail, and even letters. Cam Girl aesthetics are often stereotypically "girlish" and "cute"—they can be related to the aesthetics of Japanese *Kawaii* culture.[4] She uses pinks, purples, and other bright or pastel, nonprimary colors associated with young, feminine aesthetics. The aesthetics of "cute" reach an almost kitsch level in some of these sites: designs use an abundance of pink, hearts, stars, cartoons of pretty, young-looking, sexually developed "*manga*-esque" girls, and other Japanese influenced "cutesy" designs, such as those of the Hello Kitty brand. Other sites are aligned graphically with the Cam Girl's favorite band or musician: as *Camgirldirectory.com* creator "Mike" says he has seen many sites where the design is centered around bands such as Blink 182 and singers such as Britney Spears (Katcher 2002).

The Cam Girl rarely shows live images on the Web cam, nudity, or sexually provocative images. Her Web cam images are usually candid looking shots: the costume is casual "street clothes," and her poses are often at the computer desk, clicking on the mouse, posing from her desk chair, or sitting on her bed. She often states explicitly that her site has nothing to do with "porn" and contains no nudity. Some cam girls do display still-photo images that may be slightly more provocative—girls pose on their beds, sometimes in intimate ware such as pajamas or boxer shorts, conscious of "cuteness" but still with a candid, I would argue, purposefully unaffected tone. If the Cam Girl does seduce the viewer (although this is not an expressed objective), it is with her innocence, passivity, and naivety, in a typically feminine manner, through playful, innocent looking, and "pretty" poses and images. Mostly, cam girl images are comparatively unprovocative and visually uninteresting. They do, however, create a sense of intimacy: for example, a series of still images or footage in which slight variations are visible in each shot—head turning, subtle pouting and changes in gaze and facial expression are common (Figure 6.1, Figure 6.2). This creates the sense that we are watching her in her natural environment, unaware of the cam. When looking at the Web cam, she often looks as if she is gazing into a mirror, and we feel as though we are privy to this performance, as though we are simply watching her "be herself." In this way, the Cam Girl scenario tends to position the viewer as voyeur and thus exploits the notion of girl-bedroom-culture as "private."

The Cam Girl rarely even refers to her cam, her images, or her sexuality, although other intimacies, such as personal relationships with friends and family, are often disclosed at length. The primary purposes of her site seem to be self-expression through designs, blog writing, and socializing through her online network of friends. The Cam Girl's main displays are of her social network, of "fun" and social interaction—her "performance of popularity." The Cam Girl will often discuss her friendship groups, have links to her friend's Web sites, and display a blog or tag board that documents conversations between her and her friends. Danae from *Danae.co.nz* displays a calendar with highlighted dates that form icons showing friend's birthdays, holidays, and events on her social calendar. In a display of her "everyday," social life she may show pictures taken with friends, smiling and hugging, pulling silly faces, and so on (Danae 2004). For the Cam Girl it seems her cam and pictures are there "just so we can see what she looks like," although *why* she wants *us* (the unknown viewer, as opposed to the friend) to see is generally unclear. This repertoire, her display of sociality, ironically has the effect of making the "accidental"/unknown viewer even more a voyeur: her site is, though not explicit, a public display of the personal, and although the viewers may be invited, their position is an uncomfortably voyeuristic one.

Cam Girls often articulate a sense of power found in the freedom to express themselves without censorship or limitation. In her blog and other writings, the Cam Girl often expresses pride in the fact that she is in complete control of her site, as well as in the decision *not* to show nudity or sexually explicit material. Typically, the Cam Girl places a very high value on honesty and being

Figure 6.1 Randi from www.ohvanity.com (accessed September 1, 2006). With permission.

Figure 6.2 Randi from www.ohvanity.com (accessed September 1, 2006). With permission.

"true" to herself and often expresses pleasure, satisfaction, and pride in giving an "honest" and accurate portrayal of herself, rather than trying to be someone she is not, or construct an identity that is "not really her." As discussed above, many Cam Girls aim to present the "truth" of themselves, and connections are often made between confession and display of the self, and self-empowerment. As Foucault has theorized of the seventeenth-century culture of confession, confession of the "truth" is constructed as freedom, whereas silence is seen as an oppressive force (Foucault 1976, 60).

Cam Whores, or "the Whore Next Door": Older Teenage, 18–25[5]

The Cam Whore is generally friendly in her tone and manner, but usually presents little information about her self, and is comparatively one-dimensional in that most of her content and self-presentation is sexually provocative imagery. What she does reveal is fairly standard. For example, "J" from *Calichick.net* gives the viewer a fairly nondescript self-description by telling us that she likes cheeseburgers, rock music, and the color black ("J" 2004, "About Me," accessed August 4, 2004). The Cam Whore invites communication through online chats and e-mail, but usually for a fee, or only for those who have paid to be members of her site. The graphics and design are generally not features of Cam Whore sites. The layout is usually more functional than decorative—a way of displaying her images in the most enticing and eye-catching manner. The style of Cam Whore sites may be described as modernist and more sophisticated and "professional" looking than Cam Girl sites: slick, modern, "functional" designs such as straight lines, rectangular, and square borders around photos, and bars of color that fade from dark to light are commonly used. Typical palates feature cool colors, such as blue, white, black, and gray, to the glossier and kitsch "hot pink and black" looks typical of adult entertainment parlors.

Her still photos and Web cam images are often close-ups of specific body parts.[6] There is comparatively less emphasis on the face/head, but when this is the focus, the eyes are usually focused intently and seductively on the cam, often looking up at the cam from a lowered head, creating maximum depth of gaze. There are many images of the whole body, but usually the focus of the camera is the torso, the shape of the body, or what the body is doing (for example, touching herself). She will often be rolling around on the floor, stretching or undressing in a constructedly candid and unaffected manner. Even when the poses are "hardcore," such as shots of her touching her breasts or masturbating, she creates the illusion of naturalness, candidness, and intimacy through an aesthetic of flesh, flesh tones, and warm lighting. For example, Laura from *theothergirl.net* displays a series of shots in which she is lying on a bed, rolling around and touching herself. She is not looking at the cam, and often her head is out of view. As the shots progress she masturbates, and her flesh and the flesh-toned bed sheets fill the image (Laura 2004, accessed August 11, 2004). Here, the viewer is clearly positioned as "voyeur" rather than acknowledged audience member. Unlike both the Cam Girl and Cam Artist, who either openly display or construct their "natural" environments (their bedrooms are covered with posters, clothes, and other objects from their daily lives) the Cam Whore usually appears in an undecorated, minimal environment or against a more "neutral," sparse background, showing little of her personality or personal possessions—for example, on plain white sheets, against an undecorated wall, or in an empty room—creating an illusion of neutrality and clearly constructing herself as the object rather than the subject in the picture.

Through her casual jean-and-t-shirt style, her thin body type, images of flesh, candid-looking poses with natural colors and lighting, she constructs a mainstream, typically feminine character, that of the average "girl-next-door," or more accurately, the "whore next door." Like the celebrity we see in candid tabloid photographs, she gives the illusion of casualty and intimacy by donning costumes such as skimpy "exercise" clothes, jeans and (tight fitting) t-shirts, or lingerie. The Cam Whore is a strange mixture of constructed naivety and sexual self-awareness. Usually, she is explicit about the fact that her aim is to make profit from her site, but the sexual persona that emerges through her images is similar to that of the Cam *Girl*, or the Japanese *Shojo*: young, typically "pretty," submissive, innocent looking, and yet, sexually charged. She is "just your average" good-looking "girl/whore/celebrity-next-door."[7] She often sports a Brazilian wax job, signifying her "little girl-ness" and her (quasi) sexual naivety. However, at the same time she is the "super hero of sexy," in that it doesn't matter what she is doing, she is always perfectly groomed and "ready to go."[8]

Both visually and linguistically, her performance is one of servitude to the customer/viewer, willing submission, and friendliness. She does not show negativity, "attitude," or any opinions that may alienate her viewers. Instead, she displays compliance and friendliness towards her viewers. For example, J from *Calichick.net* writes in her daily blog,

> I'm back from the beach and what a day it was ... Have you ever been in the sun for the whole day like from morning to night, well I did. I was so sun burn and I had so much sand up my ass it was like another beach! Pretty funny don't you think. Well hopefully I'll be tan enough for you guys of maybe too tan? ...Catch you later guys! Love ya, J. ("J" 2004, Blog 8/2/04, accessed August 10, 2004)

Here, J displays both a sense of her own pleasure (in lying in the sun all day long), and at the same time titillates the imagination of the reader by expressing her willingness to use her body in service to the viewer (by burning herself so she will look tanned "for you guys"). The "performance" on which the entire profession of prostitution rests is a complex and contradictory one, of constant, insatiable sexual appetite as well as passive, willing "service" to the customer. Thus, the contradiction in the Cam Whore scenario is that her act is founded in performing her own pleasure as much as it is in servitude and submissiveness. She gives overt displays of pleasing herself both sexually and through her own autonomy—her "day to day" life as she shows it on cam. Her act is based on the premise that the viewer is not there, and she is behaving completely "naturally"—the viewer is to believe that all her actions are purely for her own pleasure. However, she is also explicit about the fact that she is there to "service" and to make money from the viewer. Her "performance" of autonomy and pleasure is an illusion, carefully constructed for this purpose.

The cam portal *Camwhores.com*, is worth mentioning briefly in this section on the genre of the Cam Whore in relation to the use of this loaded term and its multiple meanings within cam girl culture. The portal of this same name is one of the most "exclusive" cam portals, selecting its cam girls based on their looks, popularity, and, of course, the extent to which they are willingly to perform as "whores." However, I should clarify that this does not mean that girls must necessarily show sexually explicit images to get on this portal: many *Camwhore* members merely pose seductively fully clothed, some pose in underwear or naked, and some masturbate or perform other sexually explicit acts on cam. In the context of this site, the title "Whore" is a measure of beauty, sexiness, and popularity. This site is so popular with cam girls and has such a long waiting list that the site founder has started another portal called *Cam Whore Wannabes* (Frauenfelder 2002). As in popular culture at large, "whore" is now often a proud title rather than an insult, and even girls whose practices are far from anything that would be considered close to (virtual) prostitution refer to themselves in this way in a display of savvyness, if not always pride. The following quote from the fairly nonsexually explicit site of a fourteen-year-old girl is an example of the cultural climate I am describing. These comments were posted by viewers on cam girl "Natalie's" Web site, in response to her rather extensive wish list and documented by internet journalist Mark Frauenfelder:

> "Did I mention that you're the second ugliest girl I've ever seen?" and "You're site SUCKS ass because of your fucking brutal WISH list, you ain't even good-looking and yet you think people are just going to ship you that stuff?" Natalie isn't shy about how she feels about these tirades: "WAAAAAAAAAHHH people don't like me because I'm 14 and I don't know anything and I'm ugly and I have a huge Wish List and other people are stupid and I'm honest about wanting to whore my site!!! I'm a whore and you've hurt my feelings!" (Frauenfelder 2002)

The popularity of *Camwhores.com*, not to mention the casual use of this term in much popular music and culture, as well as by girls themselves, indicates the way in which complex dialectical notions and performative repertoires of selling one's self/body is often simplified, or at least taken for granted in cam culture.

The Cam Whore too has commodified "traditional" femininity and the private space of the girls' bedroom. She profits heavily from her image, which is one of "traditional" femininity—submissiveness, passivity, and sexual naivety; while at the same time, selling herself to us as only a seasoned professional can: the Cam Whore is analogous to Walter Benjamin's notion of the whore as a dialectical image of commodity and seller in one (Benjamin 1973, 171). This scenario draws on complex and heavily theorized relationships between viewer and viewed, object and subject, and also on complex repertoires of sexual performance and pornography long debated in feminism. However, the fact that in cam girl culture, the girl is seen to be in control of her image, and sexually explicit acts are presented clearly as the *choice* of the girl herself, means that often, these issues are bypassed somewhat simplistically and unproblematically.

Although it is not my intention to debate these issues at length here, it is important to point out in relation to the use of sexuality as power for girls that these debates over objectification and exploitation are far from being resolved simply because in cam culture, girls are seen to be participating in this system by *choice*. In fact, discourses of choice further complicate the situation because of the way this notion tends to depoliticize, personalize, and individualize these issues. Individualization of these issues is problematic because it takes the focus away from the wider social context of young female sexualization and makes these complex decisions into simplistic discourses of personal "freedom" and "choice." However, personalizing the issue also places a certain responsibility with the girls themselves to be aware of what part they play, if any, in relation to the broader Internet culture where pedophilia and underage pornography are major issues, to say the least. Many cam girls earn money by putting links to pornographic sites on their Web sites. Sixteen-year-old cam girl "Renee," interviewed by CBS News, says that porn sites will pay her between $600 and $800 per month for linking their site to hers (www.cbsnews.com 8/1/03, accessed September 28, 2004).

There is little awareness or acknowledgment of these larger issues in cam culture, when the decision to show explicit material, or link one's site to a porn site is expressed as a *personal choice*. However, I do not think it fair to place the responsibility for the effects of such choices in the hands of individual girls, given the contradictory messages girls receive about female power, sexuality, and success in our culture. Girls are encouraged now more than ever before through a variety of media and organizations to become "self-made," entrepreneurs, and businesswomen (Harris 2004, 74–75). They are told that they can become successful and powerful by means of opportunism, ingenuity, and self-promotion—through selling themselves. It is interesting to note that girls who do manage to become economically independent and successful in the expected ways are publicly celebrated and highly praised, while girls such as cam girls, who perhaps take this message a little too literally, are criticized and/or labeled "victims" of our materialistic, sexualized society.[9]

Cam Artists, or "Sexy Alternative/Goth/Punk/Raver/
Retro/Mod Chicks"—Older "Girls," 18–30+

Cam Artists often present a strong, sometimes arrogant or aggressive persona. The Cam Artist has "attitude"—in most cases quite a cynical and pessimistic one. For example, Raven from *Screaminginfidelities.org* commentates her images with captions such as "I feel like my head is going to explode," "I hate the world and want to burn it down," and "Some days, I really fucking hate my life" (Raven 2004, accessed August 4, 2004). Cam Artists' presentation is as dependent on text, design, and commentary as it is on imagery. Cam Artists generally have a high level of skill in their graphic design and layout. Their designs and unusual aesthetics are often the most visually interesting of the three genres I have classified. There is a palpable "alternative" aesthetic at work in many of these sites, defined by dark colors, skilful, unusual designs that feature strange, scary-looking figures, creatures, or patterns. Other Cam Artist sites contain abstract artworks, and interpretative cartoons, and some defy artistic classification. Images consist of a whole range of subject matter, from posed facial expressions, to mundane images of "everyday" life, to sexually provocative images like those of the Cam Whore, to images of the "hyper"-sexual and grotesque (as will be discussed further). In images of her face, the eyes are often the focus, often heavily, darkly and theatrically made up, with a seductive gaze working through the serious, deep-set expressions of the Cam Whore, but more exaggerated and sometimes in parody.

Her body is often costumed in unusual clothes derived from a range of subcultural fashion styles, such as gothic, raver, retro, and mod. The gothic-looking Cam Artist seems to be the most common, and she often includes elements of dominatrix wear into her costume. Corsets, latex, leather, and lace underwear or costumes are commonly featured in Cam Artists' images, as are the tattoos, piercings and other various forms of body decoration commonly sported by the Cam Artist. She will feature "taboo" objects such as guns, beer bottles, and drug paraphernalia as props in her images. The Cam Artist often combines photo images with graphic design by adding captions, text, or designs, or altering her pictures in other ways. Cam Artist writings are comparatively more personalized and, I would argue, deliberately confronting for the viewer. For example, while most girls provide answers to questions such as favorite food, color, star-sign, and measurements, Cam Artist Sarah from *Wondergirl.org* tells us her sexual orientation, places of body piercings, pubic hair style, and chest size, among other things (Sarah 2004, "My Biography" section, accessed August 4, 2004). Typical Cam Artist sites contain writings about her views on politics, alternative music, film, and literature. They may also contain links to alternative pornography sites and various other artistic or "alternative" cam girls' sites and other Web sites.

The Cam Artists' presentation of sexuality is distinctly different from the other two genres discussed. She is self-aware, self-reflective, and sometimes sexually "kitsch." She is admittedly sexual and proud of it. The intention for her site is comparatively more performative. She may be considered or compared to a performance artist, and many Cam Artists may see themselves in this way—as expressing themselves and their sexuality creatively through explicit material. Others simply see themselves as exercising their free will and *choice* and taking pleasure from doing so. Many Cam Artists state that they are unashamed to be seen/used as pornography and to make profit from their sites where possible. (Some of the Cam Artists discussed here are members of the *Camwhores.com* portal.) Words and images are "hyper"-sexual, that is, they are often over-the-top parodies, sometimes ironic, sometimes sarcastic, and demonstrate a high degree of self-awareness. For example, on her short self-description for the portal *Camtracks.com*, Jessica from *Jessiekitty. com* writes that her interests are: "Music, Cock, Intoxication," while she states her dislikes to be "the on/off lists of the average cam pig" (*Camtracks.com*, accessed September 8, 2004). Like the dominatrix, the vamp, or the femme fatale, she seduces through her display of power, control, and the sense of threat she often tries to create. It is not traditional stereotypes of femininity that we see in Cam Artist sites, but more contemporary notions of girls made popular through the "girl power" trend, of girls as highly sexual subjects, rather than objects, creative, assertive, and unashamed to demonstrate and use both their sexuality and aggression as tools.

The Cam Artist's sexually provocative shots contain a high level of theatricality. The Cam Artist *constructs* her poses explicitly, to be visually interesting, expressive, and "artful" through costume, make-up, and lighting. The illusory aspect of her performance is often made visible, and the viewer is an acknowledged audience member rather than a voyeur. In her nude shots she often looks directly into the cam and keeps her face/eyes a strong focus of the shot. Her imagery may be more "taboo" or fetishized, such as Ana Voog's close up of her vagina with a racing car in it (Voog 2004, accessed August 11, 2004). Alternatively, she may parody typical feminine sexiness, as Jessica from *Jessiekitty.com* does in Figure 6.3, with her pigtails, her innocent, wide-eyed stare, and the caption, "My bruises are sexy, right?"

Cam Artists: "Individualism" and the Death of Ideology   Like the Cam Girl, the Cam Artist prides herself on being "true" to herself, on expressing her "real" self without censorship (self-imposed or otherwise) or compromise.

Her images display power and pleasure most obviously through eye contact, and a certain kind of eye contact: her gaze is often direct, unsmiling, and

Figure 6.3 Jessica from Jessiekitty.com, July 31, 2004 (accessed August 11, 2004). With permission.

either deliberately and obviously posed as flirtatious and inviting or deliberately threatening and uninviting. Figure 6.4, which shows Jessica from *Jessiekitty.com* (accessed November 27, 2004) exemplifies an image of hostility towards the viewer.

Cam Artists often indicate a power, pleasure, and freedom in displays and repertoires of grossness and vulgarity. In a section entitled "Me = Attention Whore" Kitty (2003) from *Sinnocence.com* writes:

> I may put a cam up my cunt and show everyone my cervix.
> I may doodle on my face with a magic marker.
> I may get naked and write domain names
>   on my tits and ass cheeks.
> I may take a big dump and take a video of it and post it here.
> I may never update again or I may update every day.
> Who cares? You shouldn't.
> I am a seasoned attention whore…and I'll do
>   whatever I god damned feel like.

Kitty has also displayed an image of herself, bent over with the camera focused on her butt (accessed August 4, 2004), which is not traditionally sexy (read, skinny) but rather, lumpy looking. The "wad" of flesh (her vagina) that comes through between her legs is quite pronounced in this shot, and I would argue that this position and view is more vulgar or crass than "sexy" in any traditional sense.

Figure 6.4 Jessica from Jessiekitty.com, November 12, 2004 (accessed October 27, 2004). With permission.

But sexy or vulgar, traditionally feminine or subversive, it does not matter to Kitty. For, in "Me = Attention Whore," Kitty justifies her right to behave in whatever way she feels the whim, without necessary alignment to any principles, even her own self-stated ones. She admits that she is very hypocritical. Thus, she says that her site is for her and no one else, but also admits to being an "attention whore." She also admits to getting pleasure from "pissing people off." Further, she calls cam girls "vapid retarded bimbos." But her final claim, "I'll do whatever I god damned feel like," ensures her right to still bitch hypocritically about "vapid retarded cam girl bimbos" *if she feels like it*, and to still act like one *if she feels like it*. Any objection to her opinions or behavior is preempted with self-criticism and irony. This is DIY philosophy taken to its logical extreme. It is also reminiscent of the mentality of self-aware, "ironically" sexist advertising that currently dominates visual culture, as Angela McRobbie has noted (McRobbie 2004). It is not hard to imagine the last lines of Kitty's statement in an advertisement for Bratz Dolls or tampons, nor a t-shirt with the "Attention Whore" slogan printed across the chest.

Similarly, Jessica from *Jessiekitty.com* has shown images of herself pulling her butt cheeks taut, close-up to the cam so that her ass-hole is clearly in view, and posted images of herself with a shotgun in her mouth (accessed November 27, 2004). As she writes in her biography section: "This isn't a porn site. This is a fucking Jessie site. Im not interested in selling a better version of myself. If you can be into me in all my natural brutality, then … shit is exactly as it should be" (Jessica 2004, "Biography," accessed August 11, 2004.) Jessica claims that her performance is not for the viewer's pleasure, but for her own. However, the explicitly performative acts of displaying closeups of her vagina and anus, as well as images in which she plays with guns seductively and threateningly, leads us to conclude that her pleasure comes from performance for and titillation of an audience. At least to some degree, her pleasure is found in her own objectification. Both of these girls may provide the audience with something different from the traditional feminine sexiness/submissiveness reproduced by the Cam Whore and Cam Girl, but their images do draw on other well-established stereotypes and repertoires of femininity, such as that of the "bad girl," feminine "cattiness," as both of their names imply, and the implicit danger/evilness of the temptress/"femme fatale." They are very much in line with the current girl power culture in which powerful girls are increasing constructed as highly sexual, aggressive, "mean," and unashamedly ambitious and materialistic. However, perhaps unsurprisingly, in their tone they also depict a certain sense of self-hatred.

Kathy Bail argues that, whereas first- and second-generation feminists made an effort to present a united front despite their differences, now the emphasis is on "individual practice ... rather than group identification," and further, that this diversification and individualization of feminism have made it stronger (Bail 1996, 16). The above quotes/images from Kitty and Jessica, as well as the discourses of "personal choice" discussed in relation to Cam Whores, are evidence that the "cult of the individual" has taken a stronghold in contemporary society. But, without denying that diversity and individual pragmatism can be constructive elements in any political or cultural movement, my observation of cam girl culture and contemporary girl culture in general leads me to question whether "individualization" is just an excuse for behaving how we want, when we want, with no pressure to align ourselves to, or stick with any set of views or ideals, with no sense of any effort towards a consistent ideology, no sense of "sisterly" or even "humanly" solidarity, and very little emphasis on personal responsibility. In this sense, "Individualism" is not really about being an individual at all but, rather, a synonym for the values of mainstream consumer culture. The only consistent value I can see in current "girl-powered" culture and cam girl culture alike is the value placed on image. Therefore, the only alignment all girls have (perhaps by default) is to consumerism.

Conclusions

In this chapter I have discussed some of the current cultural conditions that help us to contextualize and understand the emergence of the cam scene, as well as some of the archetypes of femininity found in cam girl images. I have analyzed the values and powers signified in popular culture girl power narratives as those of visibility, celebrity, and consumerism;

I have discussed the ways in which surveillance, confession, and display are increasingly elevated in our culture and associated with freedom and empowerment; and I have examined the tensions and contradictions this leads to in girls' culture, which is traditionally positioned as private, invisible, and domestically located. Rather than representing an actual change in the nature of traditional girl culture, I have argued that the cam girl phenomenon makes visible traditionally invisible feminine cultures and spaces, and also actively commodifies both the girl and the private, bedroom space. I want to conclude here that in this commodification of girl's images and spaces there is both a naturalization of the female as domestically located, and a naturalization of the female-as-visual-object. Cam girls have appropriated the technology and the marketing methods of the patriarchal, capitalist system to feed their own desires. As my analysis of cam girl archetypes shows, their ability to make this system work for them seems to be dependent on a mastery and reproduction of traditional, often stereotypical, notions and images of femininity, as well as a simplification of complex repertoires of feminine representation.

I would like to finish by making a final suggestion about the cam girl generation's attitude towards image culture and objectification. Even within new and seemingly subversive representations of young femininity as powerful, assertive, "mean," and highly sexualized, there is complicity and alignment with the dominant consumerist ideology, as Angela McRobbie has noted:

> There is quietude and complicity in the manners of generationally specific notions of cool, and more precisely an uncritical relation to dominant commercially produced sexual representations which actively invoke hostility to assumed feminist positions from the past in order to endorse a new regime of sexual meanings based on female consent, equality, participation, and pleasure, free of politics. (McRobbie 2004, 9)

The major controversy and debate around the cam girl phenomenon has centered on this notion of girl's consent, participation, and pleasure in objectification. However, lamentably or not, this is for many girls a debate that is irrelevant and dead. Perhaps female objectification has become so ingrained in our culture that it is taken for granted by the next generation. When seen in this way, objectification becomes not a question of morals or ethics, or what is good or bad for girls, but simply a fact of our culture. Thus, the debate for girls today is perhaps not so much about a choice as to *whether or not* to participate in the image economy, but about how one will best survive and thrive in it.

Perhaps exploitation (of cultures, others, and self), self-commodification and "DIY objectification" for girls today is, consciously or not, celebratedly or not, about doing it to yourself before it's done to you. Much thanks to Anita Harris for her comprehensive editing and thoughtful suggestions!

Notes

1. For the purposes of this chapter, I have looked only at images available freely on cam sites and portals.
2. See Ganetz 1995 for a detailed discussion of female consumption and use of department stores.
3. As stated above, most of the research and analysis of cam girl sites used in this chapter was conducted during 2003 and 2004. Due to the transient nature of cam culture, many of the sites discussed here no longer exist, and many new cam girl sites have since appeared. The archetypes visible in cam culture now may have changed significantly since this research was done. It seems that "cam" culture has also become broader and more widespread on the Internet: with the advent and popularity of large host sites such as *My Space* and *You Tube*, there are more people in general displaying footage and images of themselves online.
4. As Katherine Mezur explains, *Kawaii* (cute) is a developed aesthetic and culture in Japan. According to Mezur, "*Kawaii* can mean variously cute, pretty, cutesy, or sweet. For example, "hello kitty" motif objects are *kawaii* with their pink little kitty icon. Things that are decorated, with delicate, frilly, lacy material or designs are *kawaii*. ... Pink dominates cute culture. ... Much of pop "girl" iconography suggests a power to seduce and transform. This cute girl image is the image that *manga* and *anime* exploit over and over again. She is a bouncing little girl, without any past. ... The anime girl is full busted, long legged, and ready for sensual or violent adventures. She is viscerally cute with huge eyes, pug nose, and tiny chin." (Mezur 2004, 77)
5. In the United States anyone who displays images depicting nudity or sexually explicit conduct (online and in other forms of representation) must be over eighteen years old, and display their name and date of birth with the material, in accordance with Section 2257 of Title 18, Part 1, Chapter 11 of the United States Code (U.S.C.). So, although many of these girls look younger than eighteen, specified ages on these types of sites will always appear as eighteen or older.
6. In Margaret Lazarus' documentary *Still Killing Us Softly*, Jean Kilbourne describes how images of women have been dismembered and split into body parts through the mass media and advertising. This is an effective way to turn a person into an object, but more so, Kilbourne argues that this kind of dehumanization and distancing is the first step towards justifying violence and brutality against individuals (Kilbourne, 1987).
7. The more recent phenomenon of turning the girl/boy-next-door into the celebrity-next-door through filming their lives in the myriad of reality TV shows brings the ideals of "celebrity" ("perfect" beauty, *constant* beauty, attention to all bodily areas such as face, hair, nails and now also pubic hair, value on exclusive and expensive brand names even/especially for "nonfashion" items such as exercise clothes, underwear, sunglasses, and keeping up with the latest fashion trends) and the quest for "celebrity-ness," as both an adjective and a product, into mainstream, suburban consciousness. As Harris writes in *Future Girl*: "TV surveillance and reality shows such as *Big Brother* and its spinoffs, for example *The Bachelor*, *Temptation Island*, and *The Villa*, open up the private sexual world for public scrutiny, and in the process this kind of programming constructs the ordinary person as a celebrity of sorts. These kinds

of shows suggest both that we can all potentially be the stars of TV programs, and that voyeurism is natural, harmless, and acceptable" (Harris 2004, 128). Not only does this programming construct the ordinary person as a celebrity, but to some degree, the ordinary girl as a whore. Cam Whores are very much linked to this cultural phenomenon; however, their combination of "everyday-ness" and "natural" sexiness, youth, and innocence feed another myth: she is not just the "girl next door" but the "whore next door"—beautiful and sexy as a celebrity, sexually charged and waiting for you just behind every suburban picket fence.

8. The cultural myth of the "sexy girl-next-door" seems to have been heavily propagated of late: along with the cultural phenomenon of soap operas such as *Neighbours* and *Home and Away* goes the idea that every girl-next-door looks like a soap star and can be reasonably "pretty" in the mainstream, plain-yet-attractive way. Also, the recent obsession with "average looking" celebrities propagated through magazine features on "stars without make-up" and the like perpetuates the idea that "anyone" can look like a celebrity with the right tools and beauty technologies, and further, that women *should* make the effort to look like a celebrity whenever they are in public, fostering other typologies such as "suburban celebrities," "yummy mummies," etc.

9. See Harris, 2004 on "The Girl Entrepreneur" for a discussion of girl power dis-courses and the recent increase in entrepreneurial organizations and competi-tions for girls.

References

Bail, K., ed. 1996. *DIY feminism*. St. Leonards, NSW: Allen & Unwin.

Benjamin, W. 1973. *Charles Baudelaire: A lyric poet in the era of high capitalism*. Transl. Harry Zohn. London: New Left Books. Quoted in Schneider, R. 1997. *The explicit body in performance*. New York: Routledge.

Christina. 2004. www.immortalized.net (accessed September 6, 2004).

Danae. 2004. www.danae.co.nz (accessed August 11, 2004).

Driscoll, C. 2002. *Girls*. New York: Columbia University Press.

Foucault, M. 1976. *The history of sexuality*. London: Penguin.

Frauenfelder, M. 2002: Cam girls. *Yahoo Internet Life*, June 2002. www.boingboing,net/camgirls.html (accessed March 25, 2003).

Ganetz, H. 1995. The shop, the home, and femininity as masquerade. In *Youth culture in late modernity*, ed. J. Fornas and B. Goran, 72–99. London: Sage.

Harris, A. 2004. *Future girl*. New York: Routledge.

Hopkins, S. 2002a. Come watch me. *Sydney Morning Herald Weekend Edition*, August 10-11, 2002, Spectrum, 4–5.

Hopkins, S. 2002b. *Girl heroes: The new force in popular culture*. Annandale, NSW: Pluto Press Australia.

"J". 2004. www.calichick.net (accessed August 4, 10, 2004).

Jessica. 2004. www.jessiekitty.com (accessed August 11, October 27, 2004).

Katcher, P. 2002. *The interview*, May 12, 2002. www.paulkatcher.com/fulldisclosure/

Kilbourne, J. 1987. *Still killing us softly*. Videorecording. Produced and directed by Margaret Lazarus. Cambridge, MA: Cambridge Documentary Films.

Kitty. 2003. www.sinnocence.com (accessed November 19, 2003).

Laura. 2004. www.theothergirl.net (accessed August 11, 2004).

Levy, A. 2005. *Female chauvinist pigs: Women and the rise of raunch culture*. Melbourne: Schwartz Publishing.

McRobbie, A., ed. 1991. *Feminism and youth culture: From Jackie to Just Seventeen*. London: Macmillan.

McRobbie, A. 2000. Sweet smell of success? New ways of being young women. In *Feminism and youth culture*, ed. A. McRobbie, 198–215. London: Macmillan.

McRobbie, A. 2004. Notes on Postfeminism and popular culture: Bridget Jones and the new gender regime. In *All about the girl: Culture, power, and identity*, ed. A. Harris, 3–14. New York: Routledge.

McRobbie, A. and J. Garber. 2000. Girls and subcultures. In *Feminism and youth culture*, ed. A. McRobbie, 2–25. London: Macmillan.

Mezur, K. 2004. Cute mutant girls: Sweetness and deformity in contemporary performance by young Japanese women. In *Alternatives: Debating theatre culture in the age of Con-Fusion*, ed. P. Eckersall, U. Tadashi, and M. Naoto, 73–87. Brussels: P.I.E.-Peter Lang.

Mulvey, L. 1989. *Visual and other pleasures*. London: Macmillan.

Munk, N. 1997. Girl power. *Fortune*, December 8. Quoted in Hopkins, S. 2002b. *Girl heroes: The new force in popular culture*. Annandale, NSW: Pluto Press Australia.

Raven. 2004. www.screaminginfidelities.org (accessed August 4, 2004).

Reid-Walsh, J. and C. Mitchell. 2004. In *All about the girl: Culture, power, and identity*, ed. A. Harris, 173–184. New York: Routledge.

Sarah. 2004. www.wondergirlmedia.com (accessed August 4, 2004).

Schneider, R. 1997. *The explicit body in performance*. New York: Routledge.

Senft, T. 2004. www.terrisenft.net (accessed September 26, 2006).

Taft, J. 2004. Girl power politics: Pop culture barriers and organizational resistance. In *All about the girl: Culture, power, and identity*, ed. A. Harris, 69–78. New York: Routledge.

Voog, A. 2004. www.anacam.com (accessed August 11, 2004).

www.camgirldirectory.shtml (accessed October 9, 2003).

www.camtracks.com (accessed September 8, 2004).

www.cbsnews.com 2003. *Kids for sale: Look, but don't touch*. January 8, 2003. http://www.cbsnews.com/stories/2003/01/06/48hours/main535423.shtlm?CMP=ILC SearchStories (accessed September 28, 2004).

7

Reflections
For Those Who Reflect

FEDA ABDO, RAYANN BEKDACHE, SAMAH HADID,
MEHAL KRAYEM, AND TARA PENGILLY

Headscarf-wearing Muslim women are the great unpeople of our day:
spoken about as though they are not in the room

Aly (2006a)

Reflections is a quarterly magazine that was born out of the frustrations young
Australian Muslim women had with the mainstream media, the comments
made by conservative, right-wing politicians, and the negative portrayal of
Islam and Muslims, particularly after the events of September 11 and the Bali
bombings. *Reflections* seeks to give a voice to "the great unpeople of our day"
(Aly 2006a), the Muslim women. Launched in September 2003, *Reflections*
is a vibrant magazine aimed toward youth of all backgrounds. By exploring
the importance of culture and identity for today's youth, it aims to educate
both Muslims and non-Muslims about the beliefs, practices, and misconceptions of the Islamic faith. *Reflections* is a publication (both online and print)
produced by a dynamic group of young Australian Muslim women from the
Sydney metropolitan area. It is produced under the guidance and support of
the United Muslim Women's Association Inc. (MWA).

The MWA is a peak community-based organization specializing in the
delivery of services to Muslim women and their families in New South Wales.
Established in 1983, the MWA provides support services in accordance with
the needs of Muslim women. The vision of the MWA is to provide Australian
Muslim women with the opportunities to actively participate in and contribute to Australia's culturally and religiously diverse society. In achieving this
objective the MWA has played a key role in identifying and developing strategies that aim at removing barriers preventing Muslim women from accessing
and participating in services that are generally accessible to all members of the
public. Strategies used in addressing such barriers have included direct support service provision, community education, advocacy and representation,
policy development and planning, religious awareness, community relations
initiatives, as well as a large focus on equipping young Australian Muslim

women with the skills to actively participate in society and have a voice. This is what led to the development and creation of *Reflections*. We were a group of young Muslim women given the chance to develop our leadership skills and encouraged by certain mentors who were long-time members of the MWA to become more involved in our community and increase the connection of young people with their community, while at the same time providing a platform for the often unnoticed voice of Muslim women. Under the guidance of mentors within the MWA *Reflections* was born and has continued to be nurtured with these aims in mind.

Stereotypes, misconceptions, and generalizations about all groups of people permeate almost every aspect of society. We will always have to contend with ignorant bigots, racists, and closed-minded people. Yet it is important to realize that we must do what we can in order to combat these views, and it is in this way that *Reflections* provides an unequivocal response to these views. We are a group of young Australian Muslim women who sought to take a proactive stance through the literary means of a magazine that seeks to debunk myths and untruths about Islam and Australian Muslims. *Reflections* magazine is a platform by which young Australian Muslim women express their identities and politics. It is also a cultural space in which connection, community, and identity are explored. The fact that there is very little space available in the media for young women to engage with on more than a superficial level is another purpose upon which *Reflections* magazine was launched. Rather than taking a fence-sitter's position in our political and social context, as a group of young Australian Muslim women we sought to take a proactive stance through the literary means of a magazine.

The title *Reflections* exemplifies the aims and objectives of the magazine, a publication aimed at spurring young people to reflect about events and issues around them. The logo is a jewel from which many colors are illuminated and ties in with the *Reflections* motto: "The lamps are different but the Light is the same: it comes from Beyond." This is a quote from the Persian poet Jalaluddin Rumi (d.1273) whose poetry and literature are widely read by Muslims and non-Muslims alike. Combined, the *Reflections* logo and motto serve to reiterate the message that at the crux of humanity, "lying dormant in the deepest roots of most, if not all, cultures there is an essential similarity" (Havel 1995). The notion that we all hold the same, if not similar, aspirations of love, humility, and peace is also central to the purpose of *Reflections*. Through the magazine, we have focused on communicating this message to the wider Australian community, focusing mainly on youth, so that there is an opportunity for change in the future, by all people.

Background to Reflections

Historically the veiled Muslim woman has been seen by the West as a silent, downtrodden, submissive, and helpless figure; she has rarely been seen as a person with intellectual thoughts, ideas, or actions. Her voice is rarely heard, as she is viewed as someone who has no valuable contribution to make and therefore nothing she says is worth listening to. *Reflections* is an attempt by Australian Muslim women to deal with the concept of "Orientalism" in our modern era and its implications for Muslim women. The magazine seeks to dispel the notions of "the Other," described as "the ways dominant groups characterize subordinate groups as problematically different" (Poynting et al. 2004). The "Other" is often seen as a foreign, threatening entity that embodies all of the things we deem as uncivilized, deviant, and in opposition to mainstream society. The concept of the Other was originally developed by Edward Said (1978), a Palestinian academic who was writing in the late 1970s, and yet the idea is just as relevant today as it was back then. The concept of Othering is based on the idea that there is a created division between populations where people begin to view a particular minority group as being the Other, in that these people are suddenly seen as something immoral and alien. This helps pin many evil phenomena on this group, with little question from the wider majority. In this day and age with the growing threat of terrorism and the moral panic that has spread, particularly throughout Australia, regarding those from the geopolitically created "Middle East," Said's idea becomes all the more obvious. The Other is different, something we cannot relate to and cannot understand; it is they who are responsible for the unexplained evil that exists in today's society. The threat of evil today seems to be looming over us like never before and with the ever growing threat of terrorism conjured up by politicians and the mass media; we feel we need to feel safe, as if the authorities are doing something about this. This adds to the need for the creation of the Other. In a time of crisis, such as terrorist attacks, we need to be able to blame it on a group of people, not an individual because of the severity and greatness of the problem. *Reflections* presents an alternative, more human aspect to this Other figure. *Reflections* is exemplary of the ways in which young women are engaging in positive cultures of change.

Thus, this much needed voice of Muslim women has manifested itself in the production of *Reflections* magazine. This is a publication that subverts the numerous labels and stereotypes that have become synonymous with Muslim women and youth. These labels include the submissive, oppressed Muslim woman who has no rights of her own and has her life dictated to her by her father, brother, or husband. These are stereotypes that really could not be further from the truth, especially for the young Muslim women of Australia, and this helps to drive the passion we have to ensure that we counteract this image. And so the existence of such a public form of expression by Muslim women immediately dispels the myth that Islam denies women the right to freedom of opinion and speech, as that is exactly what *Reflections* is. How can Islam oppress women when they are free to publish a magazine such as *Reflections*? This is just one example that argues against the stereotype that

Islam oppresses women, and through the magazine we also attempt to present articles and stories that demonstrate that if anything, Islam serves as a liberation for women. Articles such as those that discuss the prominent women of Islamic history and the crucial roles they played in their time demonstrate that Islam has always provided a platform and voice for women to be heard.

Muslim women are often the subject of mainstream discourse and more often than not, they are not given the opportunity to offer social commentary on issues that directly affect them. *Reflections* is an outlet that gives young Muslim women the necessary chance to explore relevant issues that affect them. *Reflections* magazine also serves as an alternative media outlet aimed at educating mainstream Australian society about Islam. And by discussing issues relevant to young people no matter what race or religion they are, it also assists Australian youth in the development of their identities. At the same time *Reflections* provides an insight into the lives of Australian Muslim youth. Through educating people about young Muslims this also serves the purpose of familiarizing others with what Islam is all about and conveying to them that it is not as foreign as some may think. Since its inception *Reflections* has also served as a response to the mainstream media representation of Muslims through tabloid papers such as News Corporation's *The Daily Telegraph* and commercial news programs like Channel 7's *Today Tonight* and Channel 9's *A Current Affair*, which, although they have produced some positive stories on Muslims here and there, are generally known for their distorted and stereotypical portrayal of young Muslims as hooligans who go out looking for trouble, as well as the image of the oppressed and submissive Muslim woman. This dissatisfaction with mainstream media reportage and the saturation of negative images branded in the national consciousness as a result of it fostered the need for a balance of information.

The production of an alternative media outlet like a magazine would provide this balance, help diversify, and correct the information about Islam and Muslim women within the public domain. Furthermore, as Australian Muslim women, we wanted to relinquish the "victim" mentality associated with us and gain a stronghold of the discourse and information produced in relation to what it truly means to be a Muslim, a woman, and a youth in our social, political, and cultural context. The literary form of a magazine seemed to be the most effective and accessible avenue in raising awareness in the public sphere in a creative and informative way. It also allowed young Australian Muslim women to use the media as a positive tool for generating informed knowledge. Other projects that we considered were activities such as holding a youth forum to discuss the issues of identity and other issues concerning youth, as well as writing a script for a play that discussed the issues that were relevant to us. And although these ideas were possible for us and had their own advantages we felt that a quarterly magazine would first of all provide a consistent voice for young Muslim women in the media and second that we could always do other projects in the future, which is what we did when we held a youth forum on identity in September 2003 to coincide with the launch of the magazine.

What began as an ambitious vision soon transformed into a magazine and subsequently an Internet Web site. The Web site increases the widespread publicity, availability, and readership of *Reflections*, rendering it even more accessible and appealing to a wider audience. We chose the medium of a Web site because of its viability and appeal to the technologically driven youth of today. The Internet ensures even more of a readership, as it surpasses the limits of the print magazine and has reached international spheres, with comments received from people all around the world, such as a young Muslim woman from Canada who remarked that she felt empowered and inspired by the fact that there were young Muslim women on the other side of the world providing a platform for our voices to be heard. Also, many people turn to the Internet today for research and information as well as leisure, so it was important to ensure that *Reflections* had a presence on the Web. With the support and guidance of one of the main Muslim women's organizations in Australia, the United Muslim Women's Association (MWA), a selected group of young Australian Muslim women were empowered socially and politically in harnessing this ongoing and fulfilling project.

Reflections also arose out of a New South Wales government initiative titled *Shifa*, funded by the Premiers Department and aimed at equipping Australian Muslim and Arab youth with the leadership skills to develop and maintain a community project. MWA selected a group of twenty young Muslim women who had been involved with the activities of the MWA and had shown leadership potential and a commitment to making a difference in their community to participate in the *Shifa* Leadership Camp, which was developed by the Centre for Cultural Research at the University of Western Sydney in partnership with the Premiers Department of New South Wales. The camp, which was specifically tailored to the needs of Muslim women, was held in January 2003 and was intended to give young people the chance to develop their leadership skills so that they could become more involved in their communities and neighborhoods. At the end of this camp we had to come up with a community project that would allow us to make a contribution to our community, and this is when we brainstormed a number of ideas and finally settled on the idea of the magazine. And then it was up to the dedicated workers at MWA to select from those who had attended the camp and showed potential and commitment to contribute to a magazine and mentor and guide us to developing what we now know as *Reflections*. So from January 2003 it took us nine months to put together a team and positions within the editorial team according to our individual skills and experiences and finally publish the launch edition in September 2003. In this time we came up with a theme for the edition, researched, and wrote articles, as well as sought sponsorship from various local businesses and funding from various government and nongovernment organizations that had grants available.

Reflections was a proactive response to pivotal events like September 11, which reinforced the need for the existence of such a publication. Bridging the widening gap between the Muslim and non-Muslim communities and breaking down the "us versus them" binary that exists within mainstream society was another chief objective of the magazine. Another quite significant aim for the project was that it would portray Australian Muslims as belonging and intricately woven into the tapestry of Australian society, not as an outside group. By selecting young people in the twelve to twenty-five age group as its target audience the magazine aspired to foster a sense of understanding within Australian society on a grassroots level and to pave a path of tolerance and harmony to be maintained for the future. Projecting the voice of young Muslim women would appeal to and create a connection between youth of many backgrounds. The name *Reflections* was born out of the idea of reflecting on and thinking critically about issues that have arisen from our social and political context but also evaluating one's own individual actions and position within society. The logo of *Reflections* is a jewel that accompanies the message of the magazine. The jewel is a representation of our multicultural and globalized society, as the diverse facets of the jewel symbolize the unique qualities of the human race. The array of colors that radiate from it show that individually we shine in our own distinct way and that we each have something to offer to society but when we all work together we can shine even brighter and make more of a difference. Figuratively, the differences within us come together to form a rare and precious jewel. The jewel is a unifying trademark, as is the motto of the magazine, which is a quote from Persian poet Jalaluddin Rumi (d. 1273): *The lamps are different but the Light is the same: it comes from Beyond.* This phrase was selected as it encapsulates the message of the magazine that although humankind seems to be riddled with contradicting facets, at the most basic level, we share a "light" that surpasses these superficial differences. The overriding theme of unification coincides with the magazine's vision of promoting harmony and making a positive difference within the world, for as Schuster (2006) says, "When we have the courage to speak out—to break our silence—we inspire the rest of the 'moderates' in our communities to speak up and voice their views."

Issues Addressed by *Reflections*

Reflections' readership was initially intended to be youth, for an outlet specifically for the youth to voice their opinions was something of a rarity, especially among young Australian Muslim women. However, the relevance and topical nature of the content featured in the magazine sparked an interest from a wide variety of ages, broadening not only the audience but the content as well. The widespread distribution of *Reflections* generated a range of responses that diversified the issues and subject matter discussed through the magazine. The magazines are distributed widely, from public libraries to universities and even schools; they are also handed out and available at conferences, forums, and initiatives that the writers attend. Along with subscriptions, *Reflections* has been distributed to wider communities throughout New South Wales and even globally with the help of the Web site.

The universality of the issues addressed by *Reflections* is essential in allowing the content of the publication to resonate deeply within all types of readers, young and old. Feedback received from both local and global communities reinforced the purpose and appeal of the issues raised by *Reflections*. The context of the post-September 11 era rendered the issues and perspectives the magazine highlights even more appealing to non-Muslim audiences, thus contributing to the growing interest in the magazine.

The positive publicity and exposure *Reflections* and the dynamic group behind it have received from media outlets like *ABC's Triple J* radio station and *SBS World News Television* in Sydney helped foster interest in the magazine. The magazine launch, incidentally held on the eve of September 11, 2003 received much media attention particularly from local media outlets. The coverage and feedback *Reflections* has received from an array of persons of many ages and backgrounds illustrates how the magazine speaks to non-Muslim, Muslim, young, old, male, female individuals, and groups. The launch itself initiated interest in Muslims and non-Muslims alike from across Australia.

Following *Reflections'* launch, the letters to the editor section was flooded with letters of support, for example, Brian from Canberra wrote: "I think it's great that you're taking a positive and proactive stance against mindless discrimination and I'm particularly glad to see that it's young people making that stand." (2003/04, 6)

Indeed, older Australians, usually assumed to have conservative outlooks, were intrigued by the magazine. One fifty-eight-year-old, third-generation Australian of Irish/Celtic background replied: "There are many like me who do not like the racist mood perpetrated by some in the community, on both sides and hope you achieve your goals." (2003/04, 6)

Despite a small number of criticisms related to articles, an overwhelming number of responses received were supportive. Although the magazine explores issues at the forefront of the "War on terror," the content is not exclusive to this controversial topic. The articles cover a wide scope of topics that captivate young Muslim women but have universal interest as well.

The desire to highlight the fundamental similarities that run throughout the human race was of great significance to us as young Muslim women and serves as the baseline for *Reflections* (Figure 7.1).

Thus, in the interest of unifying local and global communities, we tend to focus our content on fundamental principles of equality, tolerance, and understanding of different races, religions, and concepts. Moreover, *Reflec-*

Figure 7.1 Selected editions of *Reflections* magazines from 2003–2005 dealing with issues such as unity, education, the mind, the body and soul as well as the position of human rights in Islam.

tions allows Muslim women to vocalize their various interests, concerns, and perspectives, ranging from humanitarian concerns to the arts, science, religion, and politics. Articles tackle a number of issues; the spring 2005 issue of *Reflections*, which discussed human rights, featured articles from a range of human rights concerns and issues, for example, articles on the casualty crisis in Chechnya and Guantanamo Bay dealt with human rights violations; on a local scale, Australia's immigration policy of mandatory detention was also addressed in the edition. Articles like "Education/Exploitation System" (Mawas 2004b, 7) and "The Confused Conflict" (Mawas 2003/2004, 27) critically address debates around the education system in Australia and the Palestinian–Israeli conflict; these type of articles raise awareness of contentious issues surrounding national and international debates. Religion is explored regularly throughout various editions; we discuss the Islamic perspective as part of the featured theme of most editions, along with comparative perspectives from the other Abrahamic faiths.

Reflections accommodates the broad interests and facets of life that Muslim women participate in and reflect upon. As the makeup of the editorial team of the magazine is quite diverse, with Muslim women who study, work, and participate in volunteer work, the themes and topics represent the diverse, unique range of insights and experiences of these Muslim women. *Reflections* brings to the forefront issues of identity as experienced by Australian Muslims and the complexity that such a concept holds in their lives. The launch edition, released September 2003, was focused around the issue of identity; one such example was the feature on the *hijab*, "The Hijab: Misconceived, Mistaken, Misunderstood" (Krayem 2003, 12). This article addressed the concept of the *hijab* and what it meant to Muslim women. It explored how "the hijab helps Muslim women to make a statement about their identity, feel dignified, modest and confident" (Elghoul and Youssef 2003, 14).

Reflections sheds light on the fact that Muslim women are complex individuals and leaders in their own right, dispelling the stereotypical impressions and perceptions of Muslim women held by mainstream society. The passive, oppressive, and subservient attributes with which Muslim women are branded are quickly silenced by the existence of this magazine. *Reflections* aims to replace these grave misconceptions with the first-hand experiences and perspectives of Muslim women. The fact that such a medium is used for Muslim women to express their views and concerns, and actively participate in society's tapestry of ideas, does away with the subordinate characteristics attached to them. The writers do not shy away from controversial standpoints and topics but rather highlight the complexity of topical issues and challenge otherwise accepted truths by providing an alternative viewpoint to the mainstream. Controversial articles featured in editions included "Leaders Shmeaders" (Mawas 2003, 20), which critically tackles the leadership problem and the state of the world today; and "A Destructive Construction" (Abdo 2003/04, 8), which also deals with Israel's construction of the security wall in the West Bank, touching upon the controversies that fuel debate around the world today.

Opinion pieces like the latter based on taboo topics are prevalent in the magazine, as are issues and concerns affecting young Muslim women in the twenty-first century, such as the prevalent harassment and discrimination faced by Muslim women, along with issues of belonging and identity. *Reflections* provides the platform to critically explore these and other contentious issues; however, the editors do use their discretion as to what articles are included and excluded. Editorial decisions made in regards to highly controversial articles have sometimes resulted in the omission of certain sections of the articles, if not the entire article. Any articles that serve to be discriminative or overly defamatory to the point of damaging the image of the magazine will not be featured in the magazine. Despite this editorial policy, writers are given the freedom to explore areas of interests, whether they are controversial or not, so long as it coincides with the objectives of the magazine, but discriminative opinions or exploration of illicit matters are prohibited in the magazine. *Reflections* is also an independent media outlet that does not have any political affiliations and thus does not take part in political propaganda or campaigning.

This innovative channel allows young Muslim women to reconnect with their spiritual, Islamic principles, and Muslim women from the past who have shaped their identities and lives. For instance, the magazine explores the many different aspects of Islam, spirituality being a prominent element. Moreover explorations of the lives of past Muslim women and significant female figures in Islam, like Maryam the mother of Jesus and the wives of the Prophet Muhammad, feature regularly in the magazine; this allows Muslim women to grasp an insight into the significant role that women played in the history and development of Islam. Through this insight into the lives of various past female figures, Muslim women are able to identify with the many similar causes and struggles these women have experienced that they themselves share today.

For many young Australian Muslim women, the issue of identity seeps through every aspect of their lives, not only expressing themselves in secular societies but simultaneously dealing with preexisting notions like that expressed in late 2005 by Federal Liberal Member of Parliament, Bronwyn Bishop:

> Now, this morning on a debate with a Muslim lady, she said she felt free being a Muslim, and I would simply say that in Nazi Germany, Nazis felt free and comfortable. That is not the sort of definition of freedom that I want for my country. (Yaxley 2005)

In *Reflections* the *hijab* is discussed as an empowering expression of faith and examined in accordance with everyday experiences and perceptions of Muslim women. Often, mainstream feminist discourse criticizes the *hijab* as a symbol of patriarchal and theological oppression. Waleed Aly's article ("A Smarter Way to Fight for Muslim Women," 2006b) in *The Age* newspaper makes an interesting comparison of feminist discourse and colonial imperialism:

> To the Muslim ear, feminist discourse smacks of colonial imperialism. It echoes a broader historical polemic between the Muslim world and the West in which Western prescriptions for Muslim reform were often egocentric and hypocritical. Here one could cite Lord Cromer, the 19th century British consul-general in Egypt who advocated Egyptian women's unveiling while simultaneously being president of the men's league for opposing women's suffrage in England.

Conservative, right-wing politicians have exploited this type of feminist discourse in relation to Muslim gender relations. More recently, Prime Minister John Howard accused "some sections of the Islamic community" as having "an attitude towards women which is out of line with the mainstream Australian attitude" (Howard 2006). Since the 2002 invasion of Afghanistan, touted by the Coalition as a liberation movement from the Taliban, we have seen a growing interest in Muslim women and the veil, which generally is not attributed to a growth in feminism but rather a marked interest in the status of Muslim women in the light of a political context where Islam features regularly. Ironically, this neofeminist agenda on the part of conservative politicians serves to further alienate and exclude Muslim women from public debate. This is because when politicians and social commentators seek to speak on behalf of Muslim women, they reinforce the assumption that Muslim women are powerless and unable to represent themselves; they need to be spoken for.

Reflections subverts these misconceptions by returning the dictation of identity back to Muslim women to assert for themselves. The assertion of identity is underpinned by the *hijab* which contributes significantly to the identity of most Muslim women. However, it must be noted that not all Muslim women adopt the veil and indeed this does not necessarily exclude them from grappling with identity issues. Therefore, Muslim women who don't wear the *hijab* are just as likely to confront questions of their identity, although they are less likely to be stigmatized or discriminated against because they are not identifiably Muslim.

Although defining themselves in accordance with religious spheres is a fundamental part of the identity of Muslim women, it is not the only part of life they wish to be defined by. Australian Muslim women seek to be identified as active participants of society, whether through sociopolitical, cultural, or religious avenues. *Reflections* complements the desire for Muslim women to be influential agents of change in society by showcasing their engagement in all different aspects of society. And by giving young Muslim women the opportunity to contribute to a medium that they feel comfortable with through their writing and photography, as well as by including an article on present-day successful Muslim women in every edition of the magazine, *Reflections* allows young Australian Muslim women to pursue their many talents, interests, and passions in life, while spreading the accurate message of Islam. *Reflections* is a by-product of Islamic teachings which stress the fact that women need to have a voice, as well as ensuring that the views of young people are heard and that they are able to engage in society. These are some of the values upon which *Reflections* was built, and it is through them that we are able to confidently reassert the fact that Muslim women make up an integral part of Australian society and deserve to be recognized accordingly.

Engaging Young Women

As the world around us evolves and society changes, various groups are left unrepresented, with no platform or avenue by which to express their views. For women and young women especially there are very few avenues available that give them the freedom to express and define themselves in their own terms and not those that have been set out for them. In contemporary society, where the liberation of women is apparently a given, we are constantly faced with images of women that portray them in the same constricting roles as always. Women continue to be put into constrictive categories: either they are sex icons used for the purpose of advertising or are seen as having to be both domestic and career-driven beings. For example, many women complain that they perform the role of a modern superwoman because of the pressures mainstream society places on them to prove themselves. However, through *Reflections* we aim to broaden the notion of liberation in that it is not limited simply to the clothing one wears, or the salary one earns, or how many degrees one has earned. What liberation comes down to is choice. And if a woman chooses to stay at home and raise her children she is no less liberated than a woman who is a director of a global company or a woman who tries to achieve both. Liberation is quite a subjective notion and various articles in *Reflections* have highlighted this point through the discussion of the *hijab*, exemplifying the choices that Australian Muslim women have made and their achievements, as well as articles that have challenged the misconception that Islam oppresses women.

Although many have proclaimed that young people, particularly women, have little to say on issues that are of great importance and further that young people are not interested in being agents of change or challenging stereotypes, we argue that this is merely a generalization and a stereotype in itself. Although it is possibly true that many young people are purely interested in living out their youth and dealing with issues of adulthood when they get there, it is not the case for all young people. There are many examples of young people being heavily involved in their community with the aim of creating change; one need only look at the number of Youth Advisory Councils that are present on local, state, and national levels to see the involvement of youth in advisory roles. This aim encompasses the need to reshape the existing structures of society to allow for minority groups, young people, and women to engage in political, social, cultural, economic, and legal debate on their terms, be it through written opinion or factual pieces, a voice on radio, a segment on television, holding public forums and debates or the like.

Young people are constantly told that they are the leaders of tomorrow. In simply accepting this fact one must look at the implications that this has for the thoughts and opinions of young people. Beginning with the preexisting stereotypes of youth primarily through mass media as being associated with trouble, crime, and rebellion, "3ers ["Generation Xers"] have been bombarded with study after story after column about how bad they supposedly are … we are told, [they] are consumed with violence, selfishness, greed, bad work habits, and civic apathy" (Howe and Strauss 1993, 53), the reasons for such opinions become clear. So through *Reflections* we also try to reinforce the fact that young people do have a positive contribution to make to the community despite what many have to say that all they do is cause trouble and havoc. Through interviewing young people who are doing productive things with their lives we try to portray this fact.

Reflections challenges the stereotypes of not only youth as a misrepresented group within society, making it evident that young people do have a voice and an opinion which is just as valid as those of the older generation, but also it further enhances the voice of women from minority groups. Being comprised of young women from a minority background, *Reflections* has not only given young people a platform by which to relay their opinions, thoughts, and feelings, but also has allowed women and minority groups to be given such an opportunity. Although it may appear that *Reflections* itself operates within what some may call the narrow framework of young, female, Muslim minds, it encompasses a broad range of opinions by allowing its readers to freely contribute to the magazine in any way they like. The readership of *Reflections* is by no means limited to Muslim women, and we actually have a broad subscription base of males and females from a variety of ethnic and religious backgrounds and ages. Readers are free to contribute to the magazine through articles, poetry, photography, or any other means of expression they see relevant. We also continue to receive a lot of feedback from our readership through e-mails where they have suggested certain topics they would like to see us discuss or how they felt when reading certain articles, or even simply letting us know that they support us and look forward to reading the upcoming edition. Furthermore, *Reflections* gives all women a means by which to express their views and outline their politics on a more than superficial level, allowing them the opportunity to discuss issues beyond that of cosmetics, outer physical beauty, men, and other material and worldly subject matters. This allows women to connect in a forum where they are able to discuss and give their opinions on current government policies and further attempt to challenge the stereotypes and misconceptions of Islam by being proactive rather than reactive. *Reflections* wants young women to have their opinions heard as valid ones and provides a platform for this.

Reflections also aims to unite people of faith, by focusing on similarities between religions and showing that young people of Jewish, Christian, Buddhist, Hindu, Muslim, and other faiths have a common basis from which to work on issues of terrorism, human rights sufferings, education, the environment, the identity of young people or commonalities between religions. This allows people to identify with Islam at least on a minor level as they can see the similarities Islam has with other faiths as well as the similar attitudes Islam holds with the above-mentioned topics and that really it is not so different and thus no longer view it as a foreign or alien concept to which they cannot relate. This further helps young non-Muslims identify with young Muslims knowing that there are commonalities and that they do share the same essence of being youth with a future direction. We feel that education must begin with those who are young for they will eventually be those who run our country, change our policies, and further advance our nation into the next era and if a basic level of communication and understanding is developed at this early stage than a bright future lies ahead.

Reflections focuses on education as the process that governs change. We suggest that by slowly allowing the channels of communication to open up through education and understanding, tolerance can eventually permeate into the public arena. Although it is not the aim of *Reflections* to change the worldview of all humankind, it does seek to ensure that those who come in contact with and read the magazine or visit the Web site are likely to have a more comprehensive understanding of the Islamic issues they have dealt with. Once people begin to understand Islam and the concepts behind it they will no longer connote the word Islam with the notions of fear, terror, and barbarism.

Although *Reflections* has all these high aspirations of understanding, tolerance, and harmony, it is also realistic. The writers recognize that not all people in society share these same hopes and are actually trying to work against them. But this is what drives *Reflections* even more, with the hope that eventually and somehow this message will get out to these people in our society and it will make a difference to them. Being Muslim, being young, and being female, the *Reflections* team most likely represents the three most underrepresented and misunderstood groups in our society. But herein lies the secret of *Reflections*; because of these three components, which many would see as "disadvantages," *Reflections* is better able to be more effective in ensuring that we have a stronger voice in society and that it doesn't just echo out without response, but that it is actually loud enough and strong enough to be heard in all streams of society.

Feminism and *Reflections*

The Muslim woman, young or old, living in the East or West has time and time again been the focus of negative attention. Recent examples include the proposed banning of the *hijab* in Australian public schools by Federal MPs, as well as the banning of religious attire in schools in France. Historically the veiled Muslim woman has been seen by the West as an object of both fascination and to an extent, repulsion: Once she was a seductress of loose moral virtue, then she became the embodiment of sexual and social repression. Now she has become a security threat. ... The determinative factor is not Muslim female reality, but the Western condition. Whatever we think we are, she is always our opposite. (Aly, 2006a)

Existing as a young Muslim woman in both the East and the West spurs thoughts that our freedom of expression and speech is somehow denied because of gender and social positioning apparently constructed by our religion, Islam. Contrary to the misconception that disempowerment only applies to Muslim women is the view that this disempowerment can also be attached to women in the democratic Western world. As a matter of fact it should be pointed out that women in all countries, East and West, suffer from disempowerment, and this doesn't necessarily have anything to do with their culture or religion but is simply a problem that women face worldwide. So part of our aim through *Reflections* is to get people to stop labeling Islam as a tool for the oppression of women or to stop looking to the so-called Muslim countries where women are facing problems as the only places in which women suffer from disempowerment.

It has been asserted that Western society has its own antifeminist agenda to contend with, in particular, concepts like the glass-ceiling effect and the fact that Western, developed countries like the United States of America have not yet seen a female president. In fact, participating in a Western society does not automatically mean that rights like freedom of speech are given a platform to be voiced, and there are always barriers present. *Reflections* is an attempt to break through some of those barriers and provide a medium of communication for young women on a grassroots level. Therefore, although this could be seen as feminist in itself due to the assertion of a voice for women we do not delve into feminist theory in any explicit way. By explicit, we mean that there is no identified feminist agenda that we follow we feel that we are simply providing a platform for women which should already be there and isn't, so basically we are just trying to fill in the gaps. Issues explored and raised in this publication are kept simple in order for all young women to feel a part of *Reflections* and have their say. Considering that *Reflections* is largely aimed at correcting misconceptions about Islam and Muslims as well as providing a platform for young Muslim women, this generally overshadows any strong feminist discourse.

The establishing of *Reflections* magazine gave a voice to many young Muslim women who felt silenced and powerless, a similar liberation that many of the earliest feminists would have felt upon having the courage and means to assert their views in the public sphere. However, this being said, *Reflections* need not subscribe to any constrictive label, so as not to exclude any hopeful contributor from having their voice heard due to the fact they are outside the specified label. Young women of a Muslim background on a whole do not have great access to public expressive outlets. The media and communications industry are very influential in our society and although they report on the Muslim community frequently, seldom do Muslims have unrestricted access to such a network. *Reflections* as a magazine and the team of women behind it are able not only to express their views and correct misconceptions of Islam, but also develop skills they will carry with them throughout their lives. These skills include organization, management, communication with the public and media arenas, as well as networking abilities. We feel that strengthening the youth of the Australian Muslim community is vital in ensuring the advancement of the community as a whole.

Reflections, which is free of political subscriptions, allows a wider range of young women to have the opportunity to participate. The purpose of the magazine, creating dialogues between the Muslim community and non-Muslim public and attempting to correct misconceptions about their faith under fire, needs no name badge, as too many stereotypes have already been given to Muslims, women, and young people. These core aims overshadow any other political adherence and ensure the wideness of audience.A group of young Muslim women, definitely a minority group in the society they live, work, and study in, coming together to express views at times differing from the mainstream, has a scent that some may recognize as feminism. Although the active expression of opinion in the public sphere may be compared to the 1960s' feminists who ensured they were heard after the long and dwindling silent fifties, the outlook of the two groups is vastly different.

Most third-wave feminists tend to see religion and its institutions as their enemy, the original enslaver and dictator of oppressive roles to women; however, Muslim women far from share this belief. Third-wave feminists see religion as a rigid institution enforcing gender inequality, hence have been hesitant to engage it in their debates, remaining secular and somewhat narrowing their representation and appeal (Majid 1998). This automatically triggers the catchphrase "oppression" in the minds of feminist critics of Islam. Poor women, locked away in their houses, unaware of the freedoms many Western women are blessed with and so desperately want to give them. This view has aptly been reflected in commercial news programs like Channel 7's *Today Tonight*, which recently aired a show on Australian Muslim men who were on the hunt for second wives and wanting to engage in bigamous marriages. The Muslim women featured in these programs have often been almost shadowy figures with no apparent opinions on these issues; they have been veiled women filmed walking discreetly by their husband's side; we barely hear them or see them as other than "victims" to be rescued from patriarchal, sexist oppression.

Reflections, as an organized group of educated young women asserting their place in the world and this country, is a fine example to combat such a view. The contributors to this publication are not domesticated and timid individuals but rather they are assertive, opinionated, and progressive females on a mission as it is proven through their various articles. Current members of the editorial team include young women who are part of their local youth advisory councils and state advisory boards and are really trying to have an impact and initiate change not only within their local communities but also on a broader level. There are a number of social, psychological, and economic traditions that govern the thinking of most Muslims and refer particularly to women's status in Islam. Understanding the issues that affect male and female roles will clarify the position of feminism in Islam or the lack of need for such a system. Often ignored or overlooked is the fact that women were given many rights under Islam that women in the West waited a further 500 years to achieve. Property rights and rights to inherit were established with the beginning of Islam. Respect for women as "companions" and equal citizens in society was encouraged and upheld in the time of the Prophet Muhammad. The fact that Khadijah, a successful businesswoman on her own merit and Muhammad's beloved first (as she died before him at the age of 65) wife was the first to accept his teachings placed the standard of women as equal to men. This status of women as equals is further exemplified in this excerpt from Muhammad's "farewell address" (Sardar 2006, 71):

> O people listen to my words. … Wrong not and you shall not be wronged. You have rights over your wives and your wives have rights over you so treat them with kindness…

However, these are facts that are seldom acknowledged. Women in Islamic societies need not compete with men in society in order to be seen as equal to them. Interestingly enough, people assume this means Muslim women cannot be successful and take leadership roles in society. Our amazingly Westernized country has never had a female prime minister, yet the predominately Islamic country of Indonesia, our northern neighbors, have had a woman, Muslim at that, as leader of their nation. This example alone, along with the presence of female leaders in other Islamic nations such as Pakistan and Turkey, speaks volumes of the position of women.

This is not to dismiss or deny the human rights abuses in many pseudo-Islamic countries; however, there is evidence to suggest that Muslim women are making progress. In Iran women can vote and be actively involved in politics, as is the case with the vice president, who is a woman, as are 13 of 290 members of parliament. Jordan has also seen progression for Muslim women in the form of Queen Rania, who has contributed to empowering women. Women involved in Jordanian politics and government include the Minister of Planning who is a woman, and 12 of 165 members of the National Assembly are women. Muslim women do not think they are conditioned to accept second-class status or view themselves as oppressed, according to "What Women Want: Listening to the Voices of Muslim Women," a survey conducted in 2005 by Gallup World Poll, which interviewed 8,000 Muslim women from predominantly Muslim nations (Andrews 2006). Above all, the third-wave feminist movement must realize that, whereas in the West, religion has been seen as an opposition to their liberation, Muslim women attribute their liberation to Islam and the Quran. Hence, an intrusive voice telling them they are oppressed suggests ignorance on the part of such an organization where "even among Muslims seriously committed to gender reform, Western feminism has often presented more of a hindrance than a help" (Aly, 2006b).

Reflections goes hand in hand with its light of guidance, Islam, and this goes far beyond the sometimes narrow dimensions of Western feminism.

Active participation in the community and breaking into the media sphere by a minority group is an act feminists can relate to, yet our aims and objectives have little to do with liberating ourselves, but much more to do with liberating others from being misled in what has become an age of propaganda.

Conclusions

Finally, it is evident that there is definitely a lack of platforms for young women to express themselves, and this is even more so for young Muslim women. This is why it is so significant that a medium such as *Reflections* exists for young Muslim women to actively engage in society and have their voices heard. There are of course many obstacles to maintaining this medium and most of these come from individuals in society who are ignorant of young Muslim women and what it means to be one growing up in today's environment. However, the *Reflections* team sees this as even more of an impetus to get people to hear what they have to say.

Reflections also recognizes the fact that there needs to be communication between the different groups in society in order to have a greater impact and make a difference. This is why we need to liaise with one another and be aware of what is happening on all levels of the communities we live in. It is everyone's responsibility to take an active part in society and try and make a difference and change the negative attitudes of others. We feel that we can only communicate this message to the wider society if we work together and listen to what each person has to say. In history, women have been ignored for a long time, and today we find that young women are taking a proactive stance to ensure that this does not continue to happen regardless of what obstacles are put in our way. Yes, young Muslim women in Australia do have it tough, but this is what motivates us to create a space where we can voice their opinions, connect with the community, and form a sense of identity that is not solely based on a reactionary response to what is happening around us.

Reflections represents these young Australian Muslim women who are shaping their identities and helping to shape those identities of the youth around them and not simply waiting for someone else to do it. Young Muslim women have a lot to offer society, and *Reflections* magazine is only one means of achieving this. Through *Reflections*, young Muslim women aim to achieve a sense of understanding within the community that goes beyond a superficial tolerance of one another. It is not fair to simply *tolerate* each other, we must *understand* each other and the way we live and listen to what we each have to say.

References

Abdo, F. 2003/2004. "A Deconstructive Construction." *Reflections*, Summer Edition.

Aly, W. 2006a. Canberra's demons. *The Age (Weekend Insight)*, March 4, 7.

Aly, W. 2006b. A smarter way to fight for Muslim women. *The Age*, March 9. http:// www.theage.com.au/news/Opinion/A-smarter-way-to-fight-for-Muslim-wome n/2005/03/08/1110160824806.html (accessed June 15, 2006).

Andrews, H. 2006. Muslim women don't see themselves as oppressed survey finds. *New York Times*, June, 8, 9.

Elghoul, Z., and Youssef, F. 2003. "The Hijab: Misconceived, Mistaken, Misunderstood; Part Two." *Reflections*, Launch Edition.

Havel, V. 1995. Civilisations thin veneer. Commencement address at Harvard University Cambridge, MA (May). http://www.humanity.org/voices/commencements/ speeches/index.php?page=havel_at_harvard (accessed June 22, 2006).

Howard, J. 2006. Transcript of the Prime Minister John Howard MP, Doorstop interview. *News Room*, February 20. http://www.pm.gov.au/News/interviews/Interview1779.html

Howe, N. and W. Strauss. 1993. *13th Gen: Abort, retry, ignore, fail?* 1st ed. London: Vintage Books.

Krayem, M. 2003. "The Hijab: Misconceived, Mistaken, Misunderstood; Part One." *Reflections*, Launch Edition.

Majid, A. 1998. The politics of feminism in Islam. *Signs* 23, no. 2 (winter):321–361.

Mawas, F. 2003. "Leaders Schmeaders." *Reflections*, Launch Edition.

Mawas, F. 2003/2004. "The Confused Conflict." *Reflections*, Summer Edition.

Mawas, F. 2004b. "Education/Exploitation." *Reflections*, Winter Edition.

Poynting, S., G. Noble, P. Tabar, and J. Collins. 2004. *Bin Laden in the suburbs: Criminalising the Arab Other*. Sydney: Sydney Institute of Criminology.

Said, E. 1978. *Orientalism*. New York: Pantheon Books.

Sardar, Z. 2006. *What do Muslims believe?* London: Granta Books.

Schuster, S. 2006. *A few quotes about language and communication*. DevelopingTeachers. com, http://www.developingteachers.com/quotes/q2.htm (accessed July 24, 2006).

Yaxley, L. 2005. Bronwyn Bishop calls for hijab ban in schools. *The World Today*, ABC Radio 702AM, Sydney, August 29. http://www.abc.net.au/worldtoday/content/2005/s1448343.htm.

Part III
New Activisms: Cultural and Political

8
Connecting the Dots
Riot Grrrls, Ladyfests, and the International Grrrl Zine Network

KRISTEN SCHILT AND ELKE ZOBL

Participation in punk rock subcultures and feminist activist groups have been two separate pathways to empowerment and liberation for young women seeking to challenge oppressive norms of femininity. The emergence of the Riot Grrrl movement in the early 1990s created an opportunity for the fusion of these ideologies, merging the punk ethos of "do-it-yourself" (DIY) with a critique of sexism and patriarchy. Born out of a desire to empower women to become "cultural producers" (Kearney 1998), the Riot Grrrl movement played an important role in rewriting feminism for the twenty-first century.[1] Riot Grrrls spread explicitly feminist concerns through the circulation of politically informed punk music and grrrl zines.[2] Using these and various other means of subcultural production, this loosely knit grassroots movement combined a feminist consciousness with punk aesthetics and politics.

Despite the political message behind Riot Grrrl's form of punk rock feminism, many accounts of the movement frame it as a musical moment on the timeline of punk (see for example France 1993; Gottlieb and Wald 1994; Japenga 1992; Leblanc 1999). This framing neglects the more complex picture of how Riot Grrrl as a political movement inspired girls and young women both nationally and internationally to express resistance against restrictive expectations of girlhood, femininity, and traditional gender roles both in the punk scene—an often misogynistic youth subculture (Leblanc 1999)—and in "mainstream" society. Putting Riot Grrrl politics at the forefront of analysis, this chapter explores how the women involved in Riot Grrrl combined the DIY ethos of punk with feminist politics, creating a form of punk rock feminism that has since spread to international contexts via independent print media known as "grrrl zines" and prowomen conferences called "Ladyfests." Taking this international appropriation of Riot Grrrl politics as a case study, we argue that rather than being a moment in musical history that has come and gone, the ethos of the Riot Grrrl movement continues today through the production of grrrl zines and the organization of Ladyfests by women and girls who embody the in-your-face "anyone can do it" attitude of punk rock with a feminist twist.

This chapter draws on two sets of interviews. Kristen Schilt conducted one set of interviews with key members of the original Riot Grrrl D.C. chapter in 1998. Interviewees included members of Bikini Kill, Bratmobile, and feminist zine makers who edited early Riot Grrrl-associated zines. As the interviewees were all involved in the formation of Riot Grrrl DC, the interviews focused on the pre-history of Riot Grrrl, the formation of the group, goals for participation in the movement, and reactions from the punk scene, the feminist movement, and the media. These interviews were conducted in person, as well as via telephone and e-mail, in 1998 and 1999.

Elke Zobl conducted the second set of interviews with seventy-one contemporary grrrl zine editors and distribution service providers from twenty-eight different countries.[3] These interviews were conducted via e-mail and (overwhelmingly) in English.[4] The interviewees' zines address topics such as self-defense, women's health, Riot Grrrl, lesbian, queer and transgender issues, feminist parenting, music, and pop culture. Their zines appear mainly in print form and at least partially online, some solely as print zines and only a few are exclusively Web based. The interviews were conducted between 1999 and 2006.

Riot Grrrl Emerges: DIY, Feminism, and Punk Rock = Punk Rock Feminism

As a movement, Riot Grrrl was amorphous and nonhierarchical in structure, with no elected leaders or central organizational headquarters. This decentralization allowed participants in Riot Grrrl to actively direct the activities and meanings of their local chapter. Chapters in North America and in Europe ranged in activities from zine-making to organizing grrrl-positive punk shows to having consciousness-raising sessions about feminist politics. The movement began to attract media attention in 1992 (see, for example, Chideya 1992; France 1993; Japenga 1992) and was pronounced irrelevant and dead a mere two years later (McDonnell 1994). However, an analysis of grrrl-zine culture illustrates that Riot Grrrl was not a failed experiment in merging punk rock feminism, as suggested by Gottlieb and Wald (1994). Rather, Riot Grrrl morphed into new types of activism for both younger, new adherents and older participants ready for a different kind of punk rock feminism. In this section, we explore the rise of Riot Grrrl and connect it to the later emergence of Ladyfest and the international grrrl zine scene.

Do-It-Yourself: The Relationship of Riot Grrrl to Punk Rock

The emergence of Riot Grrrl owes much to the ethos of do-it-yourself that shaped the early punk music scene of the 1970s. At its core, the ethos of DIY is starkly opposed to mainstream visions of commercial success and aims to establish authenticity, independence, and an alternative economy. In addition to punk and art movements, this idea of producing one's own culture was key to the spread of the message of the early radical feminist movement (Echols 1989). Radical feminists published many small pamphlets and magazines about their political ideas, which can be read as early predecessors of grrrl zines. Additionally, out of necessity as well as protest, independent feminist publishing houses, presses, bookstores, organizations, independent galleries, and lesbian music festivals self-organized to challenge gender relations, to work toward gender equality, and to make women's cultural and political work visible. By doing this, radical feminists in the 1960s and 1970s created alternative spaces outside of dominant culture, just as Riot Grrrl would do in the early 1990s.

Beyond connections to earlier DIY movements, the emergence of Riot Grrrl as a political movement stems most directly from members' participation in the punk scenes of the late 1980s/early 1990s. Paradoxically, Riot Grrrl was created both out of inspiration for punk and a rejection of its sexist aspects (Smith 2003). Originally, punk held proto-feminist ideas, such as self-empowerment, and women musicians could voice their views and opinions about the traps of femininity and the erasure of female sexuality.[5] But female participation decreased as new forms of punk music, hardcore and thrash, developed on the West Coast of the United States. Former lead singer of punk band the Nuns, Jennifer Miro, follows up on this idea, discussing how in the increasingly male-dominated scene on the West Coast in the early 1980s, "Women just got squeezed out" (Leblanc 1999, 51). Despite this marginalization, teenage girls who felt alienated from the "real world" continued to flock to punk because the ideology and style of the subculture offered a way to rebel against normative views of femininity (Leblanc 1999). This created a situation in which women and girls were forced to carve out a space of their own within a subcultural location inhospitable to women, finding themselves alienated both from mainstream society and the male-dominated punk scene.

Many of the women involved in the onset of Riot Grrrl came from Olympia, Washington, and Washington, DC, two cities with punk music scenes, centered around the independent music labels Dischord (DC), K Records (Olympia), and later Kill Rock Stars (Olympia) (Gottlieb and Wald 1994). While the D.C. punk scene was largely male-dominated, Olympia had a great deal of female involvement due to a strong women's art community surrounding Evergreen College (Juno 1996). Many of the women involved in the Olympia punk scene had come from D.C. to attend Evergreen, majoring in feminist theory and women's studies. This connection between Olympia and D.C., as well as participation in feminist activism, set the groundwork for the development of what would come to be called Riot Grrrl.

The beginnings of Riot Grrrl were largely impromptu and arose in part through zine networks. In Olympia, Tobi Vail, a musician and student at Evergreen College, published *Jigsaw*, a fanzine that addressed, among other things, the issue of what it meant to be a woman musician in the punk scene. Inspired by Vail's zine, Kathleen Hanna contacted Vail and the two eventually formed Bikini Kill, a band often described as the first Riot Grrrl-associated band, with Kathy Wilcox and Billy Karren. In interviews, Tobi Vail, Kathleen Hanna, and Kathi Wilcox describe the formation of Bikini Kill as a precedent to their participation in Riot Grrrl. Vail remembers the beginning of Bikini Kill, saying:

> I had spent the last nine years trying to start an all girl band that would rule the world and change how people view music and politics and would express itself to a new generation. ... In 90–91, I was going to school full-time, had been doing a fanzine for about a year, had a radio show and two new good girl friends who I was starting a band with [Kathi and Kathleen].

The members of Bikini Kill came together from a mutual attraction to illuminating women's experiences in the musical world and the desire to make punk rock feminist music. After going on their first tour, Bikini Kill moved to D.C. for the summer of 1991. Also in D.C. at this time were Molly Neuman and Allison Wolfe, two young women interested in feminist ideology and politics who had connections to Olympia. Inspired by recent antiracist riots in D.C., these women decided they wanted to start a "girl riot" against a society they felt offered no validation of women's experiences. The name "Riot Grrrl" emerged as a name for their new zine. Speaking about the zine, Neuman says, "We wanted to do a fanzine that was fun and urgent and smart and confrontational. We passed them out at shows and had meetings with other girls to discuss issues of feminism and punk and support and skill sharing." These comments illustrate the importance of zines in the early formation of the Riot Grrrl movement not only for spreading feminist ideas in a punk format but also for bringing women together in a male-dominated punk scene that often kept them apart.

The merging of DIY and feminism emerged via Riot Grrrl D.C. in a form of punk rock feminism. Members of Riot Grrrl avoided defining the group, with some describing it as "a state of mind" and others as "a community of cooperative young women" (Leonard 1997, 231). Although there was no formal agenda of Riot Grrrl, a manifesto appeared in *Bikini Kill* zine that began with "Riot Grrrl is" and included a long list of the motivations of Riot Grrrl, such as taking back the modes of production and making more women-driven zines, music, and art. Showing the privileging of DIY, one section of the manifesto lists: "Riot Grrrl is. ... BECAUSE we know that life is much more than physical survival and are patently aware that the punk rock 'you can do anything' idea is crucial to the coming angry grrrl rock revolution which seeks to save the psychic and cultural lives of girls and women everywhere, according to their own terms, not ours" (Bikini Kill, np.p.). Riot Grrrl called upon young women to form bands, to produce shows, become DJs, start record labels and distros, design posters and organize protests and festivals. Additionally, Riot Grrrl taught skills, via chapter meetings and Riot Grrrl conventions, such as networking to put on shows, zine-making, and activism strategies; skills that women could take with them even if they did not actively participate in a Riot Grrrl chapter.

The political message of Riot Grrrl quickly spread through the underground music scene via zines and punk shows. For example, in 1991 K Records held the International Pop Underground Convention and set aside one night to be "Girl's Night." Under the motto "Love Rock Revolution Girl Style Now," Girl's Night featured exclusively all-female bands like 7 Year Bitch, Jean Smith, and Bratmobile. Girl's Night and other events, such as the 1992 Riot Grrrl Convention in D.C. opened the door for young women and girls across the country to begin to form bands, make zines, and start Riot Grrrl chapters. These chapters provided safe and supportive environments for young women to talk about issues important in their lives, similar to the feminist consciousness-raising groups in the 1970s, and to share skills. Although Riot Grrrl originated in D.C. and Olympia, the group quickly spread across the United States, into Canada, and to England (Kearney 1998).

Riot Grrrl also inspired young girls and women to create zines. The appeal of zines lies in the DIY ethos, the ability of anyone with an opinion to put pen to paper (or finger to keyboard) to create a written record of their life. These early print zines played a crucial role in bringing together girls and women across the country who shared an interest in creating punk rock feminism. Often, the initial impetus to make a zine was started by a desire to offer a critique of the portrayal of women in American society. Zines became an empowering tool for adolescent girls and women, as they had a new forum for criticizing the distorted image of women in mainstream media, traditional gender roles, daily discrimination, and sexism (Schilt 2003b). Additionally, with the rise of personal computing, many feminist e-zines developed in the late 1990s (Armstrong 2004; Scott-Dixon 1999). These e-zines allowed zine editors to reach people who might not have access to punk record stores or zine catalogues. E-zines have continued to morph and now exist more as Web logs, or "blogs"—online diaries where authors express everything from mundane frustrations of everyday life to personal struggles with depression and anorexia. However, due to the digital divide of socioeconomic class, these early e-zines also guaranteed a largely White, middle-class audience.

While print and e-zines continued to flourish, Riot Grrrl chapters and Riot Grrrl-associated bands in the United States became less common by the mid-1990s. This decrease was linked in some part to the negative image of Riot Grrrls as bratty teenagers with no real message behind their action that began to surface in the mainstream media (France 1993; Japenga 1993). In response to this misrepresentation, Riot Grrrl called for a media blackout in which participants declined all contact with the press. However, stories about Riot Grrrl continued to appear regularly (Kearney 1998). Additionally, attacks on Riot Grrrl began appearing in zines produced by a new generation of girls who learned only about the subculture through the negative mainstream media portrayal. To defend Riot Grrrl against these attacks, many chapters began to break apart, turn into new organizations or go deeper underground to avoid media attention. However, due to the preservation of zines in zine libraries, academic and popular accounts of Riot Grrrl, and the success of bands that contained members formerly associated with Riot Grrrl, such as Le Tigre and Sleater Kinney, interest in the movement lived on even as the original manifestation declined. As we will demonstrate in the next section, the DIY ethos embodied in zines currently lives on in two formats: Ladyfest festivals and international grrrl zine networks.

Riot Grrrls and Ladies Go International: The Spread of Ladyfests

Entering the new millennium, subcultural feminist movements experienced revitalization, both domestically and internationally. In addition to the reunion of Riot Grrrl-associated bands (such as Bratmobile), around forty new Riot Grrrl chapters, often initiated via the Internet, appeared in Canada, Europe, South America, and the United States.[6] Feminist art, music, and activism-oriented festivals called "Ladyfests" also emerged. These Ladyfests are explicitly seen in the tradition of and as a continuation of the Riot Grrrl movement.[7] The first Ladyfest, "a non-profit, community-based event designed by and for women to showcase, celebrate and encourage the artistic, organizational, and political work and talents of women," was organized in Olympia, Washington, in August 2000.[8] A collective of more than fifty volunteers organized performances and presentations by bands, spoken word artists, authors, and visual artists. The four-day festival attracted an audience of 2,000 and raised $30,000 for a local rape crisis charity. Ladyfest marked a new phase in Riot Grrrl-related feminist activism. These festivals were in the tradition of Riot Grrrl conventions, featuring workshops, female musicians, and female artists. However, the term "lady," used both in zine titles like *Ladyfriend Zine* (the United States) and *Ladybomb distro* (Finland), and in the festival name "Ladyfest," signaled two things: (1) a move away from the term Riot Grrrl, a label that had come to be seen as limiting by many; (2) a space for older feminists who felt they were too old to be "grrrls" and thus adopted the tongue-in-cheek usage of "ladies." Ladyfests have since grown into an international phenomenon, with 123 conferences occurring in 27 countries between 2000 and 2006 (see Table 8.1).

Ladyfests usually include a range of arts, spoken word, music, film, educational and hands-on workshops, such as bike repair, grant writing for the arts and zine-making. Red Chidgey, zinester and organizer of the Ladyfest Film Archive (United Kingdom), describes Ladyfests in the following way:

Ladyfests are DIY festivals organised by women to showcase female talents, speak out against sexism, racism and homophobia, and to encourage women and girls to become active creators of their own culture, entertainment and politics. Ladyfests incorporate workshops and discussions with bands, films, spoken word, art, diy, dancing and activism. Although organised mostly by women, Ladyfests are open forums for all genders.[9]

Panel discussions featuring alternative local, national and international musicians, authors, and scholars are also often offered. Furthermore, ladies today are increasingly devoted to supporting transgender and genderqueer rights. Great importance is placed on a trans-inclusive policy and on the concept of "self-identified" women. For example, Ladyfest attendees have been vocal forces in protesting the Michigan Womyn's Festival (MWF), the longest running women-only music festival. With roots in lesbian separatist feminism—a political orientation closely linked to hostile attitudes toward transsexuals (see, for example, Raymond 1979), MWF has a "womyn-born womyn" only policy for attendance that is designed to exclude transsexual women, people who are not viewed as "real" women (Califia 1997). Many Ladyfesters refuse to attend MWF until this outdated policy is overturned. Like in the Riot Grrrl movement, there are no guidelines or rules, beyond a push for

Table 8.1 Number of Ladyfests per Year and by Country

Number of Ladyfests (LFs) per Year							
Year	2000	2001	2002	2003	2004	2005	2006	2007
No. of LFs	1	5	12	21	25	31	28 (so far)	12 (more planned)

Number of Ladyfests by Country					
Country	No. of LFs	Country	No. of LFs	Country	No. of LFs
Argentina	1	Hungary	1	Romania	2
Australia	3	Indonesia	1	Scotland	1
Austria	2	Ireland	1	Singapore	1
Belgium	2	Italy	3	South Africa	4
Brazil	3	Litunia	1	Spain	2
Canada	16	Luxemburg	2	Sweden	6
Denmark	2	Mexico	3	Switzerland	2
England	14	The Netherlands	4	Turkey	1
Finland	1	New Zealand	1	United States	50
France	2	Norway	3		
Germany	15	Poland	1		

inclusivity and diversity, on how to organize and structure a Ladyfest; emphasis is put on process-oriented, nonhierarchical, collective action.

What the spread of Ladyfests shows is that young women still identify as feminists and are actively engaged and invested in feminist activism, art, and politics. The continued relevance of the punk rock feminism created by Riot Grrrl can also be seen in a variety of other feminist (sub)cultural productions, such as blogs, open mic performances, street theater, sound and video projects. These practices have been widely associated with a third wave of feminism (Baumgardner and Richards 2000; Bell 2002; Garrison 2000; Hernandez and Rehman 2002; Heywood 2006; Heywood and Drake 1997; Orr 1997; Piano 2002; Walker 1995). The increase of culturally productive girls and young women (Kearney 2003, 2006) has been attributed to a variety of social, political, and technological transformations, such as the greater accessibility to less expensive and more user-friendly media technologies, the explosion of media literacy initiatives, and the incorporation of production practices in media education curricula (Buckingham 2003; Kearney 2003, 18–19). The emergence of the Riot Grrrl movement and "its privileging of 'girl power' as an ideological framework for the political, social, and cultural promotion and activity of female youth" (Kearney 2003, 32) paved the way for these girl-specific forms of cultural production

Somewhat in departure from the Western focus of the early Riot Grrrl movement, however, there now is a sense of an international community in girl-based feminist production. This internationality is manifested through the bundling and linking of all Ladyfests on primarily two Web sites, namely www.ladyfest.org and www.ladyfesteurope.org. Although each Ladyfest has been different due to the specific localities and backgrounds of their organizers, all are linked by a shared name and feminist ideology and are therefore connected to the same tradition and easily found on the Internet (Groß 2006). Melanie Groß has argued that such a close network and mutual referencing system did not work with the earlier term "Riot Grrrl," as there were variant spellings of "grrrl" and of the festivals and events they organized (Groß 2006, 9). While the riot grrrl network has been of similar size, she argues, it was clearly more diffuse and difficult to research. A main reason for renaming "Riot Grrrl" into "Ladyfest" has been the mainstream, commercial appropriation of the term "grrrl" and "grrrl power" into "girlie" and the "angry women in rock" phenomenon (Groß 2006, Schilt 2003a). Learning from this exploitive lesson, Ladyfest participants nowadays are much more careful in their communication and collaboration with the mainstream press. In addition, criticism from transgender folks and women of color within the Riot Grrrl movement has been taken to heart by Ladyfest organizers. However, what unites both movements is the encouragement of the participants to move beyond passive listening and to become culturally and/or politically active and to express new ideas about feminism. This sense of international community and dedication to subcultural feminist production also is found in the zine networks.

Emancypunx, PinkPunkies, and *Grrrl:Rebel*: Zinesters Doing-It-Themselves

Largely due to increased Internet access, contemporary grrrl zines have become part of an international communication network among feminist zine editors in many countries around the world. These international zinesters produce and participate in print and online zines, distros, mailing lists, message boards, live journals, and resource sites, as well as in zine archives and libraries, gatherings, festivals and conferences, exhibits and workshops. Illustrating this international growth, grrrl zines from forty-three different countries in thirteen languages were located for this research, making it evident that the contemporary international young feminist network continues to be a vital community.

Overall, the grrrl zine community can be described as an international and geographically mobile network of like-minded and culturally productive feminist-identified young women, queer, and transgender youth of complex and plural identities and backgrounds who aim at making an impact on their own and other women's lives. Zine maker Olivia (United States) has described it as followed:

> I would call all of the wonderful women who have subscriptions to *Persephone Is Pissed* part of my grrrl zine community, and they are all very different kinds of people: mothers, artists, gardeners, rebels, anarchists, liberals, old, young, outspoken and shy alike. Mostly I guess the grrrl zine community consists of women who want to change the world, and who make art or live life in a way that expresses those desires.

The creators of grrrl zines do not necessarily have to be female-bodied. What counts is a self-identification with alternative feminist and queer youth communities and to transport a feminist, grrrl-positive message. In the past few years, queer and transgender zinesters have published numerous zines about their daily lives, personal experiences, and political opinions, and have criticized the exclusion of their viewpoints from the feminist movement.

By and large, contemporary grrrl zines cover just about anything that concerns young women and queer and transgender youth in their daily lives. Some may use zines for their personal writings; others devote themselves to political discussions. More often than not, a mix between topics, forms of writing, and art making (such as drawings and collages) are present. Some of the most prominent topics are: Riot Grrrl, music, mothering, pop culture, feminism, politics, women's rights and issues, and bisexual, lesbian, queer, and transgender issues.

Grrrl zines can take all kinds of shapes and forms: From photocopied, black-and-white, cut-and-paste, stapled zines in booklet size (e.g., *Clit Rocket*, Italy), to printed, full-color, full-size, designed (maga)zines (e.g., *Bust*, United

States) and to purely online zines, sometimes referred to as CybergURL zines (e.g., *geekgirl*, Australia). Whereas many zine makers favor the print medium for zines, others, such as Kelly, editor of *Pretty Ugly* (Australia), feel that the Internet is "the ultimate in DIY: No paper, glue, scissors, staples, photocopiers, distributors, you can do it yourself quickly and easily and affordably online." Tanja, one of the editors of *Bunnies on Strike* in the Netherlands, says that the Internet has helped her to "get the thought out to people all over the world even some who aren't aware of the zine world" and that it has "motivated some girls to start zine-writing too." At *Take Back The News* (United States), Emily collects stories from survivors of sexual violence to expose how rape is under-represented and misrepresented in mainstream media. She comments on the role the Internet has played for her zine and how it works in print:

> The internet is vital to *Take Back The News*. It allows survivors every-where to access the project, and that is an amazing thing about the medium. *Take Back The News* reaches more people through the inter-net, but is more powerful in print. Print projects generally appear in existing publications. So when readers are flipping the pages of an indy paper that [they are] used to reading, and suddenly see all of these pow-erful and horrible accounts of rape, told in the survivors own words, it's incredibly startling and moving, and real. I so strongly believe in print media, and really want to focus there for the future of the project.

Although the Internet has made DIY production and distribution easier and cheaper and a lot of young people find out about zines via the Internet, many zinesters acknowledge the fact that not everyone has access to the Inter-net and therefore continue to produce paper zines, sometimes in conjunction with e-zines. For example, as Hilde notes, the editors of *Riot Grrrl Europe* decided to create a paper zine in conjunction with their Web site and mailing list to "spread tha word":

> [...] with a website and a mailinglist you don't reach everyone on the European continent. Not everyone is interested in the internet, AND, not everyone has access to a computer. Think of remote areas (cause most city people can get access to everything) in countries like Italy, Poland, the Czech Republic, former Yugoslavia, Spain ... these people have to be reached too!

Thus, many "net savvy" grrrl zinesters are aware and address the issue of inequality and privilege in access to computers and the Internet.[10]

Zines in Relation to Punk and Riot Grrrl

The ethos of DIY holds special significance for zine makers who often come out of punk culture. Kylie explores what DIY, zine making, and the punk scene mean to her in volume 4 of her zine, *Personality Liberation Front*:

It is my strong belief that DIY zine projects affirm both a sense of self, and a sense of community. I really think that they are such an excellent medium for challenging mainstream norms and expressing radical opinions that will never make it on to the 6 o'clock news. I also think that it is so important to break down barriers between audiences/performers and consumers/creators via the Do-It-Yourself ethic. Zines truly are a great example of this DIY realization in the punk scene—when we start to become aware that what *we* say and do matters, and that we can change ourselves and others via our personal/political activities. And although I might feel fucked-off with the wider world and alienated from normal society a lot of the time, I love the fact that there is so much emphasis on meaningful communication in the DIY punk scenes. So I can feel connected with so many other likeminded people—and that in itself is such a beautiful, rad thing. (2003, 82. Emphasis in text.)

Kylie also wants to connect the punk heritage and community with the exploration of gender issues to create social change and challenges everyone—males *and* females—to share their thoughts on gender issues. In regards to lesbian sexuality and punk identity, Trent notes on the development and eventual goal of *Trippers*, "a Hardrockinmeanspittingpunkrockdykegrrrl zine from Singapore" emphasizing "grrrls that [have] made a difference in the punkrock scene:"

It wasn't a specifically punkrock zine at first. It wasn't a dyke zine either. But as the zine progresses and I mature, readers are able to journey through life with me, how I was suddenly became aware of my sexuality, how my love for punkrock intensified and things like that. Therefore I decided to turn *Trippers* into a lesbian punkrock zine.

Hence, the connections between punk and (riot) grrrl zines are still very strong. Many zine makers interviewed learned about zines in their late teens at punk rock shows, by listening to punk and hardcore music, and through friends in the local scenes. In some countries the Riot Grrrl movement introduced young women to making zines. For example, Red, editor of the zine *Varla's Passed Out* and creator of the distro *FingerBang* in the United Kingdom, "came to zine cultures through riot grrrl." Similarly, *Jawbreaker*-editor Claire from Makati City, Philippines, writes that "[r]iot grrrl captured my attention by way of zines, facing a critique from zinesters of color in America" (*Chop Suey*, n.p.). Shannon, editor of the zine *Woami* in Melbourne, Australia, was inspired by the Riot Grrrl movement as well. Although she thinks that "things happened more slowly [in Australia] than they did in Olympia" it nevertheless "changed the feminist outlook that [she] had at the time." Isabella, coeditor of the zine *Bendita: A Latin Women's Initiative against Violence towards Women* in São Paulo, Brazil, observes:

The fanzine production began over here around the late 70s, and the first women-made publications came out in the mid 80s but normally they had help from men in the editing and stuff like that. So I can't really tell when ALL GIRL zines started to come out, but I can say that since the Riot Grrrl movement established some roots around here in 1997, girl zines started popping up wildly here and there and it was just amazing, and still is, but the difference is that today girls seem to be more daring. It's not just about being indie or punk rock or hardcore or emo or artsy whatever—girls are starting to talk about art and politics so I have to say the quality is tending to increase. *Violent Playground, Água, Magazine, Grrrls Voices, Gumption, Vertigem, Garatuja* ... the names are countless. I would even dare to say that there are just as many female editors as there are male ones, and girls seem to have so-o-o much to say as there are always new zines on the stands. Thumbs up to them as they managed to pave their way in such a culture-lacking country.

Although the Riot Grrrl movement has not spread everywhere, this empowering trend seems to happen in various countries around the world. Elise, coeditor of *Grrrl:Rebel*, observes that the grrrl zine scene in Malaysia is healthy; many girls are making zines. And she says, "this would never [have happened] if it weren't for punk and Riot grrrl."

But the introduction of feminist views into the punk community is not always smooth. Yen, part of the Polish collective *Emancypunx*—a word game of "emancipation in punk rock"—observed that "the first feminist zine was a shock for the punk community" and people, even outside of the punk community, started to discuss their articles, just as the popular press had begun discussions about Riot Grrrl a decade before. Similarly, Lil from the Argentinian e-zine *PinkPunkies*, mentions that "[a] lot of guys always sign our guestbook insulting us and criticizing our punk and feminist attitude, so we always reply [to] those insults with an explanation about what we do and what we believe in." Although Kelly, editor of *Pretty Ugly*, Australia, found guys very supportive of grrrl zines, she also says, "the music/punk zines seem to be mostly written by guys, about other punk guys so things aren't in any way equal between grrls and guys in terms of content and that particular type of zine." In response, she hopes that the "*Pretty Ugly* project will help foster a stronger feminist-focused grrrl zine community in Australia." In sum, many grrrl zinesters have been and still are inspired by punk and Riot Grrrl ideologies and communities. However, because they experience the punk scene frequently as male dominated and misogynist, they create their own grrrl-friendly spaces.

Reasons for Creating Grrrl Zines

The reasons to create feminist zines today are still similar to those in the beginning of the Riot Grrrl movement. Many contemporary grrrl zinesters, such as

Elena, editrix of *It's Not Just Boys Fun* (Germany) or Carol and Elise, editors of *Grrrl:Rebel* (Malaysia) think that the hardcore and punk scenes are still strongly male-dominated with only a few female musicians and zine editors. Therefore they feel the urge to create a grrrl-positive space. Elena for example says: "i wanted to do something on my own, see more girls involved or just know where all the active girls are and what they're up to." Similarly, the goal of *Emancypunx* was "to give girls in punk access to independent feminist projects and art done by other womyn" and "to change the sexist and homophobic attitude of the punk&hc scene" in Poland. Many grrrl zinesters want to encourage women to take proactive and outspoken roles in their local punk and hardcore scenes. The editors of *Grrrl:Rebel* comment: "we want more grrrls to be active in the punk scene, we want more girls to pick up instruments and form bands and do zines and simply just play important roles in the local scene" (Elise) and "furthermore, we want to empower fellow girls that being girls is not something to be ashamed of and they should be proud of who they are, and lastly, we want to raise awareness among the girls in the punk/HC scene" (Carol). *PinkPunkies'* Lil wants to "make all the young girls who are just starting in this punk world [become conscious] about what a girl can do" and "to abolish sexism."

Many also want to act as an alternative vehicle for information and inspiration for feminist ideas, as Emca Revoluce from the zine *Bloody Mary* in the Czech Republic notes:

> We want to inform people—give them another point of view. We want to show that women have also something to say and that they can do it. We want to spread feminist/riot grrls ideas. And, we want to have fun and amuse other people as well. The zine sometimes works as a sting for it criticizes sexist behavior of male[s] in "the movement" (i mean anti-capitalist or anarchist movement which we are part of).

Describing why she makes a zine, Isabella (Bendita) from Brazil says:

> Zine making to me means creating our own channel to express just about everything we wanna say and were never given a chance. It's so empowering. Especially coz in a lot of occasions it gives a voice to marginalized groups whose voices (and lives) have never been considered by mainstream society in general. Zine making is a way to exist, really.

This quote underscores the way in which grrrls value zines as a relatively cheap and easily accessible medium for marginalized voices to express themselves, which otherwise may not be heard in society. Because it's often the voices of young women, queer and transgender folk, and feminists that are silenced in society, grrrl zinesters create their own forums. Sandra started to publish *Queer Ramblings* (United States) "because there are just a few publications that will use queer-themed material—especially queer women and trans people" (interview with author). Nikko, editor of *good girl*, Canada, notes as well:

> I was inspired by reading about the many awesome zines that have come before us—and also by my frustration because there wasn't anything with a national scope in Canada, and I felt there was a need. ... I really wanted to challenge the mainstream media and create an alternative for young women; a place where young women can create the media they want, instead of being dictated to by the mainstream.

Besides their commitment to young women's empowerment and to provide a forum for marginalized voices, international zine makers are actively engaged in transforming the feminist movement through an exploration of feminist issues in their zines:

> When I started the first incarnation of *Pretty Ugly* ([formerly] *Kill the Real Grrls)* I hoped to refocus people's attention to feminism as a valid and essential movement, the zine was also a great medium to explore feminist issues and concerns on a personal level. As the zine transformed into the *Pretty Ugly* project, a major goal of ours became to inspire young people, especially women, to write and perhaps make their own zine.

The majority of grrrl zinesters interviewed strongly identify as feminists and with feminism(s). Hilde of *Riot Grrrl Europe* says: "EVERYTHING I do has got something to do with feminism. With liberating true female powers: be it my band, Riot Grrrl Europe, Ladyfest ... just everything. The feminist movement to me is that group of people around me who are ever active and who were also involved in organising Ladyfest Amsterdam and such." Kylie, editor of Personality Liberation Front, thinks similarly:

> i see myself as a feminist—most definitely and for sure, and i see myself coming from a long and continuing history of women's struggles and women's movements for social change, and i feel very connected to current struggles. i feel part of the broad diverse feminist movement and also particularly connected to a feminism (or feminisms, if that is more appropriate) that is aligned with radical anticapitalist multiracial queer-diverse culture and community. and of course, i have a very special place in my heart for the riotgrrrl zinester diy anarcho punkrock branch of this feminist community!

Indeed, they are very knowledgeable about the diversity and complexity of the feminist movement(s). Moira from *Moon Rocket Distribution* (New Zealand), for example, writes: "I definitely identify as a feminist, though I'm always aware that people have different perceptions of feminism and what the feminist movement should be. As a feminist, I think it's important to remain critical and questioning of feminism and what people do under the heading of 'feminism.'"

Grrrl zines provide a creative and political platform for the creation of an international community of empowered women and queer and transgender people with feminist viewpoints. As such, Riot Grrrl, punk and zines also play a key role in finding like-minded people inside and outside of the local scene(s). Before *Grrrl:Rebel* Elise got involved into the Riot Grrrl and punk community in Malaysia, she "could hardly find any mutual friends, who were into feminism, punk and female bands." Now she has friends in many countries around the world.

Because in the Czech Republic there "isn't anything [like a] riot grrrl movement," Emca Revoluce from the zine *Bloody Mary* says she "can feel as a part of it just virtually, via the Internet," therefore pointing to the Internet as an important tool to form transnational connections and friendships. For Red of *Varla's Passed Out* and *FingerBang* distro (United Kingdom) the community aspect and empowerment of Riot Grrrl have been significant as well: "Riot grrrl allowed me to join a community and not stand isolated, it also gave me permission to think of myself as an active agent of social change. Sometimes I feel like I am part of a group of women who are making history right now." These examples illustrate that there is an international network of young female cultural producers who read, publish, and distribute grrrl zines in many countries around the world and are dedicated to feminist ideologies and politics. Grrrl zines are more than individualistic diary-like writings; they create a network, reach a community, and bridge the personal with the political—in short, as Red has said, grrrl zinesters become "active agents of social change."

Conclusions

Although music journalists had begun to declare the Riot Grrrl movement dead by the mid-1990s, as evidenced by the labeling of feminist bands as "post-Riot Grrrl" (Powers 1995), the punk rock feminist DIY ethos of the movement lived on, becoming subsumed under the idea of DIY feminism. As Marcelle Karp, coeditor of *The Bust Guide to the New Girl Order* noted: "We've entered an era of DIY feminism. … Your feminism is what you want it to be and what you make of it" (1999, 310–311). In 1996, Australian researcher Kathy Bail coined the term "DIY feminism" to describe young women who redefine feminism in their very own and personal ways. Bail claimed that "DIY feminists want to be identified through their interests and passions—such as music, publications or business—before their gender" (1996, 4). She found that some young women showed ambivalence towards the term "feminism" and the movement as a whole although they embody feminist ideals in their daily lives. Anita Harris (1998) criticizes such a liberal individualist approach and highlights the political aspect of grrrl zines:

> Grrrl zines demonstrate that young women's feminism amounts to more than being "fun and feisty." The erroneous conflation of punk DIY with liberal individualism has resulted in a misrepresentation of young women who produce zines as postfeminist. In fact, young women use zines as grassroots, collectivist means to promote women's rights and agitate and campaign around feminist issues. Grrrl zines are a tool and expression of feminist politics; their producers and contributors are knowledgeable about and passionately engaged with women's issues, and they use the method of DIY to communicate their feminism rather than to consume a new style or fashion. (92)

In agreement with Harris we argue that in making independent music, zines and Web sites, and organizing festivals in their very own DIY ways, many young women, queer and transgender youth consciously do, live, and integrate feminism and politics in their daily lives. As seen in hundreds of grrrl zines and musical lyrics, many identify as feminists and act on a feminist and political consciousness. Through their day-to-day actions, activities, and cultural productions, this diverse, international network keeps feminism (and the feminist movement[s]) creatively as well as individually and collectively active and alive.

Certain critiques about the limitations of this type of subcultural feminism have been raised. Stephen Duncombe—speaking retrospectively on Riot Grrrl—doubts the translation of Riot Grrrl into a lasting political movement and questions whether members really want to change greater society (1997, 70). Duncombe's question speaks to the personal/political divide, as well as to what types of political activism strategies are considered "real," "serious," or "valid." His comment seems to assume a type of activism intent on inclusivity that would attempt to reorder the existing society. With this point, he puts forth almost a Marxist understanding of cultural resistance as designed for wide scale cultural revolution. This type of widespread societal change, however, might not be the point, as not everyone has access to the type of power necessary to make this change. Going back to Riot Grrrl, an early Bikini Kill song, "Jigsaw Youth," begins: "Your world, not mine. Your world, not ours" and continues: "I'll resist with every inch and every breath." Riot Grrrl attracted participants who felt, for many reasons, outside of "greater society." Zine-making was successful precisely because of its potential to allow for expression of a voice that might be marginalized—due to gender, age, sexual identity, or race—in a forum under one's control. Rather than reproducing situations in which transgenders, queers, and young women have to defend their right to existence, zines provide a format outside of greater society to write candidly about lived experiences usually absent from mainstream cultural production. Going back to the punk roots of Riot Grrrl and subcultural feminist movements, dialoguing with greater society is not always the point; sometimes you need to have space to "resist psychic death" (Bikini Kill 1994).

That said, zine makers see their zine projects as more than just personal empowerment. Zines serve as a medium through which to communicate with others, opening a dialogue about topics usually not discussed in public. Creating this communication with zine readers, in turn, creates the potential for political awareness and action. Many grrrl-zine makers do envision their zine to have the potential to lead to political change. As Cheryl, editrix of *The Fence: A New Place of Power for Bisexual Women* (Canada), comments: zines "can educate people and raise awareness, which leads to action; and they also provide grassroots opportunities for people's voices to be heard that wouldn't normally have a place in mainstream media." This political change need not be large scale; as Kylie from *Personality Liberation Front* (Australia) writes: "at the very least they build a network of friends/community and decrease alienation in this fucked-up world. And it's good to remember that anyone can create a zine and anyone can change the world, or at the very least, the little part of it that they inhabit." Achieving this small-scale change, a political change in "one's own backyard," can makes zines, then, a "photocopied blueprint for a better world" (Kylie) for individuals who find themselves silenced in mainstream forms of political activism and discourse.

Viewed in this light, zines are a kind of backbone to subcultural feminist activism, allowing zine makers to link personal experiences to larger political activist work. As Michelle of *Echo Zine Distro* (United States) comments, "zines create both individualism and community, and that these two elements can coexist, be productive, and bring about real social change." While zines do operate outside of the mainstream, a necessity for a subcultural medium, making it unlikely that they will be able to ignite large-scale political change, this shouldn't—to return to Duncombe's question—be confused with zine makers' lack of interest in creating social change. Zines are just one piece in the jigsaw puzzle of the contemporary feminist movements which consists of a variety of (sub)cultural production, such as feminist pirate radio stations, radical cheerleading, spoken word, street theatre, and much more. Wherein zines are intrinsically ephemeral, short-lived, and personal, the process of reading, making, and distributing feminist zines, and organizing and conducting Ladyfests has an empowering effect on the personal, social, and political lives of many young women, and queer and transgender youth. Furthermore, they hold the hope for larger social and political change in the long term, as illustrated in the quotes above.

So to answer Duncombe's question "Do they really want to change greater society at all?" we can say, yes, many grrrl zinesters do indeed aim for social change and advocate so in their zines. Obviously, if they succeed is another story. Anita Harris has argued in *Future Girl* (2004) that young women involved in what she calls "border spaces" attempt to reconceptualize themselves "as new kind of citizens ... partly by attempting to shift citizenship from consumption to production, but also sometimes by trying to articulate new modes of political engagement that break with traditional frameworks" (179). Citing young women involved in resistant cultural production, she continues:

> While the enduring political efficacy of these claims is difficult to ascertain, the desire to speak, act, and agitate elsewhere, outside the normal political arenas or frameworks of older theories, suggests a strong need to take seriously new spaces for engagement and expression for young women. These provide not only sites for young women to gather, debate, and critique meanings of young womanhood in late modernity, but also potential new modes of networking and organizing. (179)

We not only need to take these new "border spaces" of young women's (sub)cultural production and resistance seriously, but also think about the possibility of enacting participatory democracy. Duncombe states, "the medium of zines is not just a message to be received, but a model of participatory cultural production and organization to be acted upon" (1997, 129). Acknowledging the uneasy relationship between revolutionary claims in free spaces (e.g., in zines) and traditional political activism, Harris (2004) argues similarly that "if we understand these [free] spaces as providing transient places to take time out and try on new identities and alliances, to network and share ideas and information with other youth away from regulation, they can be imagined as a kind of pre- or even newly figured participatory politics. At least they can be acknowledged for their ongoing use as rest stops, fissures, places for momentary reflection, and connection" (180). While we need to keep in mind that only a small percentage of young people are involved and interested in Riot Grrrl, zines, Ladyfests, punk, and feminism and have access to economic resources and the means of cultural production, and that not all zine-making women are invested in feminist ideologies, the personal and political potential that lies in participatory cultural production for young women, queer, and transgender folks needs to be looked at more closely.

In conclusion, as we have shown, the spirit of the Riot Grrrl movement continues to live today, to a large part in international Ladyfests and grrrl zines, and in other (sub)cultural, participatory feminist productions not mentioned here in detail, such as radical cheerleading, feminist street theatre, or culture jamming. The creative DIY cultural work of Riot Grrrls, ladies, and grrrl zinesters indeed has not only effected personal empowerment but also has grown into a broader international network. The immense spread of Ladyfests across Asia, Australia, Europe, and North America and of international grrrl zines in many countries around the world illustrates not only that the Riot Grrrl movement has had a lasting impact on young women's (sub)cultural production in the international realm but also that there is lasting and renewed interest in many issues that were raised by Riot Grrrls in the 1990s. Utilizing the method of DIY for their purposes, contemporary print and online (Riot) grrrl zines and feminist-oriented Ladyfests play a crucial role in the spread of feminist and political consciousness and, furthermore, connect participants in the feminist, queer, and transgender liberation movements around the globe.

Acknowledgments

Elke Zobl's work on this chapter was supported by a postdoctoral fellowship from the Austrian Science Fund and a Marie Curie International Reintegration Grant (6th European Community Framework Programme). She would also like to thank all zinesters for providing their time and thoughts so graciously!

Notes

1. It is important to note that not all women associated with what has come to be called the Riot Grrrl movement took on the label and/or identity of "Riot Grrrl." However, for the purpose of clarity in this article, we refer to women and girls associated with the ideology of the Riot Grrrl-associated bands and zines as "Riot Grrrls."
2. Zines, short for "fanzines, are homemade magazines with limited distribution that express the thoughts and opinions of the author or authors. They incorporate a variety of genres, such as sci-fi, political, music, and what has come to be called "grrrl zines," zines that focus on feminism, as well as the lives and experiences of girls.
3. Namely, Argentina, Austria, Australia, Brazil, Canada, Croatia, Czech Republic, Finland, France, Germany, Italy, Ireland, Israel, Japan, Malaysia, Mexico, the Netherlands, New Zealand, Norway, Peru, Philippines, Poland, Singapore, South Africa, Sweden, the United Arab Emirates, the United Kingdom, and the United States.
4. The interviews can be accessed at the Web site *Grrrl Zine Network:* http://grrrl-zines.net/interviews.htm.
5. See the Slits' "Typical Girls," the Raincoats' "No One's Little Girl," and X Ray Spex's "Oh Bondage Up Yours" for examples of punk lyrics dealing with the stereotypes about women.
6. Because these chapters are organized informally, come and go, and are not always represented online, it is difficult to ascertain the exact number of active chapters. For current information visit the *Riot Grrrl World Newsletter* [http://www.geocities.com/riotgrrrlworld/] and the *Riot Grrrl International Message Board* [http://users.boardnation.com/~riotgrrrlInternationalmb/].
7. As evident in many historic accounts of Ladyfests, e.g., on the Web sites of Lady-fest Belgium 2003 [http://www.anarchie.be/index/show.php?t=55], "the f word" (July 2002) [http://www.thefword.org.uk/features/2002/07/the_lowdown_on_ladyfest], or in the news such as in the *San Francisco Bay Guardian Online* (July 24, 2002) [http://www.sfbg.com/36/43/cover_lady1.html].
8. See http://www.ladyfest.org/index3.html.
9. See http://www.geocities.com/fingerbangdistro/listings.html.
10. Factors such as race, gender, class, education, language, geography, and ability privilege, play a complex role in this so-called "digital divide." The advantage of zines lies in the fact that zine makers who live in remote rural areas or in countries with less access to the Internet and education in the use of computers can create their own local networks of printed cut-and-paste zines and do not have

to rely on computers and the Internet to transport and spread their messages. Besides, people (still!) enjoy the paper quality of zines tremendously. However, we as Western researchers, feminists, and zine makers, need to be mindful of our privileges and of those who are left out of the digital loop.

References

Armstrong, J. 2004. Web grrrls, guerrilla tactics: Young feminisms on the web. In *Web. Studies,* 2nd ed., ed. D. Gauntlett and R. Horsely, 92–102. London: Arnold.

Bail, K., ed. 1996. *DIY feminism.* Sydney: Allen and Unwin.

Baumgardner, J. and A. Richards. 2000. *Manifesta: Young women, feminism, and the future.* New York: Farrar, Straus and Giroux.

Bell, B. L.-A. 2002. Riding the third wave: Women-produced zines and feminisms. *Resources for Feminist Research/Documentation Sur La Recherche Feministe* 29 (3/4):187–198.

Buckingham, D. 2003. *Literacy, learning and contemporary culture.* Cambridge, UK: Polity Press.

Califia, P. 1997. *Sex changes: The politics of transgenderism.* San Francisco: Cleis Press.

Chideya, F. 1992. "Revolution girl-style." *Newsweek,* October 23, 84–86.

Duncombe, S. 1997. *Notes from underground: Zines and the politics of alternative culture.* London: Verso Press.

Echols, A. 1989. *Daring to be bad: Radical feminism in America 1967–1975.* Minneapolis: University of Minnesota Press.

France, K. 1993. "Grrrls at war." *Rolling Stone,* July 8, 24–26.

Garrison, E. K. 2000. U.S. feminism—grrrl style! Youth (sub)cultures and the technologies of the third wave. *Feminist studies* 26 (1):141–170.

Gottlieb, J. and G. Wald. 1994. Smells like teen spirit: Revolution and women in independent rock. In *Microphone fiends: Youth music and youth culture,* ed. A. Ross and T. Rose, 250–274. New York: Routledge.

Groß, M. 2006. Das Internet als Plattform politischer Interventionen: Ladyfeste im Netz. *kommunikation@gesellschaft* 7 (4). Available at http://www.soz.uni-frankfurt.de/K.G/B4_2006_Gross.pdf (Accessed May 22, 2007).

Harris, A. 1998. Is DIY DOA? Zines and the revolution, grrrl-style. In *Australian youth subcultures: On the margins and in the mainstream,* ed. R. White, 84–93. Hobart, Australia: National Clearinghouse for Youth Studies.

Harris, A. 2004. *Future girl: Young women in the twenty-first century.* London: Routledge.

Hernandez, D. and B. Rehman, eds. 2002. *Colonize this! Young women of color and today's feminism.* New York: Seal.

Heywood, L., ed. 2006. *The women's movement today: An encyclopedia of third wave feminism.* Westport, CT: Greenwood.

Heywood, L. and J. Drake. 1997. *Third wave agenda: Being feminist, doing feminism.* Minneapolis: University of Minnesota Press.

Japenga, A. 1992. Punk's girl groups are putting the self back in self-esteem. *New York Times,* November 15, 30.

Japenga, A. 1993. Grunge r us: Exploiting, co-opting and neutralizing the counterculture. *Los Angeles Times Magazine,* November 14, 5.

Juno, A., ed. 1996. *Angry women in rock,* Vol. 1. New York: Juno Books.

Karp, M. 1999. Herstory: Girl on girls. In *The BUST guide to the new girl order,* ed. M. Karp and D. Stoller, 303–311. New York: Penguin Books.

Kearney, M. C. 1997. The missing links: Riot grrrl, feminism, and lesbian culture. In *Sexing the groove: Popular music and gender,* ed. S. Whitely, 207–229. London: Routledge.

Kearney, M. C. 2003. Girls make movies. In *Youth cultures: Texts, images, and identities,* ed. K. Mallan and S. Pearce, 17–34. Westport, CT: Praeger.

Kearney, M. C. 2006. *Girls make media.* New York: Routledge.

Ladyfest. Available at http://www.ladyfest.org.

Ladyfest Bay Area, California. 2002. Available at http://ladyfestbayarea.org/2002.

Ladyfest Film Archive. Created by Red Chidgey. Available at http://www.geocities.com/fingerbangdistro/listings.html.

Ladyfest Liege, Belgium. 2003. Available at http://www.geocities.com/ladyfestliege/info.html.

Ladyfest Olympia, Washington. 2000. Available at http://www.ladyfest.org/index3.html.

Leblanc, L. 1999. *Pretty in punk. Girls' gender resistance in a boys' subculture.* New Brunswick, NJ: Rutgers University Press.

Leonard, M. 1997. Rebel girl you are the queen of my world: Feminism, subculture, and grrrl power. In *Sexing the groove: Popular music and gender,* ed. S. Whitely, 230–256. London: Routledge.

McDonnell, E. 1994. Queer punk meets womyn's music. *Ms.* November/December, 78–79.

Orr, C. M. 1997. Charting the currents of the third wave. *Hypatia* 12 (3):29–45.

Piano, D. 2002. Congregating women: Reading 3rd wave feminist practices in subcultural production. *Rhizomes.net.* Issue 4 (spring): Cyberfeminisms. Available at http://www.rhizomes.net/issue4/piano.html (Accessed August 4, 2004).

Raymond, J. 1979. *The transsexual empire: The making of a she-male.* London: Women's Press.

Schilt, K. 2003a. "A little too ironic": the appropriation and packing of Riot Grrrl politics by mainstream female musicians. *Popular Music and Society* 26 (1):5–16.

Schilt, K. 2003b. I'll resist with every inch and every breath: Girls and zine making as a form of resistance. *Youth & society* 35 (1):71–97.

Scott-Dixon, K. 1999. Ezines and feminist activism: Building a community. Women's studies and the Internet, *Resources for Feminist Research* 27 (1/2):127–132.

Walker, R., ed. 1995. *To be real: Telling the truth and changing the face of feminism.* New York: Anchor Books.

Zines

Bendita: A Latin women's initiative against violence towards women. Isabella Gargiulo, Geisa, and other uncredited authors. Published since 2000. (Brazil). Available at www.benditazine.com.br.

Bikini kill. Various Authors. Circa 1991. (United States).

Bloody mary. Emca Revoluce. Published since 2000. (Czech Republic).

Bunnies on strike. Bunnies on strike collective. Published since 1998. (The Netherlands). Available at http://bunniesonstrike.cjb.net.

Bust. Debbie Stoller and Laurie Henzel. Published since 1993. (United States). Available at www.bust.com.

Chop suey: Stuff from ZineCon '02 & beyond. Circa 2003. Paolo, ed. 2003. (Philippines).

Clit rocket. Veruska Outlaw. Published since 1999. (Italy).

Echo zine distro. Michelle Downer. Published since 2000. (United States). Available at www.geocities.com/echozinedistro.

Emancypunx. Yen and emancypunx collective. Published since circa 1997. (Poland). Available at www.geocities.com/CapitolHill/Lobby/8522/emanz.html.

The fence: A new place of power for bisexual women. Cheryl Dobinson. Published since 2002. (Canada). Available at www.thefence.ca.

geekgirl. RosieX. Since circa 1995. (Australia). Available at www.geekgirl.com.au.

good girl. Nikko Snyder. Published 2001–2004. (Canada). Available at www.goodgirl.ca.

Grrrl:rebel. Elise, Caroline, Michelle Azura, and Rizal. Published since 1997. (Malaysia).

Idea is matches. Clodagh. Circa 1998–2002. (Ireland).

It's not just boys fun. Elena Stoehr. Published since 1998. (Germany). Available at www.notjustboysfun.de.

Jawbreaker: Hard candy for kickass pinays. Claire and Paolo. Published since 2002. (Phillipines).

Jigsaw. Tobi Vail. Circa 1988–1995. (United States).

Ladybomb distro. By Riikka. Circa 2000–2002. (Finland).

Ladyfriend zine. Christa Donner. Published since 2001. (United States). Available at http://ladyfriend.homestead.com.

Moon rocket distribution. Moira. 2000–2006. (New Zealand). Available at www.moonrocket.co.nz.

OvaryAction. Val and Ingvild. Published since 2002. (Norway).

Persephone is pissed. Olivia. Circa 2001–2002. (United States).

Personality liberation front. Kylie Lewis. Published since 1996. (Australia).

PinkPunkies. Lil and PinkPunkies collective. Published since 2000. (Argentina). Available at http://pinkpunkies.8m.com.

Pretty ugly. Kelly Elizabeth and Pretty ugly collective. Published since 2002. (Australia). Available at www.pretty-ugly.com.

Queer ramblings. Sandra R. Garcia. Published since 2000. (United States). Available at www.queerramblings.com.

Riot grrrl. Riot Grrrl D.C. collective. Circa 1991. (United States).

Riot grrrl Europe. *Riot grrrl Europe collective.* Circa 2000–2006. (Europe). Available at www.geocities.com/riotgrrrleurope.

Riot grrrl international message board. Since 2004. Available at http://users.boardnation.com/~riotgrrrlInternationalmb.

Riot grrrl manifesto. Kathleen Hanna. 1992. (United States). Available at www.tribe8industry.com/grrrls/id5.html.

Riot grrrl world newsletter. Published since circa 2001. Available at www.geocities.com/riotgrrrlworld/.

Take back the news. Emily Brandt. Since 2002. (United States). Available at www.takebackthenews.net.

Trippers zine. Trent. Published since 1998. (Singapore).

Varla's passed out and *Fingerbang distro.* Red Chidgey. 2001–2005. (United Kingdom).

Woami zine. Shannon. Published since 2002. (Australia). Available at www.geocities.com/fieryrockbabe/woami_zine.html.

(r)Evolutionary Healing
Jamming with Culture and Shifting the Power

CARLY STASKO

Art tells gorgeous lies that come true.

Bey (2003, 40)

The strongest form of power may well be the ability to define social reality, to impose visions of the world.

Gal (1995, 178)

At age sixteen I made my first zine. I did it because it seemed fun, different and a little mischievous. It wasn't as if I sat down and said, "Hmmmm, seems like the representation of women in media is doing a real number on my self-confidence. I know! I'll recontextualize those images and affirm my personal world view in a zine!" That level of deconstruction would have to wait for later.

Stasko (2001, 275)

Introduction
Making Space for Possibilities

Before we get started, let's make this a safe space, right here and now, to consider specific ideas and values that are integral to our well-being and happiness but which are too often under- or misrepresented in mainstream media. I hope to engage with you intellectually, but also to connect on a human level. Sometimes it feels dangerous to be hopeful, to be angry, or to be creative, and yet we must create places for such expression in order to grow into ourselves and build the worlds we want. In this chapter I discuss the communities and spaces both created and reclaimed that have provided me with opportunities to feel safe in an unsafe world. I'd like to make the courageous statement that we are on the verge of some exciting social transformations, and I think that this will occur primarily because of the ways that individuals and communities are driven to connect and share with each other.

Creative Resistance

In the paragraphs to follow I will combine theoretical analysis and personal narrative to cast light on the role of creative resistance communities in projects of social transformation and healing. I will draw from philosophers, psychologists, cultural theorists as well as independent producers and community activists so as to draw connections between resistance, play, and healing. I will discuss such topics as the public realm, feminism, culture jamming, consumerism, as well as do-it-yourself (DIY) and indymedia culture in order to explore healing in all its shapes and forms, and show a variety of types of activism that can contribute to the empowerment of individuals and communities in the face of apathy, isolation, illness, and oppression.

This chapter unfolds into five parts. The first section investigates the context in which young women are becoming radicalized, while the second discusses the roles of play and resistance in DIY culture. In the third section I describe how I became involved with culture jamming and DIY community organizing and activism, while in the fourth section I will explore the broader applications of jamming, such as reclaiming public spaces, and grassroots education. In the fifth and final section I discuss and define (r)Evolutionary healing, and describe how I culture jammed cancer by shifting the metaphors of illness by adapting familiar DIY storytelling strategies for the purpose of healing.

Over the past ten years I have been engaged in the inspiring world of DIY culture: producing zines (low-budget, self-published, magazines), documentaries, street art, conscious hip-hop, grassroots media literacy initiatives, public space performances, and protests such as Reclaim the Streets. Most important, I have been involved with building a vibrant community both locally and globally that inspires, educates, and empowers me in ways I hadn't believed possible. So often power is framed as a destructive and desired commodity to be owned. "Girl Power" for example, is sold as a product that promises freedom and the ability to be one's self, as though such rights can be granted rather than claimed. In my journey as a feminist community artist, activist, and educator, I have discovered that empowerment comes from feeling connected with others in authentic ways, and from being able to define one's own identity beyond the products and narratives of mass consumer culture. In other words, I have learned not to buy girl power, but instead to grow my own.

The Healing Journey

Much of my work has focused on media literacy and media activism, and it has only been recently that I began to see how this work connects with healing. I was afraid to bring my interests about broad topics such as love, healing, and spirit to the forefront, yet they remained ever present in my work—dancing in the shadows. Over the past two years I have undergone some dramatic transformations which have emboldened me to seek out new connections, as well to ask myself difficult questions. When I first set out to write this essay I was twenty-seven-years old, and midway through cancer treatments for Hodgkin's lymphoma. My whole world had quickly turned upside down and healing became my primary goal. In spite of my best efforts, I often found myself wondering why I had gotten "sick" in the first place. Was it the pollution in the environment? The toxic spray paints, markers, and photocopy toner that were my creative tools as a culture jammer and zine publisher? Was it the tear gas I was exposed to while protesting the World Bank? Or was it the stress of trying to live up to the ideals I held so deeply? I desperately wanted answers so I could have some control over the disease and prevent it from reoccurring or hurting others. I spent a lot of time looking back on my life as an artist, activist, grassroots educator, and self-titled Imagitator (someone who agitates imagination), and I found myself questioning my worldviews, guiding philosophies, and chosen methods for social change. "Had my art and activism had any true effect?" I wondered. I felt angry and vulnerable. Ultimately, what helped me to heal, to face life-changing fears, and to endure months of brutal treatments along with the tsunami impact cancer had on my life emotionally, socially, physically, psychologically, and financially, was my creative and resistant spirit.

Defiant creativity has been the thread spiraling through my life, which has both held me together and transformed me during some of my most challenging times. This creative resistance has been saving my life. Every artist and activist who has inspired me along the way has helped me to thrive and survive. Regardless of what the cynics and critics might say, creative action does change the world. Creative communities are the fertile grounds from which sprout healing medicines, sources of empowerment, and many ideas and movements whose time has come. Sharing possibilities and fueling courage and connection are some of the ways that DIY communities forge change. This change is not always tangible or predictable, which is why it requires a certain degree of courage and optimism, but I strongly believe that such communities have always played a very important role in social and environmental healing and transformation.

Movements or Markets?: The Future Isn't What It Used to Be

To appreciate the dynamic ways that young feminists are organizing DIY subcultures of creative resistance, it is best to consider the sociopolitical forces that are leading young people to become radicalized in the first place. As I will briefly discuss, an examination of the current context reveals that young people are treated more as the next generation of choice-makers and brand-loyal consumers than future citizen leaders.

"The future isn't what it used to be." This is the catchy slogan of *Strategy Magazine*'s annual "Understanding Youth" conference on youth marketing. This Canadian marketing magazine is well of aware of the billions of dollars to be spent by young people, both now and in the future. They know that many companies and corporations depend on having a profitable influence on the tastes and spending patterns of today's youth (Quart 2003). In conferences like these, the new marketer's bible is a fourteen-country survey of over three thousand teens called "GenWorld: The New Generation of Global Youth" (Medeiros and Walker 2005). This study calls today's teens "Interactivist Gen" and describes the growing desire among youth to contribute to society, to make a positive difference in the world, and to "do the right thing" both locally and globally. Yet, marketers are only interested in youth civic engagement insofar as it can be packaged into a profitable marketing campaign, rather than a genuine youth movement. In response to the complex desires of "Interactivist Gen," marketers struggle to forge links between their products and social and environmental causes—often spending more money to promote their ethics than on the issues they profess to care about. For example, Nike represents itself as a promoter of feminism in their "If you let me play" campaign featuring young girls. This "cause marketing" is criticized because of the discrepancy between Nike's feminist civil rights pitch and the exploitive ways it treats its female workers in developing countries. It has become clear to many young feminists that companies that market feminism and civil rights do not want to empower women, but only care about them when they already have power—the power to spend.

Trevor Norris, a philosopher of education who has been tracking the encroachment of school commercialism in Canada, argues that consumerism is "our new ideology, the paradigm of post-modernity." He frames it as a process which is "corrosive of political life," by which "the human being is dehumanized and depoliticized." In this brave new world, "rights" are replaced with "tastes," and young consumers find their power in their pocket books. Because of the discrepancy in spending power between private marketing institutions and public democratic or education projects, our hopes, fears, and dreams are most commonly voiced before the two-way mirror of a market researcher, while we experience a false democracy through the limited scope of our consumer "choices." As a result, consumerism has become "our primary language" such that "the act of consumption [has become] our primary mode of insertion into the world and experience of participation in something beyond ourselves" (Norris 2005a).

Me, Inc. and Rebranding the Public

While the structures and supports once offered by governments and communities are increasingly replaced by privatized "services," young people are taught to see themselves as "individual consumers" rather than as a "public citizenry." Feminist scholars Michelle Fine and Lois Weis argue that "the public sphere, the State-sponsored safety net (always frayed and inadequate), has rapidly been dismantled" such that those not privileged with power and wealth are "tossed from our collective moral community" (2000, 1139). Formerly public institutions such as hospitals, schools, and social services are being reshaped by a vision of the world in which individualism, entrepreneurship, efficiency, and free markets are the highest goods, while the social safety net and labor and environmental laws are framed as an infringement on the "liberating" forces of capitalism (Klein 2000).

For young people today, the precarious work force devoid of security, health plans, and union protection has been repackaged as the "Me, Inc." economy, where we are the creators of our own destiny—"free agents in an economy of free agents" (Peters 1997, 83). In the absence of a healthy social system, this career path is not sustainable for everyone, and it is too often women and low-income families who end up left out and made invisible (Fine and Weis 2000). Not everyone wants to be "Me, Inc.," especially when being your own boss means that you are on your own, with no safety net.

Although many young women are inspired by DIY culture, they are aware of the difference between choosing to do-it-yourself and having no other option (Figure 9.1). I became all too aware of this discrepancy when as a cancer patient I found out that the life-saving cancer drugs I needed were not covered by my public health care system. As a Canadian I believed in public health care, and I was shocked to discover that the only way I could survive would be if I was sponsored by a drug company to pay for the medicine I needed. I also found out that some of the chemotherapy drugs I was taking could jeopardize my reproductive health, but the costly treatments that could protect my fertility were also not covered by the public health care system. My reproductive health was seen as nonessential in the eyes of my government. As a young woman, the message was clear: I could have all the "girl power" I wanted, as long as I was willing to be sponsored by corporations or to pay tens of thousands of dollars for it. Thus, this reveals how seemingly powerless we're becoming as citizens: that while our opportunities as consumers are ever-growing, some of our most important needs are being transformed from rights to choices—and ironically, we have little choice about it.

Creative Resistance: The Power to Change

Today's youth are sold a narrative of individual power that is granted through choice while at the same time their ability to challenge the true powers of this world has become increasingly limited. Branded images of products and politicians are ever present in the mediasphere, as marketers seek to access public mindshare. Yet the CEOs and politicians behind these constructed and often contradictory images and messages have become dangerously inaccessible

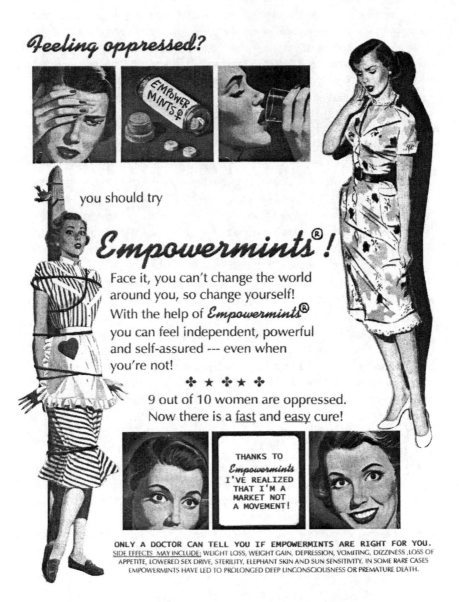

Figure 9.1 Carly Stasko, "Empowermints" from *This Magazine*, 2001. With permission.

Warning: For best results don't buy *girl power*.

Grow your own!

Figure 9.2 Carly Stasko, "Don't Buy Girl Power" from *Uncool Zine*, 2000. With permission.

(Klein 2000). Most of the world's largest decision makers are unelected conglomerates and banks who meet with elected leaders behind closed doors to design the global economic framework for the future. When members of the public protest because they are denied participation from such meetings, they are regularly met with tear gas, riot police, or worse. In such a context, many young people feel especially angered as they see that the kind of power and choice they are constantly sold has nothing to do with democracy.

How are young people able to get their voices heard beyond voting with their dollars? Increasingly, they are discovering their own powers as producers, turning their media-saturated childhoods into media literate action (Figure 9.2). Growing up immersed in consumer culture, many young people have shifted their relationship with commercial culture and have learned to deconstruct the commercial messages that dominate their environment as they explore new ways to coopt and subvert such messages to express new alternatives. A mix of emerging technologies and timeless creativity has led today's youth to connect globally and learn from each other in ways that were previously unimaginable. This kind of engagement is playful and draws its power from anger, inspiration, and critical thinking, rather than disposable incomes and "coopted" cool.

Defining DIY: "DIY 101"

If DIY 101 was a course (and often it is), it could likely be taught in a free school or the basement of a feminist bookstore. There wouldn't be just one teacher; instead people would be sharing skills, resources and, most important, being creative and making things happen. At the roots of DIY culture is the simple act of doing things independently in creative ways so as to compensate for a lack of finances, infrastructure, professional training, and often permission. DIY culture nurtures communities where people share skills, ideas, and creative expression, thereby fueling connectivity. It has been described by zinester Liz Worth as "an ever-expanding movement rooted in anti-consumerist ideals" that "gives people possibilities," and is "a way for them to take a political stance, start up a scene or accomplish something on their own terms"(Worth 2006, C1). Many people who seek to raise awareness about social and/or environmental injustices turn to DIY techniques such as zines, blogs, stencils, street performance, and hacking to get their message out. They don't own their own media conglomerates or have access to powerful politicians, CEOs, and decision makers, so they try to make up for their deficit with an abundance of innovation and hard work. DIY reflects "a certain feminist generations' (or scenes) vocabulary—one that values actions and collective creativity as a challenge to an advanced capitalist, imperialist dominant culture that would cast us all as passive isolated consumers" (Hoffman 2006, 88).

The spirit of DIY stands in resistance to the popular notion that this is just the way things are, and that we might as well get used to it because it can't be changed. In the book *We Don't Need Another Wave: Dispatches from the Next Generation of Feminists*, Jennifer Pozner calls us to action when she says "Don't like the media? Be the media. Do your own reporting on Indymedia.org web sites, make your own films with www.PaperTiger.org or DykeTV.org, and host your own college, community or cable access TV or radio show" (2006, 301). Similar to the punk-inspired Riot Grrrl movement of the early 90s, young women are moving forward and creating their own music, their own scene, and their own meaning (Gottlieb and Wald 1994, 255). They aren't waiting to be deemed experts or professionals by outside sources, but are making culture that resonates with them using the tools they have available. At age nineteen, having never made a film, I was given a super-8 camera and some film by feminist scholar and artist, Allyson Mitchell, who coorganized an event featuring first-time filmmakers. It was very empowering to be told that anyone could make a short film regardless of training. I had previously felt held back by the cost of equipment, but the DIY *ethos* of beg, borrow, or improvise refuses to let the lack of resources be a road block to creative expression.

Play Is the Way: Learning, Healing, Adapting

> Play makes us flexible. By reinterpreting reality and begetting novelty, we keep from becoming rigid. Play enables us to rearrange our capacities and our very identity so that they can be used in unforeseen ways. (Nachmanovitch 1990, 43)

Play is a key element of DIY culture and creative resistance. With enough courage we can channel our anger, fear, and pain into something as brave as play. In his book *Playing the Future,* Douglas Rushkoff (1999) provides many examples of how today's youth are responding in creative and adaptive ways to radical shifts in our chaotic society brought on by technology, globalization, and mass culture. From video games to skate boarding and surfing, Rushkoff mines youth culture for metaphors that can be guides for engaging with chaos. What is it that kids do so well that allows them to thrive and adapt in changing environments? It's what they do most naturally: play. Rushkoff describes play as "an adaptive strategy for the coming millennium" and he argues that young people are "less in danger of becoming obsolete [because] they are our evolutionary future" (1999, 7).

Rushkoff is not alone in his reverence for play as an evolutionary force. In *The Ecology of Imagination in Childhood*, Edith Cobb argues that the imagination, wonder, and the desire to make sense of the relationship between the self and world are what drive children to play, and that this instinct is rooted in survival of the species (1977). Cobb suggests that is it only through "creating and recreating perceptual worlds in a continuous interaction or communication between the bodily self and the environment that we achieve and maintain an identity of our own and are at home within our own uniqueness" (66). Much of DIY culture is organized around this very principle of creating new subcultures and cutting and pasting elements of the cultural or physical environment so as to weave a new story of self and world.

Adventures of a Teenage Media Tigress

Throughout Rushkoff's examination of play, the notion of "youth" is limited to young men, and in a glaring oversight he barely mentions the ways young women have been engaging in the same activities and evolving their own forms of adaptive play. The same terrain that Rushkoff has omitted to map—the spaces that young women have been occupying as they find new ways of connecting, engaging in, and redefining social action—is where I've been living for the past decade. I will begin to address Rushkoff's oversights by describing in more detail my own experiences of playful resistance and creative (r)Evolution, including zine publishing, culture jamming, guerilla theatre, Reclaim the Streets, alternative education, skill sharing free-schools, rave culture, as well as environmental and prodemocracy global activism. As you will see, throughout this journey I have enlisted the creative spirit of DIY culture to change how I relate with myself and the world.

Cut 'n' Paste (r)Evolution

My relationship with media first began to shift at age sixteen, when I started to cut up fashion magazines and create my own collages. Upon my request, a relative had gifted me with a subscription to *Seventeen* magazine, a teen fashion magazine that consisted mostly of ads and advice columns (i.e., advertising in disguise). In a form of trance I would consume the images with a sense of curiosity and urgency, as though my teen survival depended on it. Once I'd finished devouring the magazine I tended to feel dissatisfied with my body, clothes, lifestyle, and gender. The images and messages in the magazine reinforced my insecurities and introduced many new ones! The world of fashion magazines was (and still is) populated by very skinny, airbrushed, mostly White women, with no body hair, endless wardrobes, who are often surrounded by men approving of their beauty. Tampon ads would feature a woman from waist to knees, wearing white pants, showing no arms, face, or feet. All that was shown was the contentious area where a woman might stain her clothes if her pad leaked. Many of these ads would suggest that it was embarrassing if anyone found out I had my period and reinforced the idea that menstruation was dirty, unclean, and smelly. These were NOT the kinds of messages I needed as I entered womanhood. They filled me with shame, insecurity, and fear.

Everything changed the day I took out my scissors and glue and started cutting up my teen fashion magazines. I created a collage of a monster made up from bits and pieces of different models. Instead of looking beautiful, this Frankenstein-like model exposed what I believed to be the ugly underbelly of the modeling industry: eating disorders, dangerous plastic surgery, and self-loathing. Next I started to cut up a box of maxi-pads, changing the logo from "Always" to "Go away," with a slogan that read "Tell Manipulative Media to Go Away!" That is when the power first started to shift. I felt like I was revealing something. I showed it to friends who would laugh, nodding their heads in approval. Through this new kind of storytelling we were empowering ourselves.

I realized that in the eyes of many youth marketers, my fears and insecurities were good for business, that marketing was in fact an "Insecurity Industry"—and the product was me. Fashion magazines provoked self-loathing and then dished me up to their advertisers as a desired demographic, seemingly easy to manipulate. This inspired me to start making more collages. I covered the walls of my bedroom in cut and paste creations. These were very personal because they attempted to piece together the few empowering voices and images I could find in the media. Then I got the courage to take my other collages, the ones that expressed my anger, critique, and awareness, and began to publish them in a zine called "Quit Gawking" with some friends. Soon I began to create my own zine called "Uncool," which consisted of collages, rants, "Madvertisements," and other parodies of consumer culture. Inspired in part by the budding zine culture in the 1990s that came out of the Riot Grrrl scene, many young women have since found fun and empowerment in the act of writing and publishing their own work both in print and online. Isabella Gargiulo, a zinester from Brazil says that zines "give voice to marginalized groups whose voices (and lives) have never been considered by mainstream society in general. Zine making is a way to exist, really" (2001).

Creating Community

One publishes to find comrades!

Andre Breton

My approach to zine distribution was hopeful and chaotic. I rarely charged a fee for the zine, as I was very creative in finding avenues for free photocopying. My primary goal was to express myself and possibly forge social connections. Initially I would give my zine to friends, and if I knew that someone would be traveling I would give them a whole pile, and ask them to drop them like seeds during the course of their trip. I would leave my zine in bookstores in a technique referred to as "drop-lifting" (the opposite of shoplifting), which involves leaving creative artifacts in stores in the hopes that someone will serendipitously stumble across them and feel curious. I'd also drop my zine in cafes, at concerts, and on the subway. My backpack was always filled with zines or little stickers that I'd made. I would sometimes offer my zine to strangers with a sales pitch, adopting the tone of an advertiser, "Here is a zine, specially designed for you! It's free! It's fun! It's mind-altering! Enjoy!" I appreciated how the zine gave me a chance to engage with people beyond the normal social scripts previously available to me.

I was first introduced to "zine festivals" by some fellow zinesters who invited me to share their booth at a festival. The gathering was organized by *Broken Pencil Magazine,* which published zine reviews, ordering information, as well as articles about self-publishing and DIY culture. I started to go to zine festivals regularly. We would set up booths and sell or trade our zines with each other. It was at this stage that I really started to feel as though I was part of a community of creative people who were activated to express themselves and by-pass the advertising and money-oriented side of publishing.

Make Your Own Zine

Soon I would start bringing these zines into classrooms and smaller communities where I presented workshops titled "How to make your own zine." I've had a chance to work with a diverse community of producers, ranging from ten-year-old girls to middle-aged teachers, pregnant women living in the streets and teenage girls with eating disorders. I've come to believe that everyone has a zine in them once they've tapped into their unique truth.

During my zine workshops I like to bring in copies of my zine as well as many sample zines to share, such as "Heavy Girl Press," a zine dedicated to "celebrating the fat female experience in pop culture," promising to be filled with "exciting information" and to "be feminist in a post-preachy way" (Banks 2004). I also bring in zines by the "Blood Sisters" from Montreal, about the "serious health, environmental and psychological ramifications of the toxic feminine hygiene industry" (under "When the Private Becomes Public"), as well as copies of "Infiltration," a zine about urban exploration (infiltration. org). Other zine topics include student activism, do-it-yourself gynecology, environmental issues, abuse survivors, racism, globalization, alternative models of masculinity, and public space. In the past nine years I've traveled across North America with a small suitcase filled with a mini-zine library, showcasing the broad range of experiences and insights Indy-authors have to share. So what's your zine like? Or what will it be like? There's no time like the present so grab whatever creative tools you have available and starting playing around.

Finding and Founding the Media Collective

> Where extreme dogmatism often leads to activist paralysis, in the Media Collective, extreme activity is coupled with a striking absence of ideological fanaticism. (Klein 1997, A15)

One evening, during my last year of high school, while dropping off zines at a local café I was invited to participate in a "happening" that was going on upstairs. As I entered it felt like I was walking into a dream. There was live music, tasty food, film projections, strange inventions, collective painting on a communal canvas, and people reading aloud from journals and books. I knew then that I had stumbled across something quite fantastic. There was a sense that we could create all the fun and culture we needed ourselves. For the first time I felt like I'd found a community where I could create, share, and thrive with people who wanted to do more—and be more—than just consumers. It was through this community that I became involved with cofounding the Toronto Media Collective, a loose-knit network of artist, activists, hackers, and culture jammers, who would meet monthly to share ideas and resources. Membership was open, and there was no central mission statement or decision-making strategy. Each month some regulars would return while new people and ideas would arrive. We rarely, if ever, acted officially as a group. The monthly meetings were a place for people to share their thoughts and ideas for projects, as well as resources and assistance. One flyer listed the following topics as potential themes to be explored: "art, graffiti, zines, video, micro-power broadcasting, radio, performance art, food, street theatre, cartoons, fasting, civil-disobedience, newspapers, music, hacking, phreaking, luddism, the web, television, pirate-radio, writing, video-conferencing, elite-crashing, talking, loving, partying, reading, reporting, ranting, protesting, analysis, conferences and revolution." Naomi Klein described it as an organization where "barriers were dissolved between activism, media, and art all infused with a sense of play and creativity virtually extinct on the left" (Klein 1997, A15).

One group of women who attended meetings called themselves the "Bitch Brigade," and they would ride around town on their bikes lighting small fires inside the newspaper boxes of the *Toronto Sun*, which publishes a demeaning feature called the "Sunshine Girl" alongside right-wing editorials and sports "reporting." I felt empowered as a woman because I was able to take on a natural leadership role within the group and have my voice and opinion heard in the many debates we had. I was regularly engaging with women and men who taught me how to think critically about the representation of gender, race, and class in the mass media. From these discussions, people's zines and through our various projects, I was exposed to new ideas about feminism, social and environmental justice, and globalization. I also learned many skills through a free school we set up, structured around small learning cells directed voluntarily by members. I learned about topics such as Web design, bill-board/mountain climbing, silk-screening, bicycle repair, puppet making, and press release writing, to name just a few. Although there was no official membership or group mandate, I had found a community. The very act of meeting monthly led many of us to work and play together in ways we wouldn't have otherwise.

Culture Jamming

Soon after connecting with such a lively community, I started to take my collages and commentaries beyond the realm of my zine and began pasting, sticking, painting, and performing them around my city. I saw it as a way of reclaiming public spaces in my immediate environment, which was becoming increasingly privatized and plastered with commercial messages to the point where the "concentration of media ownership had successfully devalued the right to free speech by severing it from the right to be heard" (Klein 2000, 280).

At that time, I had been helping some friends to plan a "billboard liberation," a form of culture jamming that involves climbing up a billboard so that the original message can be altered with paint, stickers, or banners, such that the underlying message or intent of the ad becomes explicit (Figure 9.3).

The motto for our group was "Don't Get Caught," so we planned out each action carefully. In this case it was an ad for Target cigarettes located within the sight line of a public high school. Several people dressed in uniforms so that they appeared to be employees of the billboard company and began to attach a large banner to the top of the billboard. Once they had descended from the billboard, ropes were pulled and a banner unfurled to reveal new slogans for Target cigarettes, "The Target is Children" and "No

Figure 9.3 Top: Jammed gas pump on right, jammer at work in background left. "Oil Habit Suicide," 2006. Bottom: Jammed bus shelter ad, "More money is spent on marketing than on education," 2006.

More Death Ads." Footage of the "subvertising" action ran on the news later that night. While no permanent damage was done to the private property of the billboard company, more serious damage occurred to the message the advertisers were projecting into the public sphere. We had jammed their mind-share, and this was more valuable to them than any physical object such as a billboard.

Inspired by the French Situationists in the 1960s, culture jammers try to challenge, subvert, and reclaim mind-share and public space by playing with the symbols and slogans used by marketers. I frequently enjoyed jamming bus stop advertising throughout the city by writing speech bubbles coming from the mouths of anorexic looking models, that read "FEED ME." I was also inspired by a group called "Pretty, Porky and Pissed-Off" who posted stickers that read "Be a Revolutionary and Love Your Body." Through my involvement with the Media Collective I was able to work with unions, environmental NGOs, and poverty activists. However, it was culture jamming that kept me playful and optimistic, and ultimately fuelled my involvement with more traditional forms of activism. Through culture jamming I was able to express my own resistance and critical awareness so that as I traveled through my environment I could feel authentically engaged and empowered.

Spreading the Jam

The verb "to jam" has three meanings that help illustrate the distinctive elements of culture jamming. The first meaning of "jam" is to create in a spontaneous and improvizational way, as a jazz musician might jam. The culture jammer must improvise as they work within the restrictions of a preexisting situation: a billboard, an idea, or a physical space. Jamming also means to disrupt, to "jam the machinery." The culture jammer disrupts dominance and power by subverting meaning or reclaiming space. The third interpretation of jam refers to the production of a sweet preserve that can be spread on crackers or toast. In this third meaning, the culture jammer is involved with the preservation or even "cultivation of sweet things" (Norris 2005b, 22), such that new meaning and new culture is created. Thus, through improvization and disruption something new can be created and shared.

As I continue culture jamming I've come to see it as more than just subvertizing, but as a whole way of approaching creative resistance in the broadest sense. I've learned that I can jam in other ways; that my work needn't be limited to engaging with mass media. For example, I became involved with guerilla gardening: a form of "graffiti with nature" (Stasko 2002, 14). I sprout sunflowers and then, with friends, plant them in forgotten urban lots and wastelands throughout the downtown core. The planting process often becomes a spontaneous discussion with passers-by about topics ranging from urban planning to bioengineering and seed patenting.

Reclaiming the Streets: Rave Meets Activism

> Reclaim the Streeters have transposed the language and tactics of radical ecology into the urban jungle, demanding uncommercialized space in the city as well as natural wilderness in the country or on the seas. (Klein 2000, 313)

I also became involved with organizing happenings that were part performance, part protest, and part community celebration. This was a direct extension of culture jamming, which centered on reclaiming privatized spaces for the purpose of public dissent. At one point there was a wave of new people joining the Media Collective who had developed their DIY community skills through the rave scene as organizers. Many of them were interested in throwing gatherings that not only celebrated life but also built communities, opened minds, and inspired people to take action for social or environmental justice. The first time I saw the beauty of this new marriage was in Reclaim the Streets (RTS). My friend Dave Meslin (Mez) inspired us to join together and organize Toronto's first RTS party, a global street party that was meant to fuse celebration with activism. The party was set to occur simultaneously in cities all over the world to coincide with closed-door talks organized by the World Trade Organization. One of the RTS flyers read "The Resistance Will Be as Transnational as Capital."

A variety of tactics were used, combining "utopian gestures with practical displays of resistance," representing the diversity of participants (McKay 1998, 27). Some people brought astro-turf and set up faux-picnic areas in the middle of the road. Children and adults alike drew messages and pictures with chalk on the street. I organized a small troop of coed radical cheerleaders. We made pom-poms using scrap fabric we had salvaged while dumpster-diving in the textile district. Distributing flyers with the lyrics for pro-democracy cheers, we performed throughout the party and rallied others to join in. Giant floats made from bike parts carried drummers, while people on stilts waved streamers through the afternoon air. Booths were set up with free zines, stickers, posters, and flyers which could help people get involved and become more aware about a wide range of issues that include globalization, poverty, smog, racism, and violence against women. People dressed in fairy wings danced with large puppets, and small performances went on simultaneously. One of the posters for the event invited people to imagine what they'd like to see and then to create it. As a result, I was surprised and engaged by what people had come up with.

Inspired to design for actions that reclaimed space, I began organizing early morning "subway parties," which tried to brighten people's day and help strangers to interact on public transit (Figure 9.4 and Figure 9.5). My belief was that people should be rewarded for not driving, and that since the subways needed more funding we would start by giving them more "fun," and

Figure 9.4 Culture jammed bus-shelter advertisement in Toronto's Dundas Square, "Advertising pollutes my mental environment," 2006. Photo: Carly Stasko.

Figure 9.5 Subway party organized by Carly Stasko with The Toronto Media Collective, 2004. Photo: Jackie Levitt.

hope that the "funding" would follow. Both the street parties and the subway parties carry at their core the seed of a new vision of how the world could be.

Spacing

The erosion of the public spaces and institutions is a societal shift that has triggered a great deal of DIY activism. In *Disappearing Acts: The State and Violence against Women in the Twentieth Century,* Fine and Weis describe this shift as the "retreat of the State from community life," such that public spaces for "communities and schools—for poor and working-class girls and women to come together, share stories, educate and organize" are evaporating (2000, 1141). They describe how "local library branches are shutting down; streets and parks seem increasingly unsafe or are locked" and "public gardens are being sold off." In this kind of environment, DIYers have learned the importance of creating spaces as well as reclaiming public spaces through street art, performance, and protest.

Creating "spaces" is deeply catalytic. Such spaces can be simultaneously physical, mental, emotional, and even spiritual. Once a space has been created for people to gather, to create, to express, and to transform, it is almost naturally filled and used for these purposes. Aspa Tzaras, a Toronto organizer of the anarcho-techno-hippy outdoor "OM Music Festival," describes the "struggle of temporality" faced by organizers "as restrictions to gather as an autonomous community become increasingly difficult." Yet she insists that "we continually manage to assemble in new and interesting ways, marveled by the rising thinkers who bring forth new knowledge to share" (2006). Although reclamations of public space and transcendence of the status quo are usually temporary, it reminds us that alternatives are possible. Allyson Mitchell explains that "Feminist geography embellishes the politics of identity by creating theoretical space for women to claim where they are, not just who they are; it has created the politics of place" (2001, 228).

Reclaiming the Classroom

Culture jamming, activism, and self-publishing opened up a whole new world for me, connecting me with a larger community as well as to my own strong voice. I have discovered that schools are another medium that I can reclaim. Eight years ago I founded the Youth Media Literacy Project, through which I visit high schools across North America and teach workshops on self-publishing, media literacy, globalization, and culture jamming. Instead of cringing at tampon ads, I discuss them openly during media literacy workshops. I ask the students to consider why such commercials tend to promote shame and secrecy. I show a commercial featuring a person dressed in a lab coat who is pouring blue liquid onto a menstrual pad while performing "pad experiments." "Why is the liquid blue?" I ask. There will be snickering and uncomfortable stirring in the class, until someone's hand shoots up. "Because if it were red, like blood, that would be gross!" Suppressed giggles travel in a wave across the class. "I think it would be gross," I answer, "if women had blue stuff coming out of them rather than blood." An explosion of laughter ensues, followed by an open discussion about how women's bodies and natural processes are seen as taboo and how marketers exploit women's fears and insecurities to sell their products. I've discovered that while these topics may at first cause some discomfort, if I model my own comfort with the subject as we take on the powerful role of media critics, soon the students become fully engaged and excited about the topic. When we've turned the tables and look critically at commercial messages rather than scrutinizing ourselves, a new sense of confidence emerges.

I begin my workshops with a discussion about how we relate to media. Participants are asked to complete the same sentence: "My relationship with media is … ." Some people describe this relationship as "very unhealthy," "dependent," or "abusive," while others describe it as "complicated," "in transition," or "engaging." Others admit that they haven't previously considered the nature of this relationship, that perhaps they took it for granted and never assumed it could be any other way. This is the first question we consider in the workshop: "Can these relationships be different?" I'm confident that the answer is "Yes! Of course anything is possible." In these instances play is the midwife of possibility, helping people to create healing and learning experiences. Psychologist Donald Winnicott describes the aim of psychological healing as "bringing the patient into a state of being able to play" (1977, 38). I've come to see my experiences as an artist and activist as a healing journey. At first I began to heal my relationship with the media in my environment, whether it was advertising, education, or public space itself.

But these were all just a warm up, a gradual preparation for dramatic new challenges that lay ahead. More recently, it has been my relationship with my own body that has been healing. What connects these seemingly different experiences is the role of play and creative resistance as tools for transformation and invention.

(r)Evolutionary Healing

Creative resistance is a process that can be envisioned as a spiraling wheel. The cycle begins with a challenge, something that has reached a crisis point and must be addressed. It could be an absence or silence in the mainstream narrative of history, education, or media. It could be a social, economic, or environmental injustice, an illness, an unsafe space, or the shrinking of public space.

The next phase of this cycle requires individuals and communities to muster up their courage. It takes courage to believe that we can make a difference, or that creativity, which is so often disregarded as trivial, can provide new solutions for resisting and transforming what is challenging us.

The third step isn't always obvious—it is to play. Playfulness is ever present in all the various forms of creative resistance I have participated in, from zine publishing, street art, and performance to education.

The final step in the cycle is Love, which takes the form of a new vision of the world and a new sense of purpose or place in that world. For example, this is demonstrated in culture jamming by increased media literacy and a stronger sense of belonging and participation in public space.

This transformational process is what I call (r)Evolutionary Healing (Figure 9.6). With each revolution around the wheel, we pass through Challenge, Courage, Play and then Love. Rather than traveling in a straight line or repetitive cycle, this (r)Evolution is a spiral—a process such that each time around we have the potential to move closer to the central goal of wellness and communion. Similarly with each wave of feminism, challenges both new and old are engaged. This model doesn't limit us to the metaphor of a linear path; the occurrence of new challenges do not signal a failure, but instead indicate that there are still further opportunities to transform, lessons to learn, and connections to forge.

Jamming Cancer

I'm a girl with a positive vision; I'm going to laugh myself into remission!

Carly Stasko, 2005, Princess Margaret Hospital, announced to friends and health workers the day after a cancer diagnosis

I wouldn't have seen my journey as a spiral if not for my own (r)Evolutionary experience with cancer. At first this event was so frightening—and traumatic—that I could not integrate it with my earlier experiences or even future possibilities. Even more, it was so new that it simply didn't occur to me that my acts of creative resistance—or rather, my approach to culture jamming—could help me through this terrible time. But slowly, and with a courageous and playful spirit, I began to formulate a new way of envisioning such challenges. The spiral healing journey is empowering because it allows me to see a bigger picture in which all the different challenges I have faced make sense as a process—challenges ranging from political resistance to fighting for my own life.

The diagnosis was Hodgkin's lymphoma, a form of cancer that often affects young people. It requires a brutal regime of chemotherapy and radiation, but fortunately has remarkably high recovery rates. I am now just emerging from an eighteen-month healing journey that called upon all my strengths and resources and the support of my community and family. Shortly after the diagnosis I was undergoing tests in the hospital, and through serendipity I happened upon a story in *Bust Magazine* about an independent artist and filmmaker named Miranda July. The article discussed her project "Learning to Love You More" (LTLYM). The project is described as both a "web site and series of non-Web presentations comprised of work made by the general pub-

Figure 9.6 Carly Stasko. "(r)Evolutionary Healing—The Spiral Journey: Challenge, Courage, Play, Love," 2007.

lic in response to assignments that are posted online" (July 2005, 27). July's philosophy was "just make something right now, really simply, with what you have. ... Whether that's a tape recorder, a video camera, or a pencil and paper, the main thing you need is you. Be present in the moment, make something, and that thing will be true forever."

Among the examples of assignments listed in July's brief interview, one particularly stuck out. It read, "Heal Yourself." That was the first time I imagined that healing myself could be a form of art or creative expression. And yet it made perfect sense! That night I raided the hospital supply room and used medical tape and scissors to make collages out of the magazines from the waiting room (Figure 9.7).

It was a very powerful night for me, as I snuck past the nurses' desk and countless beeping machines. Because I was creating I got to be myself again and not just a "patient." This time I gave all the models bald heads, as if they had recently received chemotherapy. As I played with the images I felt the familiar shifting of power. Instead of simply reacting in fear to what was happening I felt stronger. I no longer felt like a patient, I felt like an artist, integrating and adapting to the challenges of the medium.

This time the medium was me.

Upon hearing the news of my diagnosis a friend encouraged me to say that I "was already healed," and not to call myself "sick." Something about this resonated with me. Yet I wondered if I would be trying to define my own reality in too radical a way. How could I reconcile the gravity of the moment with a playful and creative outlook? And how could I do so when everyone I cared for looked so distraught, and I was surrounded by countless patients struggling with cancer? I wanted to say "I am already healed" as a form of affirmation rather than denial, and in the end I decided to follow my courageous instincts and try it. I explained to my friends and family that I wanted to claim my power to redefine the situation, that I would refer to myself as "already healed," and that the chemotherapy and radiation treatments and the unknown path ahead of me was all part of the "Dance of Life."

However, all of the metaphors available to me for describing the healing process relied on military imagery, such as "a war in my body," mechanistic imagery such as "broken parts," and capitalistic frameworks in which the body is a "consumer of health services." These dominant metaphors remove power from the individual and reduce the body to the site of civil war, a broken machine, or a passive consumer (Martin 2001). In the true spirit of DIY, I did my own research into the biological process occurring in my body and created new metaphors that were empowering. I began to visualize my immune system like a well-run and loving community, where everything is recycled and sustainable. I would not use the word "mine" to describe "the" cancer. It was just passing through. "It's not *my* cancer," I would respectfully interrupt family, friends—and even doctors! Eventually they all began to adopt this new

Figure 9.7 Carly Stasko, "Survive to Thrive," 2005. This collage was made while in the hospital, the day after being diagnosed with Hodgkin's lymphoma. It was made with magazines from the waiting room and materials borrowed from a medical supply closet.

paradigm too! I felt remarkably encouraged as I deconstructed the language about health and disease, using all of my creative abilities to jam the situation. On several occasions I even dressed up in various costumes as the white blood cells in my immune system and did theatrical dances to help me visualize what was happening in my body (Figure 9.8).

My friend dressed up as a "Friendorphine" (a healing endorphin brought on by friendship), and by boyfriend dressed up as "Love;" acting out the supporting characters in this great drama taking place inside my body. Talk about do-it-yourself media!

Figure 9.8 Carly Stasko, "Immune System Fairy," 2005. Dressed up as a white blood cell, midway through six months of chemotherapy treatments. One end of the broom punctures the membrane of cancer cells, while the other end sweeps up the mess for recycling. Wearing a light-reflective button on chest where tumor was shrinking. Photo: Sandy Plotnikoff.

Today, eighteen months later, the dance continues. My doctors have declared me cancer-free, with excellent prospects for continued health (YAY!). I have since learned that I was engaging in an ancient, often neglected, form of prayer in which we express gratitude for what we hope for as though it has already occurred. In doing this we form a clear vision of our hopes enacted, giving them the power to become reality. I am astounded by the power of visualization and creative expression to heal. Why is it that we don't feel more entitled to do this?

Why does it take so much courage to express hope? Too often we receive messages that discourage the imagination, and instead promise us power through choosing and buying. We are surrounded by images of fetishized products and bodies, which try to define our hopes *for* us. However, the power to create has always been ours; everyone can be the artist of their imagination.

Love: Hopes Enacted

The path to love is not arduous or hidden, but we must choose to take the first step. (hooks 2000, 147)

In her book *All About Love*, bell hooks discusses how the "transformative power of love is not fully embraced in our society because we often wrongly believe that torment and anguish are our 'natural' condition" (2000, 220). I believe that healing and play are our natural conditions. We learn how to do almost everything through play, including how to heal and transform in the face of challenges. I have come to see my life as a healing journey, one that travels around a spiral path. With each new challenge, I move through the steps of courage, play, and then love. This love is expressed as a new vision of the world, accompanied by a reinvigorated sense of calling to take action and live in action so that we feel empowered to heal the self and the world. I've begun to see how our bodies are like the planet and vice versa: all of the seemingly disparate parts must work together for the greater whole, and although there are many problems there is a strong spirit which can carry the injured parts until they heal.

Most recently, at the UNESCO World Urban Festival in Vancouver, British Columbia, I had the opportunity to present my new workshop on (r)Evolutionary Healing. I began, as I begin all my workshops, with a go-around, where we all finish the sentence "My relationship to media is … ." Following this I discussed the ways I had worked to heal my relationship with media through creativity, play, and activism. I then described the ways in which I used these same creative skills as I healed from cancer. We then did a second go-around where the sentence was slightly different: "My relationship to my body is … ." I was touched by how authentic and open people were with their answers. Following this I proposed that we do one final go-around in the workshop, which would enact the same mode of positive visualization I had used when saying "I'm already healed." This time the sentence would begin with "I healed myself and the planet by … ." I assured everyone that we would need all of our collective courage to say something so hopeful aloud. The sentence was passed from person to person and completed each time. By the end of the round there was a tenable feeling of possibility filling the space. We weren't naming our fears, enemies, or challenges. We were not talking about fighting. In that moment, we were imagining a better world, in a way that made it more possible.

Heal Yourself

I have shown that as culture jammers we have learned not only to jam with the environment in order to reclaim public space, but how to jam with our inner environments—right down to the possibilities we imagine, the metaphors we use, and the way we move in this world. We *are* our environment, and reclaiming, respecting, and engaging with the inner and outer environment is at the same time personal, public, and political. I've begun to see my exploration of media activism as a healing journey, one in which I engaged fully with my environment by using my imagination and creative energy to shift relationships and power. The spirit of empowerment is only possible when we have a strong community to engage with. I credit the feminists, educators, artists, and activists who developed strategies of organization and consciousness raising, and for creating a context where I could carry on in that work in my own playful way. And I also thank you, reader, in advance, for the ways that you will heal yourself and the planet.

Acknowledgments

Special Love and Gratitude to my parents Catherine and Robert, Trevor, and my wonderful healing community.

References

Banks, W. 2004. Heavy Girl Press reader. Review of Heavy Girl Press Zine, by Kerry Daniels-Zraidy. *Broken Pencil*, no. 18. http://www.brokenpencil.com/reviews/reviews.php?reviewid=2471 (Accessed April 12, 2006).

Bey, H. 2003. *T.A.Z.: The temporary autonomous zone, ontological anarchy, poetic terrorism,* 2nd ed. New York: Autonomedia.

Blood Sisters. When the private becomes public. *The Blood Sisters Project.* www.bloodsisters.org (Accessed April 12, 2006).

Breton, A. quoted by Bransyn, G. 1997. *Jamming the media: Reclaiming the tools of communication.* San Fransisco: Chronicle Books.

Cobb, E. 1977. *The ecology of imagination in childhood.* New York: Columbia University Press.

Fine, M. and Weis, L. 2000. Disappearing acts: The state and violence against women in the twentieth century. *Signs* 25 (4):1139–1147.

Gal, S. 1995. Language, gender, and power: An anthropological review. In *Gender articulated: Language and the socially constructed self,* ed. K. Hall and M. Bucholtz, 169–182. New York: Routledge.

Gargiulo, I. 2001. An interview with two zine editors: Isabella Gargiulo from Bendita (Sao Paolo, Brazil) and Amy Schroeder from Venus (Chicago, IL). *Grrrl Zine Network.* http://www.grrrlzines.net/interviews/bendita_venus.htm (Accessed April 12, 2006).

Gottlieb, J. and Wald, G. 1994. Smells like teen spirit: Riot Grrrls, revolution and women in independent rock. In *Microphone Fiends: Youth Music and Youth Culture,* ed. A. Ross and T. Ross, 250–274. New York: Routledge.

Hoffman, J. 2006. Making space for the movement DIY-lady style. In *We don't need another wave: Dispatches from the next generation of feminists*, ed. M. Berger, 84–96. Emeryville, CA: Seal Press.

hooks, b. 2000. *All about love: New visions*. New York: William Morrow.

July, M. 2005. The force of July, by C. O'Keefe Apowicz. *Bust Magazine*, December/January, 27–29.

Klein, N. 1997. Culture jammers come to collective agreement. *Toronto Star*, March 3, A15.

Klein, N. 2000. *No logo*. London: Harper Perennial.

Martin, E. 2001. *The woman in the body: A cultural analysis of reproduction*. Boston: Beacon Press.

McKay, G. 1998. DIY culture: Notes toward an intro. In *DIY culture: Party and protest in nineties Britain*, ed. George McKay. New York: Verso Press.

Medeiros, G. and C. Walker. 2005. GenWorld: The new generation of global youth. *Energy BBDO Report*. http://www.fresh-films.com/downloads/GenWorld_TeenStudy.pdf

Mitchell, A. 2001. The writing's on the wall: Feminist and lesbian grafiti as cultural production. In *Turbo Chicks: Talking Young Feminisms*, ed. L. Karaian, A. Mitchell, and L. Rundle, 221–230. Rotonto: Sumach Press.

Nachmanovitch, S. 1990. Free play: Improvisation in life and art. New York: Putnam.

Norris, T. 2005a. Consuming signs, consuming the polis: Hannah Arendt and Jean Baudrillard on consumer society and the eclipse of the real. *International Journal of Baudrillard Studies* 2 (2). http://www.ubishops.ca/BaudrillardStudies (Accessed September 14, 2006).

Norris, T. 2005b. Cultivating sweet things: An interview with culture jammer Carly Stasko. *Orbit: OISE/UT's Magazine for Schools* 35 (2):22–24.

Peters, T. 1997. The brand called you. *Fast Company* 10 (August):83–92.

Pozner, J. 2006. Reclaiming the media for a progressive feminist future. In We don't need another wave: Dispatches from the next generation of feminists, ed. M. Berger, 287–302. Emeryville, CA: Seal Press.

Quart, A. 2003. *Branded: The buying and selling of teenagers*. Cambridge: Perseus Books.

Rushkoff, D. 1999. *Playing the future: What we can learn from digital kids*. New York: Riverhead Books.

Stasko, C. 2001. Action Grrrls in the dream machine. In *Turbo chicks: Talking young feminisms*, ed. L. Karaian, L. Rundle and A. Mitchell, 273–284. Toronto: Sumach Press.

Stasko, C. 2002. Guerilla gardening: Reclaiming cities. *The Utne Reader*, March/April, 14–15.

Tzaras, A. 2006. Interview by author. Toronto, Canada, February 27.

Winnicott, D. 1977. *Playing and reality*. London: Tavistock Publications.

Worth, L. 2006. Just do it—yourself. *Toronto Star*, August 15, C1.

10
Feminism, Youth Politics, and Generational Change

CHILLA BULBECK AND ANITA HARRIS

Introduction

As in other Western capitalist democracies, there is considerable anguish on the left, or at least the "old" left, concerning the apparently unstoppable march of economic rationalism through the public institutions, such as universities and government, and its connection to the decline in political participation among Western citizens. Young people are sometimes depicted as central to this problem of waning social movements and political activism. More specifically, young women are often blamed for the decline in women's movement activism, being accused of a more commercialized and individualized commitment to securing their own personal goals. During the 1990s, the generational cat-fight between feminists became a favourite media handle for discussing feminism, expressed in popular books as well as academic fora.

This chapter is organized in terms of this claim concerning the younger generation's political apathy, particularly as it relates to young women and feminism, but in the hope of interrupting, or at least re-interpreting, some of its general lineaments. As an older feminist academic (not quite old enough to be a women's liberationist) and a younger feminist (not quite young enough to be girl powered) who have been engaging in analysis of both the generation debate and what "feminist politics" and youth politics might now mean, we decided to write a paper in conversation with each other. Bulbeck's research is based on a survey of young South Australians, with follow-up interviews of some of the sample. Harris's research is based on young women's production of zines and other cultural forms, such as comics, art, and music, as well as their involvement in various Internet sites. Following the presentation of our research findings, we engage in a conversation concerning why we think we agree and disagree with the analysis provided by the other author. We discuss why we have "found" different things concerning young women's political activism in our research, exploring the impact of our "politics of location," our data sources, and our own theoretical frameworks and thus interpretations of our two data sets. The chapter provides a contribution to the debate concerning young people and their political involvements and debates concerning data, methods, and theories in the production of social understandings of the world.

Young Torch Bearers of Feminism

Can women "Take Back the Night" without leaving their homes? (Millar 1998, 170)

Lynn Segal (1999, 2), a British academic feminist, complains of a "declining passion for politics evident in many veteran feminists, accompanying the frank rejection of feminism by many young women" and an "exhaustion of utopian energies" since the 1980s. In academic feminism, sociology, education, psychology, and criminology, young women are represented as failing feminism, either as overachievers—delaying childbirth in favor of careers, outperforming boys in school, becoming avid consumers—or as risk-takers—girl gangs, teenage mothers, drug offenders, mental health problems: "acting like boys" (Harris 2004). Thus, some older feminists blame young women for the decline in women's movement activism, commencing in Australia with Anne Summers' "Letter to the Next Generation," published in 1993. In the 1990s, the media caricatured older feminists as criticizing younger women for their failure to be grateful for what had been achieved, their refusal to be involved in political action to maintain the movement, and their involvement in a self-interested "entitlement feminism" (Skeggs 1995, 478), in a commodified feminism rather than collective political action (Kaplan 1997).

For their part, some younger feminists like Naomi Wolf and Rene Denfeld in the United States claim that second-wave feminists are victim feminists. Victim feminism focuses on sexual oppression in heterosexual relations, on constructing women as helpless victims of masculinity or male oppression. According to this new feminism, young feminists have a more individualized feminist politics in which gender is not a central aspect of their political identity: "I *am* a feminist *but* that is not all I am" (Rice and Swift 1995, 195). Kathy Bail has coined the term DIY feminism in which young women do not define themselves by their gender, their "group identification," but by their "individual practice," their "personal challenges," and by their passions like publishing fanzines or ezines (Bail 1996, 6).

Others note that young women have absorbed feminism into their day-to-day lives, such that it might be characterized as "everyday feminism." For example, Shelley Budgeon (2001) concludes that, although the young British women in her study do not call themselves feminists, they use feminist concepts and politics in their identity work and notice and name as such the gender inequality they perceive in their surroundings. O'Brien's (1999) Australian research also finds evidence of an everyday feminism among young women who are not involved in conventional activism. She argues that feminism operates for them in the "micropolitics" of everyday life, for example, in creating supportive cultural spaces and in articulating critiques of inequity.

Ballington (2001, 13) suggests that young people have new issues that extend beyond national boundaries, such as environmental and anti-land mine campaigns, anti-globalisation campaigns and pushing for debt relief in poor nations." Nineteen- to twenty-four-year-olds in Britain are disaffected from nation and neighbourhood, although concerned about the environment, AIDS "and above all animals" (Wilkinson and Mulgan 1995, 16, 96, 106). Other research demonstrates young people's abiding interest in transnational social and political issues, such as equality and human rights, racism, migrant and refugee issues, cultural diversity, and employment and education (see Beresford and Phillips 1997; Cope and Kalantzis 1998; Aveling 2001; Vromen 2003; Bulbeck 2004; Ellis 2004). In the Australian context, the International Association for the Evaluation of Educational Achievement (IEA) Civic Education Study of 3,331 fourteen-year-olds found that 80 percent of respondents believe in participation in activities to benefit people in the community, three-quarters are committed to participation in the protection of the environment and two-thirds support the importance of promoting human rights (Mellor, Kennedy, and Greenwood 2001, xix). In their extensive review of international and Australian literature on youth participation, Elton Consulting (2003, 23) conclude that young people cannot be characterized as disengaged simply just because they do not tend to identify with political parties and feel alienated from formal political processes. They argue instead that young people are:

> highly politically aware, have high levels of interest in political issues and ... are very supportive of democracy. However, they feel unrepresented by major political parties, hence the lack of interest in joining them or voting for them, and have instead opted for new forms of organisation and political participation.

This optimistic scenario suggests that young people are engaged in an array of new forms and media, making a new kind of politics that their parents do not recognize, but which is appropriate for the globalized digitized world of the twenty-first century. This new politics is said to focus more on issues of meaning and culture than resources and power; is more likely to be local or global rather than national or oriented towards state or federal governments; and it is more likely to rely on virtual communities on the Internet than meetings and rallies.

According to Jacqueline Zita (1997, 6) the personal combines with the media of expression to constitute also the particular:

> Third wave anthologies, zines, cyberspace communities, and other modes of cultural and media production constitute a level of discourse reflective

of local practices and personal/anecdotal narratives of experience. This is a genealogical cauldron common to the creation of new feminisms.

Anita Harris (2001b, 129, 131) finds contrary evidence for the complaint that young women are interested only in individual lifestyle decisions, are "choice biographers," or are leading lives of risk and antisocial behaviors creating disengagement from citizenship. She talked to women who were moving into the underground spaces of the Internet. Kristy says "we don't always need a movement to express our politics. I think we can all start our own revolutions from our bedrooms" (Harris 2001b, 132). Women retreat from the public media space where their issues are trivialized and marginalized, or from appropriation of their ideas by Sony or Nike, creating underground magazines, alternative music spheres and "gURL" Web pages or electronic zines (Harris 2001b, 133). Many young women claim that anyone can "make a difference" by putting out a record or magazine, putting up a poster (Harris 2001b, 135; Driscoll 1999, 184).

However, there is not a great deal of statistical evidence that a large proportion of young people are plugged into political activism on the Net (for example, see Hochschild 2001, 62 and Bentley and Oakley 1999, 58, 68). In the Australian context Vromen (2004, 1) writes that "there clearly exists a 'digital divide' amongst 18–34 year old Australians, which is delineated on demographic characteristics of geography, education level, income level and occupational classification." It is problematic to ascribe agency to publishing ezines or playing in all-girl bands, especially when constructed as a measure of resistance, because those women with less access to cultural modes of production will seem less independent, less individual, less resistant (Driscoll 1999, 188) than those with Web sites, books, ezines. Thus, it may largely be those with cultural and intellectual capital who can express virtual capital, rather than those perhaps most disenfranchised from the social and political spheres. There is certainly evidence of class as well as generational differences in political involvement, as Bulbeck found for South Australians' political engagements.

The Findings: Bulbeck

Between 2000 and 2002, as part of a large Australian Research Council funded project, questionnaires were distributed to eleven schools, a social sciences university class, and one youth service in Adelaide, the main city of South Australia. The schools range from single-sex, exclusive private schools to public (government-funded) schools in working-class suburbs. The students were either in their penultimate or final year (year 11 or year 12) of school. The clients of the youth service left high school before completing their high school certificate. The school students were asked to take home a similar questionnaire for their parents to complete. There were about 320 school students in the sample (two-thirds of them female), about 110 parents (three-quarters female),

40 university students (three-quarters female), and 40 youth service clients (half female), a total sample of about 300 female respondents, whose views are discussed in this chapter. Respondents were asked about their attitudes to feminism and the women's movement as well as their own political engagements. Those students who agreed to be interviewed were asked what they understood by "politics" and quizzed concerning their own political engagements.

About 85 percent of young women and 65 percent of young men said the women's movement had achieved good things for Australian women, although only one-third of young women and one-sixth of the young men called themselves feminist. Over half the young women found feminism personally relevant, and almost a half said feminists shared their values. However, although there was general endorsement of feminism as an "ideal," many young women distanced themselves from the movement in various ways, for example as something that belonged to the past and was no longer relevant to their generation or as something that was too radical and homogeneous for them as individuals:

> Feminism is not particularly relevant to me at the moment because the worst that can happen is someone will say something sexist to me, but when I start working etc.[,] different wages etc. will affect me (female, Protestant girls school, 100111357)

On the other hand, Charmaine tries:

> [Feminism is important] to get women to stick up for themselves and stuff. And I was telling everybody about Women's Studies last year and how good it was and telling everyone to do it and whatever 'cos you learn heaps (Charmaine, open access college, 100131481).

In her interview, another student, Kate, explained generational changes in women's movement activism:

> No, I don't think it's finished or achieved its purpose—well like, it's achieved a lot. But I think it's still strong. Like, I think every woman now has enough power to enforce feminism or encourage it—whatever. And so, it doesn't need to be a movement any more. Like, you know, a group of women burning their bras. It's alive in every woman sort of thing. And it's more accepted. (Kate B., coeducational Protestant school, 100121423)

Kate goes on to suggest that her engagement with feminism is very different from that of her mother or grandmother:

> They'd be the people who were involved in the rallies or whatever. And then there's me who's just sort of benefiting from what they——. ... We have respect for those women who gave us the world we have today,

where we have basically equal opportunities. But we've never experienced what it's like before the feminist movement. We don't know what it's like not to be treated equally, so we can't really have the same passion about it that perhaps our grandmothers or mothers had about it. Also, we don't know much about it. It's just not something that's taught because I guess it's happened and we've come a long way, and so they don't really see the need to talk about it any more because it's almost a problem that's resolved, I think.

This response was offered again and again in both interviews and in the comments in the questionnaires, reciting the near equality between men and women as the reason for quiescence. Some also believed there were more important issues for young people today:

It was stronger in the past because they had to fight for something. Nowadays … it is less of an active demonstration, it's still there, but because we don't have to fight for it and there are more pressing issues now, like there's the ozone layer, there's less jobs, there's the money, there's the economy collapsing, we're on the verge of a world war again, all that sort of stuff. (Naomi, vocational public school, 10061151)

Echoing a number of other young women, one vocational public school student, Tash, demanded: "define feminism, is there some kind of bible? I'm not anything but me" (10061161). Some of the young respondents, in self-descriptions completing an "I am …" section of the questionnaire, described themselves as "not a feminist" or "against feminism," or more stridently, "I hate feminist bitches" (female, public school, 100101438). Little wonder, then, that even those identifying as feminists were sometimes hesitant:

I find that there is social stigma still attached to feminism. I often get labeled a "man hater" by both men and women when I say I'm a feminist or talk about women's issues. I do not discuss it with people any more. (female university student, 10072047)

On the whole, then, these respondents reflected some of the lineaments of the generation debate, generally seeing feminism as something that belonged to their mothers' generation and not a pressing political necessity for their own times. A number endorsed the claims of commentators, such as Kathy Bail, that feminist activism is now a personal issue, every woman's opportunity, which no longer needs a collectivist women's movement. Indeed a collective movement may straitjacket the variety of ways in which young women practice their self-empowerment.

Turning now to young women's involvement in various political activities, by far the most common form of political engagement is signing a petition. But even for this activity, only 64 percent of the young women in the whole sample had ever done so. However, in general, the university students are the most politically active sample, more so than the sample of mothers (of the school students), suggesting that lack of political engagement cannot be explained merely as the apathy of the young. Thus, 40 percent of the university students had ever been involved in activist organizations (such as neighborhood groups, Amnesty, Greenpeace). This was much higher than involvement in political parties and campaigns. Although the results do suggest that Web site and ezine design is an activity pursued by young women rather than their parents, subsequent interviews with school students revealed that many Web sites were designed as part of a school project and none were what would traditionally be defined as "political." Naomi constructed her Web site as a school project, agreeing that the "Web site was about me" rather than being political (working-class girls high school, 10011048).

The interviews explored the young women's definitions of "politics," which generally turned on three issues: whether or not the action or involvement was "big" enough to constitute politics; whether or not the activity could or did "change" people; and whether or not the action involved politicians and political parties. Those who compared "big politics" with "little politics" sometimes excluded actions like signing petitions or writing letters as too "little" to be called politics. Niki describes petitions as "A little, very tiny step" (Niki, working-class girls high school, 10011072). On the other hand, Florence said, "politics is about changing things and I think when you sign a petition you're changing something" (Florence, middle-class girls public school, 10021100).

Kristy suggested that letter writing (e.g., to a newspaper or a politician) was a form of self-expression rather than an attempt to change others (Kristy, public high school, 100101425) but Naomi felt her letter was "sort of" political because:

> Half of it was just for my own benefit, letting others see that there are people out there that do feel the same about them—have the same views and everything like that. And there's——. I wouldn't really call that——. Yeah, I think I might call it political. (Naomi, working-class girls high school, 10011048)

By contrast, Charmaine says:

> But it still like all makes a difference. Like, I might not be doing something that's affecting like heaps and heaps of women, but I'm doing stuff that like affects a small amount and then eventually that all spreads and whatever, and every little bit counts. (Charmaine, open access college, 100131481)

Another way in which the definition of politics was explored was through the notion of "cultural politics," the new, reputedly favored domain of young women's activism. Respondents were asked if a band, such as the Spice Girls or Destiny's Child, singing lyrics about women constituted a political act. Some happily answered in the affirmative, assuming the message was about women's rights or other "political" issues, or even "Yeah sure, 'cos they're girls themselves and just getting their message through" (Natasha, Catholic girls school, 10091280), or "Through music, they're telling people that this is what's happening and that women could be strong and they don't need the typical man figure to dominate them" (Niki, working-class girls high school, 10011072). For these respondents, the impact of the lyrics was not relevant to identifying whether the action was political:

> It's the way they feel, and if other people agree with it and they buy the record, and they're saying, "Yeah, well women shouldn't be treated like this," then it is becoming a bit of a political movement. It's really just saying how you feel about something. (Tash, vocational public school, 10061161)

On the other hand, Monique believed reception was all-important:

> I don't think singing about feminist things like equal pay or something, if, say it was a popular song about equal pay, I don't think people who would listen to it would think "Hey, yeah, let's go and protest about equal pay." They'd think "this is a good pop song." I think they'd know the lyrics but they wouldn't see the meaning in it. (Monique, middle-class girls public school, 10021103)

Florence agreed that "political" lyrics "would have to be pretty powerful to actually make me go and do something" (Florence, middle-class girls public school, 10021100).

When the interviewer asked whether Naomi felt that the Spice Girls' message had been commodified into encouraging the purchase of clothes and so on rather than acting on the girl power message, Naomi was critical of such superficial engagement:

> That's the kind of people we are today, there's not really much deep thought into anything. People are more likely to sit down and have a chat with somebody on the other side of the world who they're probably never going to meet and probably never going to speak to again than they are likely to sit down and have a political discussion with their best friends.

Five young women I interviewed at Mitcham had been recently urged to attend a protest for Fair Wear, against sweated labor in the making of Nike shoes. Two students found the protest "scary":

> We went to a Fair Wear march down on Rundle Mall and that was pretty damn scary. They weren't even supposed to be there and I was going, "Mum said I'm not allowed to get arrested." I had to walk away and it was the first time I'd ever been to one of them. … I was involved in some chanting. "Nike has no souls." I was kind of scared because I didn't want to get arrested that day. (Florence, middle-class girls public school, 10021100)

The interviewer asked whether it was "kind of exciting as well as being scary," and Daphne replied:

> It was very exciting because you saw all these people who were thumping and how angry they were and the signs and they had made this papier maché shoe. Choice! It was good. That was the first real political thing I've ever been involved in. (Daphne, middle-class girls public school, 10021004)

In their interview, Monique and Tiffany also discussed the Fair Wear campaign, concluding that this form of activism was not for them, because they could do little to change the situation or other issues were more important:

> *Tiffany:* I just find it horrible that people aren't getting paid properly for the long hours they work. But I can't see how my input could help.
>
> *Monique:* You think, "Yeah that's really bad" but you forget about it and it doesn't really bother you. Whereas other things to me, like, I don't really know, other issues are more important to me in other ways. … People's lifestyle and suicide and things … interests me more. All that psychological stuff. I'm really interested in helping people with disabilities and things like that. …

However, Monique went on to comment on the media's role in shaping the "importance" of issues:

> [with light dawning in her voice] I think you don't see much of it so you don't think it can be much of a problem. … Maybe because we don't have as much exposure to it every day in the media, that you don't really, aren't concerned about it. (Monique, middle-class girls public school, 10021103; Tiffany, middle-class girls public school, 10021002)

The three university students who participated in a focus group, and who were in their mid-twenties or older, adopted the refrain of some second-wave feminists in condemning the apathy of the young:

> I still believe in political activism, and I feel that there's a backlash against feminism happening everywhere. Everything in the early 1980s that we achieved is slowly being eroded. (Sharon)

> I just think there's a lot of apathy out there now, and everybody's so much more individualistic than they used to be and I think that's a bad thing, especially for women. We just don't have a level playing field anyway. (Tamara)

In the interviews, a number of students endorsed a definition of political based on influencing politicians. One young woman, Charmaine, toyed with a future that involved becoming a politician, including a feminist agenda in her political program. Niki was one of the few young people to have been involved in a political party, of which she said:

> Just numbers—through numbers. … If you have heaps and heaps and heaps of people doing it, then you get noticed more. Also, being part of a political party, you're a step in towards doing what they're fighting for.

Most of the students, however, rejected politics as "boring," Hannah (vocational college) adding that voting should be optional as "I don't want to vote." Mariah distinguished a letter she had written on behalf of Amnesty International from "really boring 'John Howardy'[1] sort of stuff." Chantah, in the same interview group with Mariah, later described politicians as "A bunch of men with pot-bellies—and men who shave their eyebrows" who "speak of things that we don't understand really." Thankfully, perhaps, Mariah does not see feminism as political, because "I reckon politics in Australia is more about taxes and how much John Howard's spent on some holiday from our taxes."

Kevin McDonald (1999, 5) noted of his research with young people living in working-class suburbs, that their lives appear "chaotic, unpredictable and unstructured." They explain their exclusion in individual terms rather than understanding structures or shared positions (McDonald 1999, 53–54). Similarly, a deep sense of frustration and disenfranchisement was expressed by the youth center clients when asked how they responded when treated unfairly. They said they could not change their situation because of "guidelines made from the law" (female, youth service, 10035305); "they don't listen to me" (female, youth service, 10035308) or "lack of confidence and getting rejected" (female, youth service, 10035311).

These young people's stories reveal the vast gulf in political and personal horizons between the university students in my sample and the youth service clients. Although both feel disenfranchised from contemporary Australian society, the university students complain of political quiescence and rampant individualism, whereas the youth center clients complain of a social security system and wider society that disregard their personal needs and situation.

In conclusion, this is not a generation with no opinions about politics, although there is widespread resistance to being self-defined as political or feminist. It is a generation that tests the meaning of politics against the traditional definitions and considers that activism does not need to involve parliaments and "men with pot-bellies." On the other hand, these young people are not generally embracing the new media of politics, the Internet, or cultural milieux, to pursue their activism. They are, however, engaging with issues that perhaps they believe belong to their generation, such as youth suicide and the environment. Charmaine was the only young person to include a specifically feminist agenda in her imagined political activism.

Arlie Hochschild (2001, 63) argues that the young face a wider array of individual traumas like divorce and losing jobs at the same time as they have far more cultural and lifestyle choices than earlier generations: "Big events collectivize. Little events atomize." Heywood and Drake (1997, 4, 11) suggest that third wavers lack time "in our own overextended, economically insecure lives" for "public activism." Michelle Fine and Lois Weis (2000, 1143, 1144) chart the disappearance of community spaces where women could come together to share stories and educate each other, as streets and parks become unsafe, as local libraries are shut down, as social services are seen as untrustworthy and regulatory (Fine and Weis 2000, 1140). Young women are forced into Web pages and cyber networks, which allow both a private protection of identity and address and a public exchange, but may preclude the re-building of a public sphere (Harris 2001b, 136).

Rather than feel the necessity to choose between either structural politics or personal empowerment, between material changes or discursive shifts, Sarah Maddison (2002) borrows Nancy Fraser's recommendation that we explore how culture and economy work together to impede or promote change, how both redistribution and recognition are necessary aspects of politics. Maddison suggests that such cultural politics

> are keeping open a political space that "belongs" to feminism and that could be repopulated at such time as the political opportunity structure becomes more favourable for other forms of feminist activism. (Maddison 2002)

Harris's Response to Bulbeck's Findings

Bulbeck's research suggests that the picture of contemporary young feminism, and indeed youth activism more broadly, is a complex one, deeply inflected by socioeconomic conditions far from conducive to political engagement. These conditions are often unacknowledged in mainstream studies of youth politics. A related problem in the debate about young people's interest in and commitment to politics, either formal institutions or social movements, is that it tends to be framed in such a way as to delimit the possibilities of a discussion of broader meanings of participation and dissent from the outset. Consistently, researchers find that young people are not engaged in politics, which is also one of Bulbeck's findings. If one wishes to "defend" young people in response to this, only two contra claims can be made: either that young people are in fact engaged in politics, but this has taken on new forms unfamiliar to "old-style" activists, or that, although it is true that they are not engaged in politics, there are compelling socioeconomic reasons why that might be so. What is interesting to investigate is why we are having this debate now, what it means about the regulation of youth attitudes and behaviors, and how generation has become the key variable in the assignment of apathy. I return to the two contra claims later in my discussion, but for the moment I want to reflect briefly on the meanings and terms of the youth politics debate.

It is important to consider why we have become interested in generational difference on this issue and to understand how young people have become marked off from adults, as though apathy and engagement are youth problems alone. This has occurred in two ways. First, much of the lamenting about young people's apathy implicitly harks back to a golden age of activism, a time when youth were deeply involved in movements for social change. However, what must be remembered about this time (1960s to 1970s) was that the majority of school-or college/university-aged young people, the same demographic that is highlighted now as the apathetic generation, was not involved in such politics (Sherkat and Blocker 1994, 821). The concept of a straightforward generational divide in terms of active engagement in political change cannot be sustained if this comparison is drawn correctly. This suggests that more is at stake in the debate about youth politics than can be ascertained from the findings alone. Second, the panic over contemporary political disengagement is rarely cast over adults, especially privileged adults, who may be just as uninterested in and yet even more responsible for current social problems. Young people, who have always been invested with symbolic hope and fear for the future, are instead the problem that must be investigated, analyzed, discussed, and fixed. Many youth researchers have identified historical moments when young people have become the site for blame and solution regarding wider social issues. One provocative conclusion is that the problem of apathy is being sheeted home to youth at this time to divert attention from the dwindling public sphere and the disengagement of adults.

These concerns frame my reflections on the issue of young people's participation in politics. To summarize Bulbeck's findings, her study indicates that young people in general do not see a need for "old-style" feminist activism any more; that few are engaged in political activity of either an "old" or "new" nature, and most find formal politics boring; that the meaning of politics itself is somewhat contested among youth, and the efficacy of "cultural politics" similarly so; and that the political issue young people feel most strongly about is the environment, and to a much lesser extent, globalization. This study echoes others in finding few young people actively engaged in political activity of any kind and only a tiny minority who is interested in sustaining "old-style" feminist activism (see for example Macintyre et al. 1994; Lean 1996; Phillips and Moroz 1996; Saha 2000; Beresford and Phillips 1997; Vromen 2003). The idea that these behaviors and attitudes are unique to this generation, however, or that they constitute a problem on face value alone, warrants further discussion. It is here that I will return to those counterclaims, that some young people are "engaged," but this engagement is not easy to discern using old measures, and that others are not engaged, but this is a problem with our current sociopolitical order, which either denies youth opportunities or is deemed unworthy of engagement. I will explore these claims and respond to Bulbeck's findings and analysis by drawing on my research.

The Findings: Harris

> maybe adults should be asking more intelligent questions instead of assuming kids can only answer stupid ones. (Nicola)

To help me think through some of these issues, I interviewed sixteen young Australian and North American women as part of a qualitative research project on third-wave feminism and the role of alternative media, in this case, zines. The interviews were held face to face, via e-mail, and sometimes in a combination of the two methods. Five of the young women who were involved in collectives chose to be interviewed together or to write their answers in a group voice. The participants were aged eighteen to twenty-nine, and a diverse mix in terms of class, sexuality, ethnicity, and rural/urban dwelling. Most of them also worked with other young people in some capacity, in various government and nongovernment services, or held workshops and events related to youth and especially young women's health, education, work, ethnic identity, and racism, safety, and cultural activities. They were invited to participate in an interview because they produced zines, both paper and electronic, that dealt with youth issues, and because many of them had expertise as peer workers. In this way, the sample was deliberately "biased."

In framing the research project, I was not interested in gauging their or other young people's political engagement, or lack thereof, as enough evidence has been gathered on this theme. More so, in part I wanted to find out how young women who were part of a youth cultural politics (zine production, distribution, and consumption) and thereby deeply engaged in communication with young people, considered the debate about youth politics. I wanted to ask them what they thought about this issue of youth politics, rather than just measure their engagement. Due to the small, qualitative nature of the project, it is not possible to generalize, or even to generate "findings" as such. Rather, I intend the data to be read as a set of diverse, informed ideas that helps us think through the terms of the debate, not as evidence for one claim or another. Ironically, much of the discussion about youth participation excludes young people from framing the issues and seeking solutions. To take seriously the possibility of young people as reflective and knowledgeable sociopolitical actors means regarding them as more than data.

Bulbeck's research finds low levels of involvement in political activity, as assessed by standard measures, for example, signing a petition, joining a party, writing to a politician. My current collaborative research project on youth citizenship has found the same lack of engagement in these conventional political activities (see Harris, Wyn, and Younes 2006). These kinds of activities have become the usual way engagement is monitored (see Torney-Purta et al. 2001; White, Bruce, and Ritchie 2000); however, many commentators have concluded that it is time to rethink measures for political engagement, and to reflect on what constitutes activity (see, for example, Beresford and Phillips 1997; Ester and Vinken 2003; Vromen 2003; Manning and Ryan 2004). For example, is it more "engaged" to sign a petition on the way through a shopping mall, or to choose not to vote from a deep reflection on the problems of the system of government? Can a negative activity, a withdrawal of support, also be registered as a political act? Further, this rethink suggests that a distinction needs to be drawn between apathy and cynicism. As Bhavnani (1991, 13) found in her UK study among youth, "the display of 'cynical' attitudes is not necessarily an indication of political apathy, or even political inactivity. Thus, cynicism may be seen as justified ... and may even act as an *impetus* for political activity." Bhavnani suggests that we need to open up what it means to be "disengaged'" and her research indicates that this position can have political efficacy.

For some young people, a lack of engagement is a result of deep suspicion of the formal political process. They feel excluded, that their issues are not taken seriously, and that the state is not likely to work in the interests of social justice. As Kristy says:

> there are many extremely intelligent young people out there with ideas that deserve to be heard. They don't want to listen to them because they think young people are ignorant. How can we fix young people's problems if we don't listen to their ideas on how things can be changed? Everything is just so fucked up and it scares the hell out of us.

Not being listened to, and frustration about how to tackle this problem when young people are so often patronized by those in power, is a theme echoed in much research on youth attitudes towards participation (see, for example, Tuhiwai Smith et al. 2002). Tokenistic solutions, which provide opportunities for some youth to speak without anyone necessarily listening or taking action as a consequence, are felt by some young people to be worse than being ignored (see Holdsworth 2000; Siurala 2000).

This is a problem only compounded by gender and class elitism. As Kylie says:

> The normal political arenas are not at all welcoming for young women—it is extremely male-dominated in there. I think a young woman expressing herself would be all but ridiculed, belittled for her seemingly petty concerns.

Michelle suggests that the use of the label of apathy, along with exclusionary tactics that ensure "politics" is the domain of the privileged, serves to purposively alienate young people from engagement. She says:

> Dominant culture goes around saying "young people aren't interested in politics, young people don't really care" and all that sort of thing. ... By saying that young people are politically apathetic, it's just a way of trying to reinforce that. And also because the language of politics is, deliberately I think, non-inclusive. So I know that a lot of young people have very valid things to say and good ideas about the political climate

but they don't have words like "framework." ... They don't have words like that to use and therefore if you're not using that particular language, does it therefore mean that what you've got to say doesn't count? ... The language of politics is deliberately exclusive, it's only supposed to be understood and be spoken by people of a certain class.

For some young people, then, lack of interest in formal politics is a reflective choice based on frustration, cynicism, and exclusion. The separation of cynicism from apathy is important if we are to understand some young people's definition of active disengagement. In a culture where youth often feel they are not listened to, lied to, belittled, and dismissed, developing a critical insight can mean separating oneself from the institutions of power, even if temporarily. We might call this a healthy disregard for formal politics and its agendas. As Kayla suggests:

As things spiral into a deeper abyss, and more and more seems intrinsically wrong with the way we are living, more and more young people are understanding that this is a ridiculous situation. It's a situation where what is wrong is portrayed to us as right, good, and what is good is portrayed as weird, evil, wrong. ... The older generation are used to it being this way, as it crept up on them. The young folk are fed this on a platter, straight up and expected to digest it without question. Increasingly, they are rejecting the meal, and the word and idea is spreading. Most young people are cynical, and now we are seeing that cynicism used for good rather than apathy.

The key is in understanding how this cynicism might be harnessed for "good" and what this might look like. If cynicism produces other ways to engage in politics and build community, to develop new strategies and create new networks for sociopolitical action, it may be a valuable step. There is some evidence that this process is occurring (see, for example, Melucci 1996; Hetherington 1998; Klein 2000), although not among all youth and in the face of considerable challenges generated by the radical reshaping of the Western state and civil society of the late twentieth century.

Of course, this does not always happen, and individualization and self-interest are other possible outcomes. The material and cultural exclusion of young people from politics can lead to a kind of apathy that takes shape in "self-interest." One of the ways in which current socioeconomic conditions deny young people the opportunity to participate is through devolving responsibility for social rights onto individuals. As Walther (2001) argues, new youth "transition" policies that emphasize training and employment as individual responsibilities undermine young people's opportunities and motivation for participation. The retreat of the welfare state and the demand for individual self-sufficiency in a disappearing youth labor market put different pressures on young people today from those experienced by the 1960s' generation. The difficulties of surviving in an economically rationalized risk society face young people in ways that require them to change their relationship to politics. As Sabrina says:

> I think that young people are a lot more serious and sometimes they actually react in many different ways. Some people are a lot more harsher, I mean this society's like a lot more violent, some people just become really apathetic ... and so sometimes they just look like they're not doing anything with their lives ... but I think it's like hard in this society today.

Given this, are young people really able to exercise their political rights to gain their civil rights when the state no longer takes responsibility for their social rights, to use Marshall's (1950) tripartite classification of citizenship rights?

In this way, we can see how the socioeconomic context in which young people are operating has a significant impact on their capacity to engage politically and on the ways in which they value and define participation. As Bulbeck suggests, class may be a more compelling explanatory variable than generation in understanding participation. In any case, as Mel says, "It is dangerous to generalize. Many older people are apathetic too." And Kirsten elaborates:

> I know the dominant view seems to be that young people couldn't possibly be interested in radical politics. ... A lot of the people I am in contact with are in that youth demographic of 16–25 or so and nearly everyone I know is involved in radical politics, feminism, activism, movements for social change. ... However, I am also aware that people I know through things like work don't give a toss about social issues. ... I guess a lot of these kids are not interested in fighting oppression and living for equality, but most "normal" adults aren't either.

Finally, is it a problem that young women in particular do not seem to be taking up the feminist baton? Elsewhere I have argued that part of meeting this challenge lies in moving the debate away from generational conflict and the embrace of the word "feminist" towards an acknowledgment of the diversity of feminist practices that young women are engaged in today (Harris 2001c). I believe it is encouraging that 85 percent of young women in Bulbeck's study agreed that the women's movement had achieved good things and do not find it deeply disheartening that only a third describe themselves as feminist. As Aapola, Gonick, and Harris (2005) write,

> Some commentators argue that too much of a concern with labels interferes with our perceptions of the feminist work young women are actually engaged in. For example, Baumgardner and Richards (2000, 48) say, "Third Wave women have been seen as nonfeminist when they are actually living feminist lives. Some of this confusion is due to the fact that

most young women don't get together to talk about 'Feminism' with a capital F." And as Jowett (2001) demonstrates, when they do get together to talk about feminism, it becomes apparent that feminism is not perceived as a fixed state that one is either in or not in. Rather, it is a set of complex ideas and practices that contain contradictions and ambivalences, and it is shaped through dynamic relationships.

Currently, a critical mass of young women retains hold of a feminist agenda in a diverse range of ways, and, given the lack of public spaces in which feminism can be discussed, enacted, debated, and "done," this is commendable. We could see this activity as merely keeping feminism in a holding pattern, waiting for clearance to land, as Bulbeck here and Maddison (2002) suggest. Alternatively, we can explore the possibilities offered by Melissa, Jade and Tamara, who say:

> to suggest that young feminist women are politically apathetic is saying that generations after the earlier feminists are not aware, that we as young women are submissive and blind to the social realities of today. Perhaps our political motivations cannot be categorised or defined by frameworks of older theories circa 1960.

And we can try to move towards the development of better categories and better definitions to understand their political motivations. This does not mean there is no pressing need for a renewed public sphere, and nor does it mean we cannot ask hard questions about what such young women might offer. However, it does involve a more active engagement, a mutual participation, on the part of adults and researchers as well as youth.

Conclusions

Our research indicates the impossibility of capturing a single take on young people's opinions of politics. It suggests that without careful attention to the social and economic stratifications that inform lived experience, we lose sight of the real issues that shape opportunities for participation. Writing this chapter in conversation with one another has revealed that even while we agree on many issues, for example, the more difficult and very different economic and political environments facing young people, there are many insights to be gained from the differences in our approaches and analyses. For example, Harris's research reveals forms of refusal to engage in mainstream politics as a form of politics, as possibly very politically savvy in the present climate. It reminds us to read the silences in the discourse, as Louis Althusser (1971) argued, what is not said and done as well as what is said and done. It also indicates how understandings of young people's political engagements continue to be read against the yardstick of 1970s' definitions of politics. Harris's perspective on young women's politics shows not only that feminism can be done in bedrooms and on Web sites, but that this is not an inferior precursor to doing feminism on the streets or in boardrooms. On the other hand, Harris's respondents reveal the ongoing purchase of the generation debate, even if only symbolically. For all that they reject the tag of political apathy, they also define their political orientations against the older generation. Their "active disengagement" is based on a better understanding than their parents that "what is wrong is portrayed to us as right, good, and what is good is portrayed as weird, evil, wrong." This suggests that our task is not only to deconstruct the notions of "generation" and "youth" in our own theoretical frameworks, but also how these terms are used by young people themselves.

One of the most productive results of putting together our two projects has been the realization that the generation debate may well have run its course. The differences in our interpretations and findings seem less about age-related frameworks and more about theoretical perspectives and practical experience. Thinking through the differences in each other's results has therefore allowed us to displace the idea of "youth" from the center of not only our own analyses, but also perhaps to begin to do so from young people's perspectives as well. Just as we suggest that young people should be encouraged to refuse the "deficit" model of politics (young people's activism is a shadow of their parents'), our research also suggests that younger and older women who want a better world for women (and men) shrug off the generation debate and its unhappy connotations of family debt and succession (e.g., see Bulbeck 2006). The generation debate has helped to make a space for the "third wave." Once that space is claimed, it can be vacated as women—young and old, poor and privileged, mainstreamed and marginalized—seek productive interventions in our contemporary political and economic landscape. Creating a forum for our work to speak to each other has made clear that the current challenge regarding politics and activism has little to do with issues associated with an age-based demographic as such. It is to attend to the lack of sociopolitical structures that provide opportunities for meaningful participation for all members of the community.

Acknowledgments

Chilla Bulbeck would like to thank the participating school students, parents, and teachers. Anita Harris would like to thank the participants in her research for their time and thoughtful consideration of complex issues.

Note

1. John Howard was the Prime Minister of Australia at the time of the research.

References

Aapola, S., M. Gonick, and A. Harris. 2005. *Young femininity: Girlhood, power and social change*. London: Palgrave.

Althusser, L. 1971. *Lenin and philosophy, and other essays.* Trans. Ben Brewster. London: New Left Books.

Aveling, N. 2001. "Smarter than we're given credit for": Youth perspectives on politics, social issues and personal freedoms. *Australian Association for Research in Education conference paper.* http://www.aare.edu.au/01pap/are01300.htm (Accessed August 12, 2003).

Bail, K. 1996. Introduction. In *DIY feminism*, ed. K. Bail, 3–17. St. Leonards: Allen and Unwin.

Ballington, J. 2001. Youth and political participation: Tuned in or tuned out? *Development Bulletin* 56:11–13.

Baumgardrer, J. and Richards, A. 2000. *Manifesta: Young women, feminism and the future.* New York, Farrar, Straus and Giroux.

Bentley, T. and K. Oakley. 1999. *The real deal: What young people really think about government, politics and social exclusion.* London: Demos.

Beresford, Q. and H.C.J. Phillips. 1997. Spectators in Australian politics? Young voters' interest in politics and political issues. *Youth Studies Australia* 16 (4): 11–16.

Bhavnani, K. K. 1991. *Talking politics: A psychological framing for views from youth in Britain.* Cambridge: Cambridge University Press.

Budgeon, S. 2001. Emergent feminist (?) identities: Young women and the practice of micropolitics. *European Journal of Women's Studies* 8 (1):7–28.

Bulbeck, C. 2004. The "white worrier" in South Australia: Attitudes to multiculturalism, immigration and reconciliation. *Journal of Sociology* 40 (4):321–340.

Bulbeck, C. 2006. Explaining the generation debate: Envy, history or feminism's victories? *Lilith* 15:35–47.

Cope, B. and M. Kalantzis. 1998. "The frail cloak of colour": Young people speak about identity and the making of a new Australia. *Education Australia* 39:8–12.

Driscoll, C. 1999. Girl culture, revenge and global capitalism: Cybergirls, riot grrls, spice girls. *Australian Feminist Studies* 14:173–193.

Ellis, S. J. 2004. Young people and political action: Who is taking responsibility for positive social change? *Journal of Youth Studies* 7 (1):89–102.

Elton Consulting. 2003. *Youth and citizenship interim report.* Canberra: National Youth Affairs Research Scheme.

Ester, P. and H. Vinken. 2003. Debating civil society: On the fear for civic decline and hope for the internet alternative. *International Sociology* 18 (4):659–680.

Fine, M. and L. Weis. 2000. Disappearing acts: The state and violence against women in the twentieth century. *Signs: Journal of Women in Culture and Society* 25 (4): 1139–1146.

Harris, A. 2001a. Not drowning or waving: Young feminism and the limits of the third wave debate. *Outskirts.* http://mmc.arts.uwa.edu.au/chloe/outskirts/ (Accessed May 29, 2007).

Harris, A. 2001b. Revisiting bedroom culture: New spaces for young women's politics. *Hecate* 27 (1):128–138.

Harris, A. 2001c. Riding my own tidal wave: Young women's feminist work. *Canadian Women's Studies Journal*, Special issue: Young women: Feminist, activists, grrrls (winter/spring) 4 (1):27–31.

Harris, A. 2004. *Future girl: Young women in the twenty-first century.* New York: Routledge.

Harris, A., J. Wyn, and S. Younes. 2006. *Youth, citizenship and identity.* Unpublished paper presented at the Australian Sociological Association conference, University of Western Australia, Perth, December 4–7.

Hetherington, K. 1998. *Expressions of identity: Space, performance, politics.* London: Sage.

Heywood, L. and J. Drake. 1997. Introduction. In *Third wave agenda: Being feminist, doing feminism,* ed. L. Heywood and J. Drake, 1–24. Minneapolis: University of Minnesota Press.

Hochschild, A.R. 2001. A generation without public passion. *Atlantic Monthly,* February, 62–63.

Holdsworth, R. 2000. Education in Asia: Schools that create real roles of value for young people. *Prospects* XXX (3):349–362.

Jowett, M. 2004. "'I don't see feminists as you see feminists": Young Women Negotiating Feminism in Contemporary Britain', in A. Harris, ed. *All About the Girl: Culture, Power and Identity,* New York and London, Routledge.

Kaplan, E.A. 1997. Introduction 2: Two essays—Feminism, aging, and changing paradigms. In *Generations: Academic feminists in dialogue,* ed. D. Looser and E.A. Kaplan, 13–20. Minneapolis: University of Minnesota Press.

Klein, N. 2000. *No logo.* London: Flamingo.

Lean, A. 1996. Attitudes of youth towards politics and politicians. *Legislative Studies* 10 (2):52–63.

Macintyre, S. et al. 1994. *Whereas the people: Civics and citizenship education.* Report of the Civics Expert Group. Canberra: Australian Government Publishing Service.

McDonald, K. 1999. *Struggles for subjectivity: Identity, action and youth experience.* Cambridge: Cambridge University Press.

Maddison, S. 2002. Bombing the patriarchy or just trying to get a cab: Challenges facing the next generation of feminist activists. *Outskirts* 10. http://www.chloe. uwa.edu.au/outskirts/archive/volume10/maddison (Accessed May 29, 2007).

Manning, B. and R. Ryan. 2004. *Youth and citizenship.* Canberra: National Youth Affairs Research Scheme.

Marshall, T. H. 1950. *Citizenship and social class and other essays.* Cambridge: Cambridge University Press.

Mellor, S., K. Kennedy, and L. Greenwood. 2001. *Citizenship and democracy. Students' knowledge and beliefs, Australian 14 year olds and the IEA Civic Education Study.* Canberra: Commonwealth of Australia.

Melucci, A. 1996. *Challenging codes: Collective action in the information age.* Cambridge: Cambridge University Press.

Millar, M. S. 1998. *Cracking the gender code: Who rules the wired world?* Toronto: Second Story Press.

O'Brien, S. 1999. Is the future of Australian feminism feral? In *Australian youth subcultures: On the margins and in the mainstream,* ed. R. White, 102–112. Hobart: National Clearinghouse for Youth Studies.

Phillips, H.C.J. and W. Moroz. 1996. Civics and citizenship: Research findings on students' perceptions. *Youth Studies Australia* 15 (1):13–19.

Rice, E. and M. Swift. 1995. Beyond "talking about my generation": What Anne Summers isn't hearing. In *Women, culture and universities: A chilly climate?,* ed. A. M. Payne and L. Shoemark. Proceedings of the national conference on the effect of organisational culture on women in universities, 193–197. Sydney Women's Forum, University of Technology, Sydney.

Saha, L. 2000. Political activism and civic education among Australian secondary school students. *Australian Journal of Education* 44 (2):155–174.

Segal, L. 1999. *Why feminism? Gender, psychology, politics.* New York: Columbia University Press.

Sherkat, D. E. and T. J. Blocker. 1994. The political development of sixties' activists: Identifying the influence of class, gender, and socialization on protest participation. *Social Forces* 72 (3):821–842.

Siurala, L. 2000. *Changing forms of participation.* New forms of youth participation (Round Table). Council of Europe, Biel, May 4–6.

Skeggs, B. 1995. Women's studies in Britain in the 1990s: Entitlement cultures and institutional constraints. *Women's Studies International Forum* 18 (4):475–485.

Summers, A. 1993. The future of feminism: A letter to the next generation. In *Refractory voices: Feminist perspectives from Refractory Girl,* ed. Refractory Girl, 192–197. Sydney: Refractory Girl Feminist Journal.

Torney-Purta, J., R. Lehmann, H. Oswald, and W. Schulz. 2001. *Citizenship and education in twenty-eight countries: Civic knowledge and engagement at age fourteen.* Amsterdam: International Association for the Evaluation of Educational Achievement.

Tuhiwai-Smith, L., G. H. Smith, M. Boler, M. Kempton, A. Ormond, H.-C. Chueh, and R. Waetford. 2002. "Do you guys hate Aucklanders too?" Youth: Voicing difference from the rural heartland. *Journal of Rural Issues* 18:169–178.

Vromen, A. 2003. "People try to put us down ...": Participatory citizenship of "Generation X." *Australian Journal of Political Science* 38 (1):79–99.

Vromen, A. 2004. "Generation X" retrieving net-based information: Political participation in practice. Paper presented at University of Melbourne Centre for Public Policy, *Australian Electronic Governance Conference.* April. http://www. publicpolicy.unimelb.edu.au/egovernance/papers/40_Vromen.pdf (accessed September 23, 2005).

Walther, A. 2001. *Youth transitions, youth policy and participation.* Unpublished paper *Youth: Actor of social change?* Symposium, Council of Europe, Strasbourg, December 12–14.

White, C. S., Bruce, and J. Ritchie. 2000. *Young people's politics: Political interest and engagement amongst 14-24 year olds.* Layerthorpe: York Publishing Services.

Wilkinson, H. and G. Mulgan. 1995. *Freedom's children: Work, relationships and politics for 18–34 year olds in Britain today.* London: Demos.

Zita, J. N. 1997. Introduction. *Hypatia* 12 (3):1–6.

11
Young Women and Social Action in the United Kingdom

DEBI ROKER

This chapter describes the experiences of British young women, who are engaged in a variety of youth action activities. It draws on data from four studies undertaken by the author and colleagues, each looking at a different aspect of volunteering, campaigning, and social action. The chapter highlights the diversity of social action roles that have been created by young women in the United Kingdom and the impact of this action on the young women themselves, other young people, and youth policies and services. I will argue that there are now new movements and groupings of young women in the United Kingdom, who are promoting social change and significantly changing perceptions of young women and the social issues that affect them.

The chapter is structured as follows:

- Youth social action in the United Kingdom—research and policy background
- Theoretical perspectives
- The author's research in this area—four studies
- Research findings—young women and social action
- Conclusions

The author has undertaken, both alone and with different colleagues, a number of studies into young people's experiences of social action. It should be stressed that most of these projects did not have a specific gender focus, in terms of involving only young women or only men, or the analysis being based primarily on gender. However, there are a number of themes that have emerged from these projects, in relation to the views and experiences of young women in particular, which can help to shed light on gendered experiences of social action. This is what is reported in this chapter.

Youth Social Action—Research and Policy Background

Before turning to the author's research, it is useful to consider some of the issues around young people and social action in the United Kingdom, particularly in relation to young women.

One of the most significant features of debate about British young people in recent years has been the view that they are apathetic about, and alienated from, politics and decision-making processes. It is claimed that young people are disengaged and disconnected from national politics and distanced from mechanisms designed to give people a say in decision making.

The 1990s witnessed a very public debate in the United Kingdom about young people, their values, behavior, and integration as citizens (see, for example, Fogelman 1995; Haste 1996). Much of this discussion has reaffirmed a negative image of youth, with this age group portrayed as alienated, apathetic, and disaffected. Roche and Tucker (1997, 1), for example, describe how "youth today is seen as a problem. Young people are beset by predominantly negative images ... as either a source of trouble or in trouble." One well-publicized report, which was influential in government and policy circles, described young people today as a "wholly apathetic generation," possessing a "potentially explosive alienation" (Wilkinson and Mulgan 1995). Although this view has been challenged by many (for example, Roche and Tucker 1997; Roker, Player, and Coleman 1999) the view remains pervasive.

A key feature of recent debate about British youth concerns low levels of engagement in formal politics. Although rates of voting in elections, for example, have been declining among all age groups, the decline for the under 25s has been particularly acute. There is evidence of low levels of interest in national politics among young people, high levels of mistrust of politicians, and a sense of distance and disengagement from the political process (White et al. 2000). Further, there is evidence that, although many young people feel strongly about many local and national issues, they have little knowledge about how they can influence policies and practices in these areas, or indeed little confidence as to whether such mechanisms can be effective (Roker, Player, and Coleman 1999). During the 1980s and 1990s, therefore, these concerns about youth alienation led to the introduction of policies aimed at developing young people's knowledge, attitudes, and skills in relation to politics, participation, and citizenship.

Various policy initiatives have been established as a result of this concern, in an attempt to engage young people in the political process and to encourage them to participate more actively in their communities. These include the establishment of a Youth Parliament, campaigns by the British Youth Council and the Ministry of Sound, and activities by organizations such as Community Service Volunteers and the Carnegie Young People Initiative. The most significant educational innovation in this respect has been the introduction of citizenship lessons in schools, which started in 2002.

A notable feature of this debate has been the focus on what young people are *not doing* or *do not know* in relation to politics and participation. The main focus is therefore on young people's high rates of political apathy and mistrust, and low rates of voting among the under 25s. What is missing from this debate is any information about those young people who *are* engaged in participation and politics and who are attempting to bring about change in society. Yet understanding the views, motivations, and experiences of this group is essential if strategies to encourage youth participation are to be successful. Such information will also help to challenge the predominantly negative stereotype of young people in British society. This is what the research projects described in this report aimed to explore.

It is interesting, in reporting this literature, that there has been little gender-specific literature published in relation to young women, or young men, and social action. This chapter, along with the others in this book, aims to redress this balance.

Theoretical Perspectives

As well as having its roots in practical and policy concerns, the projects described in this chapter have origins in academic debates about young people's development, particularly in relation to the development of political and ideological views. The author believes that many traditional models of adolescent development are of limited use in understanding young people's involvement in social action. Traditional socialization models (and in particular many models of political socialization) suggest a passive process of development, with young people socialized into a society's particular way of thinking and behaving (Dawson et al. 1977). Studying youth social action requires models that accept the dynamism of development, with young people as active in the development of their identities, and influencing the world around them in the course of that development.

The main theoretical framework for the studies described in this chapter is derived from social-psychological theories of identity development and social identity. A key focus of the studies was on exploring the ways in which participating in social action impacts upon young people's developing identities, both in terms of their views of themselves and their perceptions of the sociopolitical world more broadly. The author was very influenced by the work of Yates and Youniss (1996a, 1996b), who identified how American youths' experiences of community service can stimulate identity development, encourage reflection on political organization and socioeconomic relationships, and develop a sense of agency in relation to social change. However, the work by Yates and Youniss focused on a group of young people participating in a compulsory program within a school context, which included time for structured feedback and reflection in the classroom. The studies reported in this chapter looked more broadly at young people's social action, generally in community settings.

The theoretical framework above focuses on the developing identities of individual social actors, and the social identities of the groups in which young people are involved. An additional theoretical framework for the studies concerns the organizational and structural aspects of social action and voluntary groups (see, for example, Handy 1988; Zeldin et al. 2000). The focus here is to identify the organizational structures, processes, and mechanisms that most effectively enable young people to participate in their communities, and to influence policies and practices in the world around them. A key aspect of the author's work has therefore been to explore the interaction among these three elements—the identity development of individual social actors, the social identities of social action groups, and the organizational processes within which these developments take place.

The Author's Research in This Area—Four Studies

The author has undertaken, both alone and with different colleagues, a number of studies into young people's experiences of social action. As stated earlier, most of these projects did not have a specific gender focus, in terms of involving only young women or only men. However, there are a number of themes that have emerged from these projects, in relation to the views and experiences of young women in particular, which can help to shed light on gendered experiences of social action.

This section outlines the aims, methods, and samples involved in each of the four studies. The section is necessarily brief, and readers interested in full details can contact the author or look at the publications listed.

Project 1: Young People and Volunteering/Campaigning

This project, undertaken in the mid-1990s, explored a topic that at the time was a very underresearched one, young people's positive contribution to society. It focused in particular on young people's involvement in voluntary activities and campaigning, effectively what young people do to benefit others. It involved young people aged fourteen to sixteen, and involved a questionnaire survey of 1,165 attending three diverse schools in the United Kingdom, and individual interviews with 103 of this group. The findings (discussed below) generated a lot of interest, with articles published in a number of national newspapers. The study was funded by the Jacobs Foundation.

Project 2: Social Action by Young People with Disabilities

This project also took place in the mid-1990s, and aimed to challenge the image of young people with disabilities as *receivers* of care and social action, and instead highlighted the way in which they are *givers* of care and action. Two methods of data collection were used: First, a U.K.-wide survey of organizations was undertaken, to identify the ways in which young people with disabilities are involved in volunteering, campaigning, and social action. The organizations that replied were then followed up with a telephone or face-to-face interview. Second, two case studies of particular organizations were then undertaken, including a school for children and young people with special needs, and a social action group involved in campaigning about disability issues. This study was funded by the Gulbenkian Foundation.

Project 3: A Longitudinal Study of Youth Social Action

This project aimed to provide a better understanding of youth social action groups. The aim was to identify and compare the motivations, experiences, and outcomes of young people's participation in different types of social action. There were two main elements to the design of the study. The first was a national review, undertaken to explore the remit and extent of youth social action in the United Kingdom. Several hundred groups were identified. The definition of social action used in the study was: *Groups of young people who meet on a regular basis, with the aim of bringing about change in policies and/or practices, or raising awareness, at a local, national, or international level.*

The sorts of groups identified in the study included: youth branches of Amnesty International and Greenpeace, young carers' groups, youth councils, peer education groups, disabled young people's groups, and youth–police liaison groups.

The second part of the study was a year-long study of eighteen youth social action groups. In total, seventy-four individual interviews were undertaken at the first time point, with fifty-seven follow-up interviews conducted at the second time point. Group interviews were also undertaken at several points during the year, and fifty-two observations of groups were also undertaken. The study was funded by the Economic and Social Research Council.

Project 4: A Survey of "Support and Campaigning" Groups in the United Kingdom

Following the completion of project three above, the author was particularly interested to find out more about young people's "support and campaigning" groups. These groups were primarily for disadvantaged or marginalized groups, such as young disabled people, young carers, and gay and lesbian young people. These young people initially came together for information and advice, and peer support. These groups then moved on to undertake campaigning and social action. This new role involved trying to challenge policies, practices, or provision that affected members of their group. The research aimed to find out more about these groups.

There were three stages to the research. First a flyer was sent out to a wide range of organizations in the United Kingdom, asking for information about support and campaigning groups. In total 106 were returned from across the United Kingdom. Second, these 106 projects were sent a detailed questionnaire, or were interviewed over the phone. In total information was received from seventy-one projects. Third, five case studies were undertaken of different projects. This involved a Trust for the Study of Adolesence (TSA) researcher visiting the projects and meeting with workers and/or the young people involved. The project was funded by the Carnegie UK Trust.

Research Findings—Young Women and Social Action

This section summarizes the main findings from each of the four studies above, focusing on the views and experiences of young women involved in different forms of social action.

Project 1: Young People and Volunteering/Campaigning

As stated in the previous section, this study was undertaken at a time when very little attention was being paid to young people's positive contribution to society. The results of the survey therefore received significant attention, when they showed that a significant proportion of the young people had been involved in volunteering and/or social action. Some of the quantitative findings demonstrate this point well. Thus, for example, 90 percent of the sample had given money to charity, 35 percent had helped out (voluntarily) with mentoring or tutoring younger children at the school, 70 percent had signed a petition, and 17 percent had written to a Member of Parliament. One in ten of the young people was also a member of a campaigning group, as diverse as Amnesty International, environmental groups, fair trade groups, antivivisection groups, etc.

In the context of this chapter, there was a significantly higher level of engagement in volunteering and social action among the young women in the survey. Thus, for example, a greater proportion of young women had been engaged in all the activities listed above, and they were more likely to be members of campaigning groups. There were a number of reasons for this, identified both by school staff, and by the young women themselves. First, school staff explained the different levels of engagement as follows:

> Yes it's pretty obvious [that more girls than boys do voluntary and campaigning activities]. You see it in everything we do, I think. The girls are keen. Often more mature, more thoughtful about the issues, and I think more genuinely concerned to help out

Another tutor picked up on the theme of maturity and thinking about others:

> The boys, you know, they're quite self-obsessed at this age, you know thinking about their mates, and sport and stuff. The girls, well they are more mature, they do start to really care about things, causes, other people. That's why we have a lot more girls in [our voluntary activities].

The young women in the study also talked about why there were more young women than young men involved in some of the activities:

> Well, like, this group [peer sex education project] we talk about things that a lot of boys get awkward about. You know, sex, feelings, emotions, things like that. The girls, well, we can do that. The boys just get embarrassed. So the peer educators are all girls.

Another young woman said:

I'd say no, boys don't like this sort of stuff [tutoring younger children].
It's all seen as a bit girlie (laughs).

As will become clear later in this chapter, it should be stressed that the
young women's experiences of social action were very diverse. Some experiences were very positive and others less so. Some activities were more successful than others, in terms of having the impact the young women wanted. For
example:

It was excellent [an open day] we really got people to listen, and you
know, sign up to action.

... well we did it [a presentation at the Council] but I don't think they
were really interested. It was all "yes yes very interesting." But you know,
we said our bit.

Some of these themes are picked up further below.

Project 2: Social Action by Young People with Disabilities

The key finding from this next study was that there are a large number of
young people with disabilities in the United Kingdom who are involved in
giving care and undertaking social action. The young people were involved
in volunteering projects, mentoring other young people, peer education, peer
support groups, and campaigning activities in relation to disability issues, the
environment, and local youth facilities. The full report on the project details
the different types of issues that the groups were addressing and some of the
organizational issues that the groups faced in terms of taking action on a variety of social issues.

The majority of the groups found that they attracted more young women
than young men to their project. This reflects the findings of the previous
project. One worker explained this as follows:

We've always struggled to get young disabled boys and men in to the
project. It's just not seen as a cool thing for boys, you know, campaigning and dealing with these sorts of social issues [the environment]. I
don't know how we change that.

It was significant, therefore, that many workers identified the greater attraction of their project to young disabled women. Two things were notable from
their comments: First, that many of the young women were involved in setting
up the project in the first place:

... [name] really got it going ... she approached us and said "look I
wanna do something about this" [a disability rights issue]. I've heard
that many groups start like that. Often a girl comes to us and gets it

going. They're often more confident the girls, I think, and keener to do something for others.

Second, workers described the ways in which many marginalized young women had been supported by education and other systems to address issues that affect them. As one worker said:

It's partly about greater equality. Disabled people generally are more visible, more vocal. The young women we work with reflect that. They've been encouraged to get involved.

This comment was supported by a young woman in the group:

The school, my special school, they said just do it [set up an environmental campaign]. They always said, like, just do things.

The experiences of the disabled young women in this study were very diverse. Success (where it was achieved) was most often managed at a local level, with, for example, groups managing to secure disabled access to buildings, or having advertising materials changed to include images of disabled people. The young women found it much more difficult to have influence at a national level, or in terms of broader public opinion or policy. As this young woman said:

We, like, we can get Local Councils to listen, and do things here. But like the law, no we can't change that.

This was particularly the case where other aspects of discrimination and disadvantage were evident. As this worker said:

… it is difficult to keep spirits high. Some of these young women face major disadvantage—disability, being an ethnic minority. We can't help them to change the world.

Project 3: A Longitudinal Study of Youth Social Action

As stated earlier, this research involved a longitudinal study of eighteen youth action groups. In order to discuss the young women's experiences of these groups, it is useful to first identify some of the characteristics of the groups. These were as follows.

First, the majority of the social action groups were not "free-standing" associations of young people. More commonly, they were groups organized and supported by other organizations. These organizations included youth and community departments, local councils, schools and colleges, social services, and national bodies like Greenpeace, Amnesty International, and trades unions. The support of the "parent" group was often crucial to the success and continuance of the groups.

Second, the groups were not evenly distributed across the United Kingdom. There was wide variability in numbers and types of groups across counties, regions, and areas. Some parts of the United Kingdom had considerable numbers of youth social action groups, in particular around cities in the northwest, southwest, and London. It is possible that these areas have local authorities and youth policies that actively encourage young people's involvement in decision making and in broader issues, and that this has led to the establishment of (and support for) youth social action groups. Further, there were more groups in urban and town areas, with fewer in rural communities.

Third, most of the groups had one or more adult facilitators, such as teachers, youth workers, social workers, and youth participation workers, who supported and facilitated the groups. These adults had a wide variety of roles and were often crucial in maintaining and promoting the group. The majority of these individuals were in paid employment in statutory bodies, with only a handful of volunteers involved. It was clear from the start that these adults were essential to the existence and longevity of the groups involved.

Fourth, the groups were very diverse in terms of the characteristics of the young people participating in them. Challenging the notion of youth social action groups as predominantly White and middle class, the groups represented young people from a range of localities, social backgrounds, and ethnicities. However, more young women than young men were involved in these groups (this point is explored further below).

Fifth, it was clear that many groups were in a precarious situation, near to collapse or only existing intermittently. The main reasons for the collapse of a project, or its activities being suspended, were lack of funding, lack of members, and no adult facilitation.

As mentioned above, we also explored the characteristics of young people involved in social action groups. Some interesting class and gender issues emerged. There is a common image of mainly White middle-class young people participating in social action. However, our national review and the groups selected for the longitudinal study very clearly demonstrated a diversity of young people in terms of socioeconomic backgrounds and ethnicity, who were involved in social action. This is in itself important, challenging the predominant stereotype of those who are "involved." We did, however, find more females than males in the groups that we identified. It is unclear why this is, but indications from the individual and group interviews suggest that social action activities were more acceptable for females, in particular in areas such as peer education. This picks up on the findings of the two studies above. As some of the young people described it:

> ... the methods [this group] use are very nonmacho. (youth council)

> It's the image thing again. I think girls are less worried about the image than boys. (community action group)

The greatest concentration of young men in this study were in the youth councils, which some of the respondents believed had a more "masculine" image.

It is useful here to think about the young people's routes into social action. Youth political and social participation is often described in terms of young people "seeking out" a social action group, because they have strong feelings about an issue, and want to take action. This was not the case for the majority of the young people in this research. Rather, most became involved in a more informal manner. Many first heard about a particular group through flyers and advertisements or through teachers or youth workers; others were invited to join through family and friends. The issues involved were often of general interest to them, but they also saw involvement in the group as a source of fun, a social life, support, and an opportunity to develop new skills that would be of value in the labor market. Many were very open about the fact that boredom and a lack of things to do led them to get involved in their group.

More specific examples of routes into social action are given below. First, young people became involved via contact with professionals:

I think it was probably when [the secretary of the local youth council] came and gave a talk to an assembly about voting, and he asked me why I wasn't on the youth forum and why the school wasn't sending anyone, I said I didn't have a good reason, so he said to come along to a meeting and have a look and see what you think, so I did. And I have been going ever since. Probably just over a year ago. (youth forum)

Second, other young people joined primarily through their own initiative, as a group "looked interesting." For example:

I saw posters up all over the place and then they [the youth service] said that they thought the deadline had gone, then they said that there were two spare places, so we applied. (peer education group: sexual health)

Third, a significant number of young people were influenced by friends and/or family:

Through my sister. At first she was uncomfortable with me coming ... but eventually she said I could come. (community action group).

It is interesting to note that all three routes above were particularly common for the young women in the study, that is, boredom, looking for something to do, looking for social interaction, etc. It should be noted, however, that most of the young women then developed a clear commitment to their group and the issue involved. This was particularly noticeable at the second interview, where it was clear that people were more "embedded" in the aims of their group. Also, a minority of the young women were motivated primarily by the *way* in which the group undertook its activities, for example by using photography and cartoons, or through peer education workshops with other young people.

Four of the groups in the research, however, were noticeably different to the young people described above. These were young people who joined self-help and support groups, specifically for young people with disabilities, gay and lesbian young people, and young carers. These groups of young people often felt isolated and marginalized and came together for support. Each group, however, then decided to broaden the aim of the group to include campaigning and social action. These groups had a particularly high representation of young women as members. As these young women explained:

> I felt often that young people today tend generally not to have much of a voice in society, they generally tend to be dismissed. And when you're a sub-set of a sub-set, you know, you're young and you're gay or lesbian or whatever, or bisexual then you get pushed aside. So I thought it would be interesting to seek out as much advice as we could actually gain, if there were more of us we could actually achieve a chorus. (lesbian, gay, and bisexual forum)

> When I was a kid I used to think I was the only one [a young carer] and there was only me, like I'm one in a million ... but there's quite a lot when you look ... So you meet people of your own status, your own sort. (young carers' group)

> I hadn't really come into contact with other disabled people, and it was a chance to meet young disabled people ... it's kind of a great place to learn because you grow up conditioned on how society, you know, reacts to disabled people. [This group] shows you that it's society's fault and not yours, you know, your disability. (young disabled people's forum)

This is clearly a much more personal route into social action than is the case for others involved in the project. It was evident that the views and experiences of young people in the four support groups were different to those involved in the other groups. This group of young people had a much more personal connection to the "topic" of their group, and it was clear that involvement had a significant impact on their health and well-being. The young women in these groups in particular talked about a need for support and belonging. However, they also talked about how the group was engaged in looking forward too, at how young women (and young people in general) in their situations could change policies and practices that affect them. These issues are explored further in Project 4 below.

A key feature of the research was to look at the impact of social action groups and the extent to which young people are able to participate in decision making and bring about change. However, the issue of success and achievement in these groups was a complex one. Most of the young people certainly believed that they had "made a difference." For example one of the groups considered that it had helped to reduce crime in the local area, in particular street muggings in which young people were the victims. Support for this came from comments by the local police. Other groups experienced positive feedback from workshop participants, who said that they found the workshops useful, whether through knowledge gained about sex and relationships, or about how to tackle racism. Other groups said that they could identify the impact of their group nationally and internationally, and these comments were often backed up by adult facilitators. The young women in the research were particularly keen to "talk up" the impact of their social action activities. For example, one young woman made the following comment:

> We ended up doing two workshops with this youth group, at the end of the workshop … one of the lads, he had been really quiet for the last two weeks, he said something we had mentioned in passing but he remembered it. It was to do with sexually transmitted diseases, and I thought if he goes away and remembers that and its useful to him then yes [we have made a difference]. (peer education group: sexual health)

It was of note, however, that definitions of success and the impact of these groups were very different, depending on who was involved. The different perceptions of adults and young people were particularly noticeable. For example, as part of a participant observation the researcher on the project watched a workshop by one of the groups, a peer education group on sexual health. The workshop was planned and run by the group's members. The workshop proved to be very disorganized, with members often contradicting each other, and obvious tensions between group members. The researcher felt that the workshop had gone badly. However, by the end it was clear that the young people participating in the workshop had found it very useful, and the group had achieved their aim of getting the young people to think about relationships and different cultures. The issue of how to define and measure "success" or "outcomes" in social action is an important one. This can be equally applied to young women's experiences of the groups—social support and personal development were as important as impact on policy.

The results of this research demonstrates that participation in social action does impact on young people's sense of who they are, their skills and abilities, and their plans for the future. This influence was most notable in three areas, on young people's confidence and self-worth, on their sense of who they are and their personal identity, and on the development of skills and abilities, including employment-related skills. This was particularly notable for the young women in the study, who frequently commented on the importance of the group in their lives.

The interviews and the observations demonstrated that group participation impacted, first, on young people's confidence and sense of self-worth. As one young woman described it:

> When I was at school I was shy and quiet. I didn't really talk to anybody. Then I finished school and had just enough confidence to go to College

on my own with no friends from the school. Then I joined Sex Action and now I'll try anything, it doesn't bother me. I went on the training weekend on my own, but I would never have done that before Sex Action, I'd have been too scared. (peer education group: sexual health)

Similarly:

I appreciate stuff [the group] has done for me. It's given me confidence to be who I am today. It's made me realize I can make a difference. It only takes one person with an idea. (youth council)

Further, many young women described how they learned to deal with difficult issues or people and that this boosted their confidence:

... we done a presentation in a safety group. We done like the female's one and there was one guy in the audience and he was giving us like a lot of hassle saying that it was girls that caused it all [street violence] because we were like making the boys want to fight each other ... just being really horrible to us and all that. We just kind of answered him back and at the end he was being nice again. (territorialism project)

The second way in which group membership affected young women directly was in terms of personal identity, their sense of who they are and their place in the world. A key result from the individual and group interviews was that experiencing different perspectives, encountering people with different backgrounds, and engaging with conflict and difference, impacted on young people's political and social identities. A good example from the research is a young Black woman, talking about her participation in a youth–police liaison group:

I've grown up with [the group] so I've seen people's different views of Black ... cos like I haven't just been around that one type of person, I've been around different people, different race people ... and it's made me see from their experiences of being Black, it's not just my eyes, it's other people's eyes as well. (police liaison group)

This young woman talked extensively about how being part of the group had provoked her into thinking more about herself, her cultural views and values, and her relationships with others, including the police. Her experiences are reflected in many other interviews, across all the groups. In this respect, it is also significant that for some individuals, their participation in the group led them to develop a more critical view of their community, or society more generally. As one member of Amnesty International described it:

I used to have a very naive view that Britain, that countries like Britain and America were very good and everyone lived in freedom and that's not true, and also that the world was generally a very lovely place where everyone grew up and was happy. Well it wasn't that simple but I knew there were horrible things going on, but it's made me realize the power of money, and the power of government and how an entire country can be controlled by just one or two people and they can pretty much do anything they want. (Amnesty International member)

Third and finally, group participation led the young people to develop a variety of skills and abilities. These skills and abilities included use of information technology, organizational skills, team-working, negotiation, and conflict resolution. Numerous examples of this could be identified, including:

it's got me experience of dealing with people who aren't very nice, and who aren't very willing to deal with you. It's progressed my journalism skills and my IT skills. I can ... I'm probably better at speaking in public now, I can probably co-run meetings. (peer education group)

Similarly:

It's given me lots of opportunities. I got to sit in on interviews, I've just dealt with the media, I've dealt with newspapers and radio ... we're doing a video now, so you learn new skills and you develop parts of your personality that you might not otherwise have. (youth council)

A key finding from this project is that participation in social action develops young women's personal and life skills. Almost all the young people in the project identified a range of skills and abilities that they had developed as a result of participating in the groups. Some made a direct connection between the skills and abilities they had developed via the group and their career opportunities and plans. In addition, group membership and participation has a significant impact on young people's political and social views and their developing identities.

As demonstrated above, participation in social action does impact on young people's sense of who they are and their understanding of political and social issues. Being involved in a youth social action group challenges young women's understanding of their relationships and the sociopolitical world and the degree to which they can influence it. Many of the young women quoted above demonstrate this very clearly. Their experiences also persuaded the young women that they can get things changed. For example:

Generally you do need a group or some kind of way in for someone to listen to you, because they are going to tell you to get lost if you're an individual. They're going to get pissed off if you keep saying "well I don't like this, I like that." Generally you have to do it in a group. (youth council)

The majority of the young people believed that they could effect change at some level, and they could identify concrete changes their group had made. A clear pattern that also emerged was a difference between what the young people believed they could achieve *locally* compared with what they could do *nationally*. Many felt that significant change and development could be achieved by a group locally, while nationally (and internationally) change was much harder to secure. As two young women described it:

> I reckon if you get together with a group of people that agreed with you, you can make a difference locally. I don't think you can make a national difference unless you're a member of an organization. … You do need a group or some kind of way in for someone to listen to you, because they're going to tell you to get lost if you're an individual. (youth council)

> I think everybody could influence politics if they tried hard enough. As singles, no, but if they can influence the people around them and you all speak as one, perhaps they'll listen. (environmental group)

Many adults were seen as dismissive and critical of the groups' activities, often deliberately blocking their involvement or influence. The young people often commented that, although some adults were supportive and respectful of the young people, other adults were dismissive or deliberately obstructive. Significantly, many of the negative comments that the young people received were from adults who were not involved with the groups. As one young person from a peer education group commented, on the reaction to a stall the group had at an event:

> One old lady walked past the stall and kind of came back and she said "this is disgusting, it's absolutely ridiculous. I teach my daughter to keep her knickers on, not off." … And all we had was leaflets and information and it was like … They hadn't even said anything to her. (peer education: sexual health)

Many of the young people talked about the tension that they experienced in their relationship with adults. In general, the role of adults as gatekeepers, facilitators, and advocates for the groups proved crucial to their success. With more and more young people's projects being set up under the "youth led" banner, it is important to further explore what this means in practice. This is a key issue for future research.

Project 4: A Survey of "Support and Campaigning" Groups in the United Kingdom

Finally in this results section, some findings are given for the most recently completed project, a survey of "support and campaigning" groups. This was defined earlier as a group of young people initially set up for mutual support (for example, for young carers or for refugees) which then takes on a more outward looking, campaigning role.

The research showed that there are a growing number of support groups for vulnerable, disadvantaged, and marginalized young people. This relatively small-scale survey identified over one hundred such projects. These groups exist in all four countries of the United Kingdom, although they are concentrated in large towns and cities. Further, the groups involved were diverse and included projects for young refugees, those who have experienced sexual abuse, young disabled people, young carers, young mothers, those living in temporary accommodation, the siblings of those with disabilities, and young people with mental health difficulties.

These support groups provide a valuable lifeline for many of Britain's most vulnerable young people, for example, those who have experienced domestic violence or sexual abuse, gay, and lesbian young people, those with mental health difficulties, young refugees and asylum seekers, and those looked after by the state. Despite providing a key lifeline to vulnerable young people, many groups struggle to survive and continue, largely due to shortage of staff, lack of suitable resources, and lack of funds. As this worker said:

> … these young people are so vulnerable. It's appalling that there's no structured support for them. They get so much from this [refugee support] group.

Many of these groups had expanded their role in recent years, thus, not only do they provide support to young people, but they work with young people to take on a campaigning and social action role. In this role the groups aim to challenge people's perceptions of young people in their circumstances, and/or to change aspects of practice and policy. For example:

> … we want more support for young carers. We do so much and don't get anything. We should get more help and support.

Many of the groups could demonstrate the many ways in which they had impacted on perceptions and policies; this had been achieved via such activities as lobbying and letter writing, presenting at conferences, peer support, and peer education, contributing to Web sites, writing articles, and newsletters, and putting on events.

Involvement in the groups was also found to have a significant impact on the young people involved. Young people were identified as developing in self-esteem and self-confidence, making new friends and social skills, and acquiring new practical skills (computer use, producing presentations, letter-writing, etc). For example:

> I've got so much from being here [a disability group]. I've made lots of friends here, learnt how to use computers, that sort of thing. It's been great.

Conclusions: Young Women and Social Action

This chapter has described the experiences of British young women, who are engaged in a variety of youth action activities. It drew on data from four studies undertaken by the author and colleagues, each looking at a different aspect of volunteering, campaigning, and social action. The chapter has highlighted the diversity of social action roles that have been created by young women in the United Kingdom, and the impact of this action on the young women themselves, other young people, and youth policies and services. This final section of the chapter offers some general conclusions about young women and social action and highlights some of the overarching themes emerging from the four studies that have been described.

In the first part of this chapter, it was mentioned that very little of the British literature in relation to young people and social action has a specific gender focus. This is surprising, given the importance of the topic. The findings from the four projects also challenge much of the existing literature, and in turn many of the stereotypes of young people as disaffected, selfish, and uninterested in the world around them. The four studies looked at different issues and involved different groups of young people from very different backgrounds. However, a key finding from all the studies was that there was a high level of engagement by young women in a range of "action": volunteering, campaigning, promoting change, challenging discrimination and disadvantage, etc.

There are a number of overarching themes that come out of the four studies described. First, that in all the studies there was found to be a higher level of engagement in social action among young women than young men. This is interesting, in that at the formal level of political engagement in the United Kingdom (such as Members of Parliament), there is a gender imbalance in favor of men. Thus, the author's studies show that it is young women who dominate more informal and community-based action. There were a number of explanations for this given by the participants in the studies, including young women's earlier maturity, greater levels of confidence, and capacity and willingness to deal with emotional and personal issues. Some also commented on the sea change in how society views women, and in particular the existence of programs and educational experiences that actively promote the empowerment of women.

Second, what was clear from these studies was that it is some of the most marginalized and disadvantaged young women who are getting involved in action. This includes, for example, young women with disabilities, lesbian and bisexual young women, young carers, and those who have experienced abuse. Many of the support projects and action groups described in these studies have enabled these young people to find a voice and further, to be heard. Many of the individuals and groups described here have secured positive and long-lasting changes in their communities and more widely. They have, crucially, challenged stereotypes of what it means to be a young woman in British society.

Third, the studies described here have raised issues about notions of success in social action and the developing identities of those involved in social action. Thus, in each of the projects, young women talked about their aims in relation to social action, the things that they were trying to achieve or change.

Many of these ambitions were not achieved, although crucially, some were. However, what was clearly important to many of the young women was the processes involved. Thus the young women talked about receiving social support from other group members, about the skills they had developed, about the fun they had in social action activities, and about how their involvement led to them changing their ideas, views, and identities. These are key outcomes of involvement in social action for many young women.

Finally, a key theme that has emerged from these studies is that of organizational and institutional support for those young women engaged in social action. It was clear from the studies that many young women struggle to engage in social action independently, and indeed would not want to. Most want and need the support that belonging to a social action group can offer. For this to happen, the support of adults and organizations is important. Thus, the provision of meeting facilities, adult facilitation, and support is essential if many of these young women are to be able to continue to engage in youth social action in their communities.

In conclusion, this chapter has aimed to highlight the positive contribution that young women make to society, via undertaking social action. It has highlighted the successes for many of these young women and how their experiences of youth action has impacted on their developing identities and sense of place and purpose. It is appropriate to close the chapter with the view of a disabled young woman:

> You can think, like, as a girl, or as a disabled person, I can't do anything. But that's not true. Look at what we've done here. We've made a real difference.

References

Dawson, R. et al. 1977. *Political socialization*. Boston: Little Brown.

Fogelman, K. 1995. Why is citizenship so important? *Citizenship*, 4, 19–23.

Handy, C. 1988. *Understanding voluntary organisations*. London: Penguin.

Haste, H. 1996. Communitarianism and the social construction of morality. *Journal of Moral Education*, 25, 47–55.

Roche, J. and S. Tucker. 1997. *Youth in society: Contemporary theory, policy and practice*. London: Sage.

Roker, D., K. Player, and J. Coleman. 1999. *Challenging the image: Young people as volunteers and campaigners*. Leicester: Youth Work Press.

Wilkinson, H. and G. Mulgan. 1995. *Freedom's children*. London: Demos.

White, C., S. Bruce, and J. Ritdire. 2000. *Young people's politics: Political interest and engagement amongst 14–24 year-olds*. Chicago: University of Chicago Press.

Yates, M. and J. Youniss. 1996a. Community service and political-moral identity in adolescence. *Journal of Research in Adolescence* 6:271–284.

Yates, M. and J. Youniss. 1996b. A developmental perspective on community service in adolescence. *Social Development* 5:85–111.

Zeldin, S., A. McDaniel, D. Toptzez, and M. Calvert. 2000. *Youth and decision-making*. Madison: University of Wisconsin-Madison.

Contributors

Feda Abdo has graduated from a Bachelor of Arts program (Media and Communication) at the University of Sydney and currently works at the United Muslim Women Association Inc. She has also been involved in a number of committees and advisory boards, such as the Canterbury Bankstown Community Harmony Round Table and the Multicultural Youth Network with the Community Relations Commission for a Multicultural NSW.

Angie Colette Beatty is a Black feminist/scholar/activist/poet/beatbox artist whose scholarly and organizational works center on racialized constructions of gender and representations of violence in popular culture (especially hip hop culture), Black women and girls as both agents and recipients of violence, and the relationship among power, language, and identity. Committed to meshing art, activism, and scholarship, Beatty exploits her talents as a performance artist to create safe spaces for young people and engage them in discussion about their relationships to media institutions, consumer activism and activism through art, racialized constructions of gender, sexuality, homophobia, and violence. A founding member of the Progressive Women's Caucus, Beatty is an assistant professor of Communication and African American Studies at Saint Louis University, and she is the 2006 recipient of both the Kramarae Outstanding Dissertation Award and Foote Distinguished Dissertation Award, as presented by the Organization for the Study of Communication, Language and Gender and Department of Communication Studies at the University of Michigan, respectively.

Rayann Bekdache is a journalism student from the University of Technology, Sydney. She has written and had articles published on issues relating to Muslim women. While studying, she also volunteers with the Bankstown Youth Development Service.

Dorothy Bottrell is a senior research associate in Child and Youth Studies in the Faculty of Education and Social Work, University of Sydney. Her background is in secondary teaching, juvenile justice, youth, and community work and as a teacher of community services and welfare studies.

Chilla Bulbeck holds the chair of women's studies at Adelaide University's School of Social Sciences in Australia. She has taught overseas at Beijing Foreign Studies University and the University of Tokyo, where she was the professor of

Australian Studies in 2002–2003. She has published widely on issues of gender and difference, including *Re-Orienting Western Feminisms: Women's Diversity in a Post-Colonial World* (1998), Cambridge University Press; *Living Feminism: The Impact of the Women's Movement on Three Generations of Australian Women* (1997), Cambridge University Press; and *Australian Women in Papua New Guinea: Colonial Passages 1920–1960* (1992). Her work has been translated into Korean and Polish. Her contribution to this chapter arises from a large Australian Research Council-funded project on young Australians' attitudes to feminism, gender, and other social issues.

Amy Dobson writes in both performative and academic genres. She completed her Honours Degree in Performing Arts at Monash University, Australia, in 2004, for which she researched and wrote her thesis on teenage Internet cam girl communities. She is currently researching online performance by young women for her Ph.D. at Monash University.

Michelle Fine, Distinguished Professor of Social Psychology, Women's Studies and Urban Education at the Graduate Center, City University of New York, has taught at CUNY since 1990. Her research focuses on theoretical and practical questions of social justice in schools and prisons. Contemporary work focuses on participatory research methods, policy work on educational and prison reform, and youth activism. Her publications relevant to young women's sexuality include "Sexuality Education and Desire: Still Missing After All These Years" (with Sara McClelland), *Harvard Educational Review*, 2006; and "The Politics of Teen Women's Sexuality: Public Policy, and the Adolescent Female Body" (with Sara McClelland), *Emory Law Review*, 2007. Her recent books and monographs include Weis, L. and Fine, M. (2004), *Working Method: Social Research and Social Injustice*, Routledge; and Fine, M., Weis, L., Powell Pruitt, L., and Burns, A. (2004), *Off White: Readings on Power, Priviledge, and Resistance*, Routledge.

Samah Hadid has been involved in various youth advisory bodies and groups like the Bankstown Council Youth Advisory Committee and the National Youth Roundtable. Moreover she is part of the Bankstown Community Participation Taskforce and is currently studying political science at University of Sydney in hope of getting involved in public policy.

Anita Harris is a research fellow at the Centre for Critical and Cultural Studies, University of Queensland, Australia. Her previous books include *Future Girl: Young Women in the Twenty First Century* (2004), Routledge and *All About the Girl: Culture, Power, and Identity* (edited) (2005), Routledge.

Leslie Heywood is professor of English at State University of New York, Binghamton. She is the author of, among others, *Built to Win: The Female Athlete* *as Cultural Icon* and *Pretty Good for a Girl* and is the editor of *The Encyclopedia of Third Wave Feminism.*

Mehal Krayem is studying for a Bachelor of Arts at Sydney University, majoring in sociology and government and international relations. She is also the current editor of *Reflections* magazine.

Sara I. McClelland is a doctoral candidate in psychology at The Graduate Center, City University of New York. Her research concerns the definition and regulation of female experiences of sexual desire and satisfaction. Her work has appeared recently in journals including *Harvard Educational Review, Emory Law Journal, Social Justice Research*, and *Qualitative Inquiry.*

Susan Nussbaum is a long-time disability rights activist and founder of the Empowered Fe Fes, a support, sexuality, and disability identity group, which has served over three hundred girls. The Fe Fe model will soon be replicated in ten other U.S. cities. Susan is also a playwright and was recently published in the anthology *Beyond Victims and Villains: Contemporary Plays by Disabled Playwrights,* edited by Victoria Lewis.

Tara Pengilly is currently studying for a Bachelor of Arts/Law at the University of Western Sydney, majoring in history.

Debi Roker is codirector of the Trust for the Study of Adolescence (TSA), a charity based in Brighton, United Kingdom. TSA aims to support professionals and organizations that work with young people and families. The organization undertakes research and evaluation, training and professional development projects, and produces publications. Debi's role extends across all three of these areas. Prior to working at TSA, Debi worked in the university sector, doing teaching and research in relation to youth and family issues.

Kristen Schilt received her Ph.D. in sociology from the University of California, Los Angeles, in 2006. She is currently a postdoctoral research fellow at Rice University in Houston, Texas. Her recent research focuses on the workplace experiences of female-to-male transsexuals.

Carly Stasko is an artist, activist, writer, and self-titled imagitator who teaches media literacy, culture jamming, and women's studies workshops in various high schools, universities, and community centers in Toronto and abroad. Her varied, playful, and interdisciplinary interests include imagination, semiotics, DIY communities, consumerism, (r)Evolutionary healing, transformative learning, and creative resistance for environmental and social justice. She publishes her own zine titled *uncool* and performs as a "superhero makeover consultant" and spoken word artist. To collaborate or connect, contact www.intrinsik.net

Elke Zobl completed her doctorate at the Academy of Fine Arts, Vienna, Austria, and pursued postdoctoral studies at the University of California at San Diego. She is now continuing her research on female youth-produced media at the International Centre of Culture and Management in Salzburg, Austria.

Index